CAMBRIDGE
EXAMINATIONS
PUBLISHING

OBJECTIVE
first certificate

Annette Capel   Wendy Sharp | **Teacher's Book**

CAMBRIDGE
UNIVERSITY PRESS

PUBLISHED BY THE PRESS SYNDICATE OF THE UNIVERSITY OF CAMBRIDGE
The Pitt Building, Trumpington Street, Cambridge CB2 1RP, United Kingdom

CAMBRIDGE UNIVERSITY PRESS
The Edinburgh Building, Cambridge CB2 2RU, UK
40 West 20th Street, New York, NY 10011–4211, USA
477 Williamstown Road, Port Melbourne. VIC 3207, Australia
Ruiz de Alarcón 13,28014 Madrid, Spain
Dock House, The Waterfront, Cape Town 8001, South Africa

http://www.cambridge.org

First published 2000
Fifth printing 2002

Printed in the United Kingdom at the University Press, Cambridge

Text typeface Minion 11/13.5pt System QuarkXpress®

ISBN 0 521 62576 9 Student Book
ISBN 0 521 62574 2 Workbook
ISBN 0 521 77801 8 Workbook with Answers
ISBN 0 521 62575 0 Teacher's Book
ISBN 0 521 62573 4 Class Cassette Set

Cover design by Dale Tomlinson

Produced by Gecko Limited, Bicester, Oxon.

Contents

Map of Objective First Certificate Student's Book

TOPIC	LESSON FOCUS	EXAM SKILLS	GRAMMAR	VOCABULARY
Unit 1 **Fashion matters** 8–11 Fashion; describing people	1.1 Speaking and listening 1.2 Grammar	Paper 5 Speaking: 2 Comparing photographs Paper 4 Listening: 3 Matching Paper 3 Use of English: 3	Comparison Adverbs of degree	Appearance and clothing Phrasal verbs
Exam folder 1 12–13		Paper 3 Use of English: 3 Key word transformations		
Unit 2 **Only for nerds?** 14–17 Computer games; the Internet	2.1 Reading 2.2 Grammar	Paper 1 Reading: 1 Skimming and scanning; matching headings	Review of present tenses -ly adverbs	Computers Compound nouns Positive and negative adjectives
Writing folder 1 18–19		Paper 2 Writing: 1 and 2 Informal letters		
Unit 3 **Going places** 20–23 Travel	3.1 Listening Pronunciation: word stress 3.2 Grammar	Paper 5 Speaking: 2 Paper 4 Listening: 2 Sentence completion Paper 3 Use of English: 3	Modals 1: Obligation, necessity and permission	Travel and holidays Verb–noun collocation Expressions with *do* Prepositions of location
Exam folder 2 24–25		Paper 3 Use of English: 5 Word formation		
Unit 4 Our four-legged friends 26–29 Animals; pets	4.1 Reading 4.2 Grammar and vocabulary	Paper 1 Reading: 4 Matching	*as* and *like*	Animals and pets Compound adjectives Expressions with *time*
Writing folder 2 30–31		Paper 2 Writing: 1 Transactional letters 1 (formal)		
Unit 5 Fear and loathing 32–35 Narration: frightening experiences	5.1 Listening Pronunciation: past tense endings 5.2 Grammar	Paper 4 Listening: 1 Short extracts Paper 3 Use of English: 2	Review of past tenses: Past simple Past continuous Past perfect	Fear Irregular verbs
Exam folder 3 36–37		Paper 3 Use of English: 2 Open cloze		
Unit 6 **What if?** 38–41 Winning prizes	6.1 Reading 6.2 Grammar and vocabulary	Paper 1 Reading: 3 Gapped sentences Paper 3 Use of English: 1	Review of conditionals with *if* Adverbs of frequency	Winning Phrases with *in* Parts of speech
Writing folder 3 42–43		Paper 2 Writing: 2 Stories 1		
Revision Units 1–6 44–45				
Unit 7 **Life's too short** 46–49 Sport	7.1 Grammar 7.2 Listening Pronunciation: question tags	Paper 4 Listening: 3 Matching Paper 3 Use of English: 3 and 5	Gerunds and infinitives 1 Question tags	Sport Phrases expressing like and dislikes
Exam folder 4 50–51			Paper 3 Use of English: 1 Multiple choice cloze	

TOPIC	LESSON FOCUS	EXAM SKILLS	GRAMMAR	VOCABULARY
Unit 16 **Good, plain cooking** 102–105 Food and drink	16.1 Listening and reading 16.2 Grammar	Paper 1 Reading: 3 Gapped sentences	The article Possession	Food Prepositions of time
Writing folder 8 106–107		Paper 2 Writing: 1 Transactional letters 2 (informal)		
Unit 17 **Collectors and creators** 108–111 Hobbies	17.1 Speaking and listening 17.2 Grammar Pronunciation: contrastive stress	Paper 5 Speaking: 2 The long turn Paper 4 Listening: 1 Short extracts Paper 3 Use of English: 4	Relative clauses	Hobbies Phrases with *look* Phrasal verbs with *lo*
Exam folder 9 112–113		Paper 4 Listening: 4 Choosing from two or three answers		
Unit 18 **What's in a book?** 114–117 Books	18.1 Reading 18.2 Grammar	Paper 1 Reading: 2 Multiple choice Paper 3 Use of English: 2 and 3	*enough, too, very, so, such*	Books Phrasal verbs with *co* and *go*
Writing folder 9 118–119		Paper 2 Writing: 2 Question 5 The set book		
Revision Units 13–18 120–121				
Unit 19 **An apple a day ...** 122–125 Health and fitness	19.1 Grammar 19.2 Listening Pronunciation: silent letters	Paper 4 Listening: 4 Multiple choice Paper 3 Use of English: 1 and 5	Modals 3: Advice and suggestion *have/get something done*	The body *It's time* Phrases with *on*
Exam folder 10 126–127		Paper 1 Reading: 1 Multiple matching		
Unit 20 **No place to hide** 128–131 Crime and punishment	20.1 Speaking and reading 20.2 Grammar	Paper 5 Speaking: 3 and 4 Shared task and related discussion Paper 1 Reading: 1 Summary sentences	Gerunds and infinitives 2	Crime Verbs with a change i meaning: *try, stop, re* *remember, forget, me* *go on*
Writing folder 10 132–133		Paper 2 Writing: 2 Stories 2		
Unit 21 **To have and have not** 134–137 Shopping	21.1 Listening and vocabulary 21.2 Grammar and reading	Paper 4 Listening: 3 Matching Paper 1 Reading: 1 Headings Paper 3 Use of English: 3	Clauses: Concessive clauses Purpose, reason and result clauses	Money Goods and services Adjective-noun collocations Phrasal verbs with *cu*
Exam folder 11 138–139		Paper 1 Reading: 2 Multiple choice		
Unit 22 **A little night music** 140–143 Music	22.1 Speaking and reading 22.2 Grammar	Paper 5 Speaking: 2 Paper 1 Reading: 3 Gapped paragraphs Paper 3 Use of English: 4	Complex sentences	Music and concerts
Writing folder 11 144–145		Paper 2 Writing: 2 Reports 2		

Content of the First Certificate Examination

The Cambridge First Certificate examination consists of five papers, each of which is worth 40 marks. It is not necessary to pass all five papers in order to pass the examination. There are five grades: Pass – A, B, C; Fail – D, E.

As well as being told your grade, you will also be given some indication of your performance i.e. whether you have done especially well or badly on some of the papers.

Paper 1 Reading 1 hour 15 minutes

There are four parts to this paper and they are always in the same order. Each part contains a text and a comprehension task. The texts used are from newspaper and magazine articles, advertisements, fiction, guides, manuals and reports.

Part	Task Type	Number of Questions	Format	Objective Exam folder
1	Multiple matching	6 or 7	You must read a text preceded by multiple matching questions. The prompts are either headings or summary sentences.	**10** (126–127)
2	Multiple choice	7 or 8	You must read a text followed by multiple choice questions with four options A, B, C or D.	**11** (138–139)
3	Gapped text	6 or 7	You must read a text with paragraphs or sentences removed. You need to use the missing paragraphs or sentences to complete the text.	**12** (150–151)
4	Multiple matching/ multiple choice	13–15	You must answer the questions by finding the relevant information in the text or texts.	**13** (164–165)

Paper 2 Writing 1 hour 30 minutes

There are two parts to this paper. Part 1 is compulsory, you have to answer it. In Part 2 there are four questions and you must choose one. Each part carries equal marks and you are expected to write between 120–180 words for each task.

Part	Task Type	Number of Tasks	Task Format	Objective Writing Folder
1	Question 1 a transactional letter • formal/informal	1 compulsory	You are given a situation which you need to respond to by letter. You may be given two or three different types of information which you need to use in your answer.	**2** (30–31); **8** (106–107); **15** (194–195); **Exam folder 15** (188–189)
2	Questions 2–4 • an article • an informal non- transactional letter • a letter of application • a report • a composition • a story Question 5 Writing one of the above types of task on a set book – choice of two questions	4 choose one	You are given a choice of topics which you have to respond to in the way specified. Articles **5** (68–69); **12** (156–157);	Compositions **4** (56–57); **13** (170–171); Reports **6** (80–81); **11** (138–139); Letters of Application **7** (94–95); **14** (182–183); The set book **9** (118–119); Stories **3** (42–43); **10** (132–133); **Exam folder 15** (188–189)

Paper 3 Use of English 1 hour 15 minutes

There are five parts to this paper, which test your grammar and vocabulary.

Part	Task Type	Number of Questions	Task Format	Objective Exam folder
1	Multiple choice gap-fill mainly testing vocabulary	15	You must choose which word from four answers completes each of the 15 gaps in a text.	4 (50–51)
2	Open gap-fill, testing mainly grammar	15	You must complete a text with 15 gaps.	3 (36–37)
3	'Key' word transformations testing grammar and vocabulary	10	You must complete a sentence with a given word, so that it means the same as the first sentence.	1 (12–13)
4	Error correction mainly testing grammar	15	You need to identify any extra words, which are wrong, in a text containing some wrong lines and some correct lines.	5 (62–63)
5	Word formation	10	You need to use the right form of a given word to fill the gaps in a text containing 10 gaps.	2 (24–25)

Paper 4 Listening about 40 minutes

There are four parts to this paper. Each part is heard twice. The texts are a variety of types either with one speaker or more than one.

Part	Task Type	Number of Questions	Task Format	Objective Exam folder
1	Multiple choice	8	You hear short, unrelated extracts, each about 30 seconds with either one or two speakers. You must choose an answer from A, B or C.	6 (74–75)
2	Note-taking or sentence completion	10	You hear either one or two speakers and this part lasts about 3 minutes. You must write a word or short phrase to complete the notes or sentences.	7 (88–89)
3	Multiple matching	5	You hear five unrelated extracts with a common theme. Each lasts about 30 seconds. You must choose the correct answer from a list of six.	8 (100–101)
4	Choosing from 2 or 3 possible answers	7	You hear either one or more speakers talking for about 3 minutes. Task types may include yes/no; true/false; 3-option multiple choice; who said what, etc.	9 (112–113)

Paper 5 Speaking about 14 minutes

There are four parts to this paper. There are usually two of you taking the examination and two examiners. This paper tests your accuracy, vocabulary, pronunciation, and ability to communicate and complete the tasks.

Part	Task Type	Time	Format	Objective Exam folder
1	The interviewer asks each candidate some questions.	3–4 minutes	You are asked to give information about yourself.	14 (176–177) Complete speaking test (Parts 1–4)
2	Each candidate talks to the interviewer for about 1 minute.	3–4 minutes	You have to talk about two pictures and then comment on the other candidate's pictures.	see above
3	Candidates have to discuss a task together.	3–4 minutes	You are given some material – diagrams, pictures, etc. to discuss with the other candidate.	see above
4	Candidates offer opinions relating to the task they've just completed.	3–4 minutes	The interviewer will join in with your discussion.	see above

UNIT 1 Fashion matters

Unit topic	Fashion and describing people
1.1	
Exam skills	Speaking Paper 5 Part 2
	Listening Paper 4 Part 3
Vocabulary	Appearance and clothing
	Phrasal verbs
1.2	
Grammar focus	Comparison
Grammar extra	Adverbs of degree
Workbook contents	
1	Spelling
2	Phrasal verbs
3, 4, 5, 6	Reading – comprehension,
	superlatives, vocabulary
7	Grammar – comparison
8	Use of English – Part 3

1.1 SB pages 8–9

Throughout the unit notes, approximate timings are given for guidance. These relate to two lengths of lesson: **SV** (short version), corresponding to a lesson of 60–70 minutes, and **LV** (long version), for a lesson of around 90 minutes. Below these timings, there is always an indication of what to cut out of the lesson (and set for homework) for the short version or, conversely, what to develop in the long version. Relevant suggestions for extra activities are included in the notes.

Lesson plan	
Speaking	30–40'
Listening	15–20'
Vocabulary	20–30'

SV   Spend less time on topic vocabulary in 2; set 9 for homework.

LV   See notes below for 1, 7 and 8.

1   Much of this lesson is conducted as pairwork. Explain to students that for the First Certificate Speaking test they will be in pairs, with two examiners present. Refer students to pages 6 and 7 of the Student's Book for further information about this and other parts of the examination.

Allow students around five minutes for this initial discussion, which is an opportunity to warm up the topic and talk about something familiar. If this is a new class, the activity will also give you a chance to walk round and make a quick assessment of their level and speaking ability. It is normal at this stage of an FCE course for students to be nervous about speaking, so do encourage them. Explain that by the end of the course, their confidence will be sky-high!

Write up some useful sentence starters on the board:

Likes
I really like …
I prefer to wear …
What I absolutely love is …
Dislikes
I hate …
I wouldn't be seen dead in …

Extension activity

As an additional ice-breaker, bring in various items of clothing, both men's and women's; if possible, try to get hold of some obviously less fashionable items. Hold the clothes up one by one, asking what they are and eliciting student preferences.

2   Ask students to describe people in other parts of the classroom. This can be done as a guessing game, where one student in the pair describes what a certain person is wearing and the other says who is being described. For a weaker class, start the activity off by describing someone briefly in a couple of sentences and asking the students who you are describing.

Students can then work in pairs or groups brainstorming topic vocabulary. Ask them to make their lists using the headings given. Allow enough time for this (at least five minutes), as a lot of the vocabulary will be needed for the subsequent speaking task and listening material. Make sure students include the following vocabulary:

Clothes: jeans, jacket, t-shirt, polo shirt
Footwear: trainers, boots, sandals
Jewellery: earrings, necklace, ring
Headgear: baseball cap
Materials: cotton, silk
Hairstyle: straight, shaved, loose, tied back
Appearance: casual, untidy, fashionable

Refer students to the Vocabulary spot and suggest that headings can be a useful way of learning topic vocabulary.

3 In pairs, students take it in turns to describe each of the people in the photographs. Allow them up to three minutes for this and remind them to use the vocabulary they have just listed. They should not compare a pair of photographs yet.

4 Ask students to read the Exam spot. These tinted boxes contain important information or advice about the exam.

Students now make comparisons between the people in each pair of photographs. Refer them to the examples given, but encourage them to use their own ideas too.

5 Elicit some of these ideas and summarise what has been discussed in pairs by writing up a few sentences about each pair of photographs. Try to use different comparison structures on the board. Explain that the next lesson (1.2) will have a grammar focus, where all these structures will be looked at and practised.

6 Tell students that they are going to hear five short recordings, as an introduction to the matching task in Paper 4 Part 3. These will contain a variety of accents, as in the real exam.

The first recording is used as an example and students look at picture 3b while they listen. Then suggest that they read the transcript and think about the words in bold, to make them aware of the need to listen carefully. Before repeating the recording, explain that the checking of answers is an essential activity at second listening in the exam.

Tapescript

Speaker 1: I'm not a suit man – even for work, I can get away with casual stuff, though I still like my clothes to look smart. I love shopping – my favourite place is Paul Smith in Covent Garden. I bought a really nice woollen shirt there recently. Clothes are important to me, but they need to be comfortable as well as stylish.

7 Ask students to listen to the four remaining extracts and match the correct photos to the speakers. They should do this on their own and only compare answers when they have finished. Only play the tape a second time if they need to check their answers. (They will listen to the four extracts again in 8.)

> **Answers**
> Speaker 2 – 2a   Speaker 3 – 1a   Speaker 4 – 4b
> Speaker 5 – 3a

Tapescript

Speaker 2: I started working this year, so I'm able to get new clothes more regularly than before, when I had to save up for months. I buy a lot, I must confess. My mum thinks I should cut down a bit on what I spend, but my image is really important to me: if someone sees me in something once, I don't like to go out in it again – well, not for a while, in any case. I like to wear bright colours and always dress up when I go clubbing. I buy a big range of styles and I do try to keep up with the latest fashions. Sometimes the things are a bit outrageous!

Speaker 3: Shopping for clothes isn't really my scene, if you know what I mean. I don't really mind what I wear, to tell you the truth. I'm the least fashion-conscious person I know! I suppose if anything I favour the casual look. I've got two pairs of jeans and I wear them mostly, with a T-shirt or something. I have got one favourite top, which a girlfriend gave me. It's red and it's got a sort of abstract design printed in navy blue on the back. She said she gave it to me so I would always stand out in a crowd!

Speaker 4: My clothes have to be comfortable, make me feel relaxed as soon as I slip them on. I often put together outfits from stuff I find in street markets – they're less expensive that way. Second-hand clothes can be real bargains, and usually, they've hardly been worn! I'll change the look of my clothes quite frequently, you know, sew in a new piece of material, swap buttons, dye something a different colour, just for a change. I make a lot of my own jewellery too.

Speaker 5: My friends take far less trouble with clothes than I do – sometimes they wear the tattiest things ever! As my job involves dealing with people, I have to make an effort to look good all the time. I like to present a classy, sophisticated image. I go shopping for clothes about once a month, though if I see something by chance, I'm quite likely to go for it there and then. I think I've got good taste and I very rarely make a mistake when I buy clothes. I did take a jacket back last week, but that was because it was badly tailored.

Students can benefit from working with tapescripts, especially at the beginning of a course. Make copies of the extracts for Speakers 2–5 and ask students to underline the key words or phrases that gave them the correct answers. They can also use the tapescripts as an alternative way of finding the nine phrasal verbs in 8.

8   Start by checking how much students know about phrasal verbs. Explain that these are very common, particularly in informal, spoken English. Play the tape for Speakers 2–5 again and ask students to write down the phrasal verbs they hear. Elicit these and write them up on the board. Then ask students to match them to the short definitions. (The numbers in brackets refer to the Speakers.)

> **Answers**
> **a** stand out (3)   **b** put together (4)   **c** take back (5)
> **d** dress up (2)   **e** save up (2)   **f** cut down (2)
> **g** slip on (4)   **h** go out (2)   **i** keep up with (2)

9   This exercise can be set for homework if time is short. If done in class, ask students to work through the note in pairs, completing the answers. Remind them to use each phrasal verb once only, and in the correct tense.

> **Answers**
> **1** went out   **2** put on/slipped on   **3** dressed up
> **4** put together   **5** stood out   **6** keep up with

Following the discussion, ask students to report their ideas to the class.

1.2 SB pages 10–11

> **Lesson plan**
>
> Grammar focus   60-80'
> Grammar extra   10-10'
>
> **SV**   Set 7 for homework.
> **LV**   Spend longer on discussion in 1; include the Extension activity at the end.

1   Ask students what the photo is illustrating: it is the finale of a Vivienne Westwood fashion show. Elicit some other names of fashion designers and ask if students know any British or American designer labels, for example Paul Smith (mentioned in 1.1 Listening), Vivienne Westwood, Donna Karan.

Ask students to read the short text individually. Check understanding of difficult vocabulary:

emaciated – extremely thin, usually because of illness or lack of food
desirable – attractive
attainable – achievable, possible

Elicit students' views on the text. Is it still true that the fashion industry prefers to use the skinniest models? Why is this?

Point out that the text contains a number of superlative adjectives, for example: *the youngest, the most emaciated, the least attainable.*

2   In this course, the approach to grammar is an inductive one. Students at this level have generally been taught all the basic structures and now need to review what they know. In most grammar focus lessons, students discuss examples and formulate explanations or rules. They can then check their understanding is correct by referring to the Grammar folder at the back of the Student's Book.

Ask students to look at the comparison structures given and discuss answers to the three questions in pairs. Allow them up to ten minutes for this, encouraging them to explore each question fully and make notes if appropriate. Refer students to the Grammar folder, page 198.

> **Answers**
> ● Single syllable adjectives add *-er/-est*; longer adjectives use *more/the most*
> ● Some two-syllable adjectives, e.g. common, likely, narrow, pleasant, simple, stupid
> ● Adjectives ending in a single vowel and consonant double the consonant (slim → slimmer); adjectives ending in *-y* change to *-ier/-iest*

3   Ask students to complete the table, working in pairs. Remind them to be careful about spelling.

> **Answers**
>
> | | |
> |---|---|
> | larger | largest |
> | thinner | thinnest |
> | dirtier | dirtiest |
> | quieter | quietest |
> | more/less casual | most/least casual |
> | | most/least outrageous |
> | better | |
> | | worst |
> | farther/further | farthest/furthest |

4   Allow students two or three minutes to complete the sentences. Check their answers.

> **Answers**
> **a** larger   **b** the most outrageous   **c** more casual
> **d** the dirtiest   **e** thinner   **f** the furthest/farthest
> **g** brighter   **h** better

Grammar extra

In this course, these short sections cover additional small grammar points. They include some explanation and examples. There is usually a short exercise to practise the point, which can be set for homework if necessary.

Answers
a a bit; much
b a great deal/a bit; much
(*much* can be used with both comparative and superlative adjectives, as in the final example.)

---

5 Explain to students that the structure *not so … as* is less common in everyday English nowadays. Allow them up to three minutes to compare the cars, using the words given.

ⒺEⓍtension activity

In pairs, students can compare other 'designer' objects, such as computers (Apple iMac, now available in five colours/grey PCs) or chairs (comfort/elegance).

---

6 Ask students to read the short article and identify the comparative adverbs. If they need help, remind them that most adverbs end in *-ly*. This will help students to locate them.

Answers
more commonly; less strictly; more readily

Refer them to the Grammar folder, page 198 or ask them to read this after class.

The discussion on unisex clothing can be initiated by eliciting examples of popular items of unisex clothing, for example, jeans, trainers, sweatshirts.

7 Explain that this exercise is an exam task from Paper 3 Part 3, Key word transformations. This task type is introduced in detail in Exam folder 1, which follows Unit 1 (pages 12–13).

Make sure that students read the rubric carefully and remind them that they cannot use more than five words, including the word in bold.

Note that these transformations are below the level of the exam, as a first introduction to the task format.

Answers
1 were cheaper/less expensive 2 the most talented designers 3 as old as 4 is a lot quicker/faster than 5 less difficult (to play) than 6 more elegantly dressed than 7 is less interesting than 8 less smartly when

---

Exam folder 1

Paper 3 Part 3
Key word transformations

SB pages 12–13

Remind students that there is a full description of the exam on pages 6–7 of the Student's Book. Paper 3 Use of English has five parts and candidates have an hour and fifteen minutes to complete the paper.

The Exam folders can be studied by students on their own outside class, but notes are given below for a mini-lesson in class.

1 Ask students to read the exam instructions carefully. They should then look at the example and the notes in italics.

Explain that there are two marks available, relating to the two parts of the answer. Therefore, even if students do not produce the whole answer, they can still get a mark if one element is accurate.

2 Ask students to close their books and to discuss in pairs what advice to give on this part of the exam. Allow them a couple of minutes to do this and suggest they make notes.

3 Now ask students to compare their notes with the advice given in the bullet points.

Stress that the key word must not be changed in any way. Check that students understand the information about contracted forms.

4 This task can either be set as homework or done in class.

Answers
1 told Sally about a new 2 took it back 3 make an effort 4 were not / weren't as fast as 5 was the worst concert 6 do not / don't dress up 7 much more easily if / when 8 far the best writer / author 9 highly priced that 10 is possible / acceptable to wear

It may be worth pointing out to students that in 10, 'is allowed to wear' would be incorrect.

UNIT 2 Only for nerds?

Unit topic	Computer games; the Internet
2.1	
Exam skills	Reading Paper 1 Part 1
Vocabulary	Compound nouns
Grammar extra	*-ly* adverbs
2.2	
Grammar	Review of present tenses
Vocabulary	Positive and negative adjectives

Workbook contents

1, 2	Reading – skimming and scanning
3, 4	Grammar – present tenses
5, 6, 7	Vocabulary – topic words and phrases

2.1 SB pages 14–15

Lesson plan

Listening	10–15'
Reading	35–45'
Grammar extra	10–10'
Vocabulary	10–20'

SV Shorten discussion in 1; set sentences in 7 for homework.

LV See notes below for 1 and Teaching extra.

1 As an optional warm-up activity, find out what experience the class has of playing computer games, either at home or in an arcade. Encourage them to talk about examples of the different types of game illustrated, e.g. fantasy, combat, sport.

  Refer students to the dictionary definition for *nerd* taken from *The Cambridge International Dictionary of English* published by Cambridge University Press. Check understanding of this. Then ask them to discuss in pairs for about three minutes, saying whether they agree with the statement.

2 Play the tape, explaining that this is a non-exam listening activity, where students are listening for general or *gist* meaning. Explain that even though they may not understand every word, they should listen

carefully to the opinions of the main speaker, a university lecturer.

Tapescript

Interviewer: I have here with me now Dr Mark Griffiths, senior lecturer in psychology at Nottingham Trent University. In a recent article for the journal *Education and Health* he says some rather surprising things about computer games … or video games, to call them by their other name. Dr Griffiths, computer games get a lot of bad publicity, but you don't see them quite so negatively, do you?

Dr Griffiths: Indeed not. The trend in society is to label computer games as mindless and antisocial. But there is another side to the argument, because computer games actually help some people to develop relationships and improve their social skills … They make people feel better about themselves, too.

Interviewer: Yes, and you mention in your article that therapists are using computer games to help children with problems … children who are perhaps aggressive … but don't most people think that computer games make people more aggressive? Some of these games are very violent, aren't they?

Dr Griffiths: That's true, but you see the aggressive content of these games doesn't seem to have a negative effect. In fact, games like this actually allow the players to release their own aggression in a non-destructive way, so they can work positively on anyone with problems. And of course, introducing 'shoot-em-up' games at an early meeting allows the therapists to get through to these kids … you know, they win their confidence, their friendship even.

Interviewer: Well, that's good news … and your article is called 'Video games: the good news' … Dr Griffiths, stay with us and after this short break we can talk further about your work …

Elicit the main views Dr Griffiths expresses:
- Computer games can have a positive effect on people: building relationships, improving social skills, increasing self-esteem.
- They are being used to help children with behavioural problems.
- They give people a way of releasing their aggression in a non-destructive way.
- Therapists use them to win the confidence of children under their care.

Summarise useful vocabulary from the recording on the board, eliciting related words where shown below in italics:

aggressive, aggression
destructive, *destruction*
confident, confidence

3   Refer students to the Exam spot and explain that the skills of skimming and scanning are essential for Paper 1 Reading.

Ask students to scan the four articles to find the answers to a–d. Check that they only looked at the information at the bottom of each article.

Answers
a 4   b 2   c 4   d 3

4   Divide the class into groups of four and tell each person in the group to skim a different article. Give a strict time limit of one minute and then allow students to briefly describe the games to each other.

5   Ask students to do the matching task on their own, underlining as suggested. They can then check their answers in pairs.

Answers
1 B   2 D   3 A   4 C

Explain that in the real exam task, there are more headings than this, and that there is always one extra heading that is not used.

6   Explain that this vocabulary exercise requires closer reading of each article.

Answers
a clone   b cliché   c goes downhill   d ammunition
e thrill   f demanding   g joyless   h elaborate
i stomp around   j at the mercy of

7   Elicit the meaning of *downside*: the disadvantage or less positive side of something. Explain that compound nouns like this one are often formed from phrasal verbs and are sometimes hyphenated. Ask students to look at the eight nouns given and decide which three are used in computing. For these three, elicit examples of how they are commonly used.

Answers
upgrade (software/memory)
back-up (disk/system)
downloading (a file/from the Internet)

Check understanding of the other words, encouraging use of a monolingual dictionary if necessary. Then ask students to complete the sentences a–h.

Answers
a let-down   b back-up   c downloading   d set-up
e upturn   f breakdown   g upgrade   h crackdown

Grammar extra

Students can discuss this in pairs, referring to the Grammar folder, page 198 if they need help.

Answers
endless: regular: add *-ly*
tragic: add *-ally*

NB This applies to all adjectives ending in *-ic* apart from 'public', which becomes *publicly*.

remarkable: lose *le*; *-ly*
easy : lose *y*; add *-ily*
true: lose *e*; add *-ly*

a   I didn't sleep much.
b   I found it difficult to sleep.
c   There have been a lot of good films recently.
d   We arrived after the film had started.

2.2 SB pages 16–17

Lesson plan

Grammar focus	60–70'
Speaking	5–15'
Vocabulary	0–5'

SV Limit the discussion in 5; set 6 for homework.
LV See notes below for 5.

1 Allow students ten minutes to discuss the examples and complete the statement. Refer them to the Grammar folder, page 198 only after they have finished.

Answers
1 The present <u>simple</u> tense is used for permanent situations (examples <u>d</u> and <u>h</u>) or to talk about actions which are habitual or repeated (examples <u>a</u> and <u>c</u>). This tense is also used in time clauses, introduced by words such as *if, until, once, as soon as,* <u>when</u> (example <u>a</u>). Note also that it is used in both parts of zero conditional sentences, as in this example and in example <u>f</u>.

On the other hand, the present <u>continuous</u> tense is used for temporary situations (example <u>b</u>), situations that are changing or developing (example <u>f</u>), and for events or actions happening now (example <u>g</u>). This tense can also be used to talk about the future (example <u>j</u>).

2 Ask students to read sentences a–f carefully and correct any errors. Explain that some sentences are correct. They should give reasons why the corrections need to be made.

Answers
a ✓ b is selling (temporary) c ✓ d use (time clause)
e get (zero conditional) f ✓

3 Ask students to work through the sentences on their own and then compare their answers in pairs.

Answers
a finish, get b are improving c is coming out
d flies, explodes, hit e is becoming f take g make
h crashes, lose, are working, save

Background information

At the time of writing this Teacher's Book, Bill Gates, the owner of Microsoft, is worth more than the entire country of Singapore. He is the richest man in the world.

4 Before reading the review, ask students whether they have used either of the two Internet browsers mentioned. Explain, if necessary, what a browser does: it allows you to access the Internet more easily, by displaying the information in categories and providing search tools.

Ask students to skim the review for general meaning and then do the gap-filling exercise on their own. Remind them to use a suitable present tense in each space. When they have finished, they should compare answers and discuss the questions below the review.

Answers
'put' is the extra verb.
1 is changing 2 communicate 3 allows 4 has
5 need 6 share/are sharing 7 includes 8 believes
9 does/is doing 10 means 11 read 12 sound
13 send 14 seem 15 comes

Both tenses can be used in spaces 6 and 9:
    In 6, there is no change in meaning.
    In 9, the continuous tense makes the situation sound more changeable.
Stative verbs used in the review: believe include mean seem sound

Refer students to the list of stative verbs in the Grammar folder, page 199.

5 Allow students up to ten minutes to discuss the statements in small groups. If time is short, allocate one statement to each group and restrict the discussion to three minutes. At the end of the discussion, summarise class opinions and any useful vocabulary on the board.

6 Ask students to work in pairs to sort the adjectives, using a dictionary if necessary.

Answers
Positive: brilliant, elaborate, excellent, popular, sensational, sophisticated, terrific, tremendous
Negative: appalling, demanding, joyless, useless

Explain that they will need to use some of these adjectives later for the Writing folder task (SB pages 18–19). Refer students to the Vocabulary spot. Encourage them to keep a vocabulary notebook and discuss the different ways it could be organised, for example, alphabetically, by unit (and topic), by meaning, or by part of speech.

Writing folder 1

Paper 2 Informal letters

SB pages 18–19

In Paper 2 Writing, students must write in a register appropriate to the task set. The Part 1 transactional letter can be either formal or informal, depending on the reader and purpose specified. In Part 2 of the paper, there may be an informal, non-transactional letter, for example, a letter giving advice to a friend.

1   Ask students to decide in pairs which two of the extracts are informal. Elicit informal words and phrases from these extracts and write them on the board.

> **Answers**
> A – get-together, It's a pity …, terrific, Why not …?
> C – Anyway …, Well …, weird guy, at my place

Refer students to the Exam spot. Stress the importance in the exam of identifying the reader and the purpose of the letter. Then ask students to discuss possible writers, readers and purposes for extracts A–C.

> **Answers**
> A – departmental secretary to staff in department; invitation to next get-together.
> B – department head to staff; report on the last meeting and a reminder about the next one.
> C – friend to friend; invitation to stay for a party.

2   Ask students to find the style clues in the extract. These are: *Guess what?*, *splash out*, *a bit more*.

3   Explain that in the exam, candidates are assessed not only on accuracy, but on content, range of vocabulary and structure, organisation, register and format. Ask students to read the sample answer and discuss reasons for the low mark in pairs.

> **Answers**
> ● failure to answer the question set (answer ends up talking about something different)
> ● inconsistent register (paragraphs 1 and 3)
> ● poor organisation: long middle paragraph with an absence of linkers
> ● language errors in middle paragraph.

Ask students to quickly correct the errors in paragraph 2: you can't decide <u>whether</u> to buy; not as cheap <u>as</u>; choose <u>a</u> computer game; spend the money <u>on</u> something else.

The improvements to style in paragraphs 1 and 3 can be discussed quickly and written up after class if time is short.

4   Suggest that students plan their own letters in pairs, working through the ideas given under the C-L-O-S-E headings. Refer them also to the lists of phrases on page 19, which relate to this planning phase. Students often complain that they don't know what to write about. They need to think around the subject and plan what to say. This does not mean writing the whole piece in rough first. Stress that students don't have time to do this in the examination and it is not advisable – hurrying over a fair copy leads to words and even sentences being missed out, and leaves no time to check for errors.

> **Answers**
> Informal expressions in 1–6:
> 1   Initial greetings: 1, 3
> 2   Congratulations: 1
> 3   Opinion: 2, 5
> 4   Advice/Suggestion: 1, 2, 4, 7
> 5   Linkers: 2, 3, 5, 6, 7
> 6   Endings: 1, 3, 4
> 7   Opening and closing a letter:
>
> Dear Jayne … Love (informal)
> Dear Sir … Yours faithfully (formal; use when the reader's name is not known)
> Dear Ms Jones … Yours sincerely (formal)

Ask students to write the letter for homework, reminding them to write between 120 and 180 words.

> **Sample answer**
>
> Dear Jan
>
> Thanks for your letter and well done for passing that exam. Your parents sound much more generous than mine!
>
> I'm not sure that you need any more computer games, do you? If I were you, I'd save up for a bit longer and then buy some clothes. In fact, why not get something special, like a new pair of boots or a coat? There are some lovely winter coats in the shops, and many of them are quite a bargain. Also, you said you needed a new coat last year – well, now's your chance.
>
> I think a charcoal grey one would suit you really well, especially something stylish and well-cut. Make sure you choose wool, and find one with nice, deep pockets, to stuff all your bits and pieces in. I'd go for a longish one, below the knee or even full-length. Then you'll be nice and warm when the snow comes!
>
> Let me know what you decide and have fun shopping.
>
> Lots of love

UNIT 3 Going places

Unit topic	Travel
3.1	
Exam skills	Speaking Paper 5 Parts 2 and 3
	Listening Paper 4 Part 2
Vocabulary	Travel vocabulary
	Travel collocations
	Expressions with *do*
Pronunciation	Word stress
3.2	
Grammar focus	Modal verbs 1: Obligation,
	necessity, permission
Grammar extra	Prepositions of location
Workbook contents	
1, 2	Vocabulary – prepositions of
	location, travel quiz
3, 4, 5	Writing – register and phrasal verbs
6	Grammar – modals

3.1 SB pages 20–21

Lesson plan

Speaking	5–10'
Listening	30–40'
Vocabulary	15–20'
Pronunciation	15–20'

SV   Set 7, 8 and 9 for homework.
LV   See notes below for 6.

1   The aim of this part of the unit is to get the students thinking about the subject and to find out what vocabulary they already know and what gaps they may have. The photos also act as an introduction to Paper 5 of the examination, when students are each asked to discuss a photo. One photo is of someone hiking in the Himalayas, the other of people on a cruise.

Ask students to work in pairs. They should talk generally about the photos and then compare them, not describe them in detail, as this is not required for the examination.

2   Decide which student is A and which is B. Student A talks about the type of people these holidays would appeal to. Student B discusses the advantages and disadvantages of each holiday.

3   Ask students to talk about their own holidays and where they usually go. This can be broadened into a whole class discussion or kept as pairwork.

❶eaching extra

Any vocabulary should be put up on the board during this part of the lesson, organised into phrases, nouns, verbs (especially phrasal verbs), collocations, etc. This will make it easier for students to get used to organising vocabulary in their notebooks.

4   In groups, brainstorm vocabulary connected with cruises. Some words which they will need are:
   to take a cruise, ship, captain, crew, cabin, deck, passenger, seasickness, a tourist party, to be seasick, on board
   trip, voyage, journey, expedition, to go on holiday

Ask students what they know about the Antarctic and any words they know connected with it. For example:
   iceberg, scientific bases, penguins, to thaw, to melt, to freeze, the polar ice-cap, the South Pole

5   Refer students to the Exam spot. In Part 2 of the Listening paper students are often asked to complete a sentence. Ask students to read through the questions 1–10 very carefully and try to predict what kind of answer they think is required. They should listen to the tape twice. The answers are in the order they hear them.

Play the tape once. Students should write down their answers. Play the tape again while students check that their answers are correct.

Tell them that there is **no** need to change the words they hear, i.e. they don't need to make tense changes or change verbs to nouns.

Answers
1 7 degrees   2 Explorer   3 under the bed   4 American
5 stormy   6 animals   7 research station   8 buildings
9 rubbish   10 wildlife

Tapescript

Interviewer: Good morning, everyone. Well, in the studio today we have Steve Jackson who's going to tell us about his recent trip to the Antarctic. So, Steve, what was it like? Did you freeze?

Steve: No, I didn't. The temperature was about seven degrees most days and I must say I found it quite comfortable. You should take warm clothes though and you really need a good windproof coat.

Interviewer: Now, tell us a bit about the ship you were on.

Steve: It was called the *Explorer*, and it was built only three years ago. The cabins are very small and at first I did wonder where I was going to put all my stuff. However, whoever designed the ship thought of just about everything a passenger would need and I eventually found plenty of cupboard space under the bed.

Interviewer: What were the other passengers like?

Steve: Oh, the atmosphere on board between the passengers was really great. The crew really tried to get everyone to mix. I was invited to eat with the expedition leader, he was American, on the first night, and then after that I sat at a different table for dinner every night, but you don't have to if you don't feel like it.

Interviewer: Did you get seasick at all?

Steve: Some of the passengers did – the weather can be stormy in the Antarctic. Of course there is a doctor on board and he gave anyone who needed it an injection for seasickness – luckily, I didn't need one and the others got over it pretty quickly once they'd had the injection.

Interviewer: I bet that was a relief! What's your best memory of the trip?

Steve: Well, that's hard to say, but probably it's of the animals we saw – whales, penguins and seals. One day we set off to a place called Cuverville Island, which is famous for its birds. There were ten of us in a tiny rubber boat – that was a bit hair-raising I can tell you! Anyway, once there we had to climb up a steep, icy hill, but the view from the top was terrific.

Interviewer: Did you come across any people apart from your fellow tourists?

Steve: Yes, a few of the scientists at a research station. They gave us coffee and biscuits one morning! There used to be a thriving fishing industry in this area at one time, but all that's left are some deserted buildings.

Interviewer: Did you feel guilty about disturbing such an untouched region?

Steve: Well, yes and no. Cruise ships are not allowed to dump rubbish or to go where they like, and they have to carry scientists to lead the excursions. Only small parties are permitted to land in one area at a time and you've got to keep away from the wildlife. So, all in all I felt that well-run trips, like this one, would do more good than harm. I also felt completely changed by the experience – it was like going to another world.

Interviewer: Well, thank you for telling us about your trip, Steve. Now next …

Photocopiable tapescript activity (**⋯⟩ page 181)**

Ask students to write questions for answers 1–8 below, using the tapescript for reference.

1 about seven degrees
2 only three years ago
3 under the bed
4 with the expedition leader
5 it can be stormy
6 an injection for sea-sickness
7 its birds
8 ten

> **Answers**
> 1 What was the weather like?
> 2 When was the *Explorer* built?
> 3 Where did you keep your stuff?
> 4 Who did you have dinner with on the first night?
> 5 What is the weather like in the Antarctic?
> 6 What did some of the passengers need?
> 7 What is Cuverville Island famous for?
> 8 How many people were in the rubber boat?

6 Round off the listening with a discussion of green tourism/ethics.

Extension activity

This activity can either take five minutes, or, if time and interest allows, can be broadened out into a prepared talk. Divide the class into pairs and explain that each person is going to give a short talk to his/her partner. Allow them each five to ten minutes to prepare a one/two-minute talk on the subject of tourism, A speaking for the subject and B speaking against. Give help with any extra vocabulary that may be needed and then time each speaker exactly. The following are ideas for the talks:
Tourism has done more harm than good.
There are some places in the world which should be protected from tourists.

7 It is a good idea to do the first example, (a) boats, as a whole class activity so that students feel comfortable with the exercise.

> **Answers**
> a **boats** – canoe, ferry, liner, yacht
> b **movement** – journey, flight, crossing, voyage
> c **seaside** – cliff, shore, coast, sand
> d **people** – courier, travel agent, holiday-makers, sightseers
> e **accommodation** – campsite, caravan, hotel, bed and breakfast

8 Refer students to the Vocabulary spot. Collocations are increasingly being tested at FCE level and it is important that students become familiar with verb/noun, verb/adjective, verb/adverb combinations.

Answers
take – a trip, a ship, a plane, a flight
book – a trip, a hotel, a flight
catch – a plane, a flight
set – sail
board – a ship, a plane, a flight
get – a plane, a tan, a hotel, a flight
go – skiing, sightseeing

---

9 Students will be aware, both from the listening and from the discussion, of the expression *to do more good than harm*. Confusion often arises between expressions with *do* and *make*. Students should try to learn them as fixed vocabulary items as there is no one easy rule to follow except that *do* is often combined with actions and *make* with constructing or creating.

Answers
a do business with   **b** do for a living   **c** do military service   **d** do the shopping   **e** did me a favour
f do my best, do my homework

---

10 It is a good idea before you begin this part of the unit to check that students understand what a syllable is and are able to break words up into syllables.

In pairs ask students to divide the words up into syllables before they underline the parts which are stressed.

If necessary, either play the tape from 'Good morning' until 'freeze' or read it aloud.

Ask students to form pairs or groups to decide on the stress on the words in their book. Then play the interview again to check answers.

Answers

RECENT	EXPEDITION	DESERTED
TEMPERATURE	INJECTION	UNTOUCHED
COMFORTABLE	SCIENTISTS	EXCURSIONS
PASSENGER	BISCUITS	PERMITTED
ATMOSPHERE	INDUSTRY	EXPERIENCE

ⓣeaching extra

Below are some **very general** basic rules. (As ever, there are exceptions! Also it is important to be aware that word stress can move depending where the word is within a sentence or phrase.)

1 In words ending in *-ic*, *-ive*, and *-tion* and most words of two syllables, the stress is on the second syllable from the end, e.g. realistic, brochure.
2 In words ending in *-ity*, *-logy*, *-graphy*, *-cracy*, *-sophy* and usually, *-tory* as well as words of three syllables or more, the stress is on the third syllable from the end, e.g. history, university, philosophy
3 In words ending in *-iator*, *-ary*, *-acy*, *-mony* and most words of four syllables, the stress is on the fourth syllable from the end, e.g. literacy, honorary
4 In words with foreign endings, such as *-oo*, *-ette*, *-ine*, *-esque*, *-eer*, *-ique*, *-ese*, etc., the stress is on the last syllable, e.g. hotel, cigarette, picturesque, auctioneer, Japanese

---

11 Ask students to mark the word stress on the words in italics in the dialogue. They then should read out the dialogue, each taking turns to change roles. Tell students that they should not stress a negative prefix attached to an adjective (patient, impatient; happy, unhappy; responsible, irresponsible).

Tapescript

Travel Agent: Good morning, can I help you?
Customer: Yes, have you got any *brochures* on *Africa*? I'm a keen *photographer* and I'd like to spend some time *photographing* the *animals*.
Travel Agent: Well, we can offer you *various package* deals. What kind of *accommodation* would you prefer?
Customer: Oh, a good *hotel*. I don't like to be *uncomfortable* – I'm not the camping type.
Travel Agent: Well, I think we have *something* here to suit you. Let's see. We have two weeks in *Kenya*. It looks very *attractive*, I don't think you'll be *disappointed*. They also *guarantee* plenty of *wildlife*.
Customer: That sounds good. Thanks. I'll take the *brochure* and have a look at it tonight.

12 Play the cassette to check pronunciation.

3.2 SB pages 22–23

Lesson plan

Grammar	60–70'
Grammar extra	10–20'

SV Omit 5 and set 8 for homework.
LV See notes below for Grammar extra.

1   Refer students to the Grammar folder, page 199.

Check students understand the explanations 1–6. Ask them to give examples of each, for example:

It's forbidden. – smoking in the classroom
It's a good idea. – to use an English-English dictionary.

All the examples in this exercise are taken from the listening in 3.1. Ask students to discuss which of a–g means 1–6. (There is more than one answer for 1.)

Answers
a 6   b 2   c 5   d 3 and 1   e 1   f 4   g 1

2   Let students try to work out the differences between the sentences, but explain the differences if they are finding it difficult. Refer students to the Grammar folder on page 199.

Answers
a   The speaker is telling him/herself to do something. (Obligation comes from the speaker.)
b   Someone else is telling the speaker what to do. (The obligation doesn't come from the speaker.)
c   Use of *must* for laws, notices and rules, where there is no choice of action.

Another point to mention:
Must is often used in a friendly way in conversation, e.g. You *must* come to dinner sometime.

3   This activity is to give free oral practice in using *must*, *have to*, and *don't/didn't have to*. Ask students to look at the example. Then they need to imagine what they would say about transportation, accommodation, food, activities, entertainment and people if they were on a holiday in the places in the photos.

Refer them to the Grammar folder, page 199 and check they all know that:

●   the past of *must* is *had to*

●   *must* is used in the present tense, *have to* is used for all other tenses.

4   In this exercise students have to decide which of the alternatives is correct. It is a good idea to ask them to not only give their answer, but also to explain why they chose that one.

Answers
a needn't   b aren't allowed to   c mustn't   d have to
e is compulsory   f have to

5   This gives students more speaking practice using *need, have to, must, should, don't have to*, using all tenses. This exercise could be followed up with a writing exercise. Ask students to write five sentences on *d, e* and *f*.

Check that they know that the past of *should do* is *should have done*.

6   Check that students know that *to permit* and *to allow* are followed by an infinitive with *to*. *Can* and *to let* are followed by an infinitive without *to*.

Answers
a allowed/permitted   b can   c let   d permitted/allowed

Ask students to work in pairs. At the end of the discussion put up examples of what their parents let them do, and what they are allowed to do at the age of 18, on the board.

7   The aim of this exercise is to clarify the difference between *didn't need to do* and *needn't have done*. Check students know that in the present tense there is no difference in meaning. However, in the past there are differences.

Didn't need to do just means that it was unnecessary and we don't know whether you did it or not.

Need not have done has the idea that you did it, but it was a waste of time, totally unnecessary.

Refer students to the Grammar folder, page 199.

Ask them to think about some examples of when they *didn't need to do* or *needn't have done* something.

8   This is examination practice for Paper 3 Part 3. Check students know that they cannot change the word given and that they shouldn't use more than five words. Contractions are counted as two words. Refer them to the Exam spot.

Answers
1 had to change   2 needn't have gone to
3 didn't let me go   4 aren't permitted to swim
5 should get health insurance   6 don't have to have/get

Grammar extra

For this exercise students need to visualise where exactly things are. A way to introduce this is to elicit which prepositions might be used in these cases:

1 a line (e.g. a road) on, off, across, along, over, etc.
2 a point (e.g. a bus stop) to, from, at, etc.
3 an area (e.g. a neighbourhood or park) into, out of, across, within, around, in, etc.
4 a volume (e.g. a building) into, out of, around, etc.
5 a surface (e.g. a table) onto, off, over, under, across, etc.

Ask students to say where exactly things in the room are, e.g. a picture, a clock, their shoes, a window, their chair, a dress label, etc.

Extension activity

Give half the class a map of a small country or island (real or made up), which you have drawn. It will have features such as villages, forests, roads, rivers and mountains. Tell them to keep it hidden. The rest of the class has a map with very few features on it, or completely blank, if you prefer. The aim is for the information about the location of the features to be transferred only by speaking and listening. The student with the completed map tells the one with the blank map exactly where everything is positioned, and the student draws in the features on their map. Pointing isn't allowed!

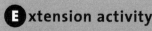

Exam folder 2

Paper 3 Part 5 Word formation

SB pages 24–25

Explain that the word formation task is the last part of the Use of English paper. The whole paper takes 1 hour and 15 minutes to do and students should aim to spend about 15 minutes on each part. This may seem to them too short a time at first so stress that they will become faster with practice. There are 10 questions in this part of the test. Students should be encouraged to read through the whole passage before they start trying to do the answers.

1 Introduce the idea that words can be made negative by putting a prefix at the beginning. Try to elicit some examples to put on the board before students do the exercise. Notice that *il-* is usually in front of words beginning with *l* and *ir-* words beginning with *r*. *Im-* is often before words beginning with *p*, but not always.

Answers
a dissatisfied   g uncomfortable   m displeased
b irrelevant   h dishonest   n unrealistic
c impatient   i unpopular   o imperfect
d incomplete   j illegible   p irregular
e illegal   k inaccessible   q illiterate
f impossible   l irresponsible

2 Not all prefixes are negative. Put students in groups and get them to try to work out what the prefixes in a–i mean.

Ask students to look at the exercise and give some more examples.

Answers
a very small skirt   b without stopping   c to train again
d under the road   e undo action   f not cooked enough
g against/to stop freezing   h very conservative
i to live longer than someone/something

mini = small *mini-cab, mini-bus*
non = not *non-smoker, non-stick*
re = again *re-grow, replace, redo*
sub = under *submarine, subtotal, substandard*
un = not/reversing action *unlock, untie, unable*
under = not enough *underfed, underwatered, undervalue*
anti = against *anti-government, anti-war, anti-smoking*
ultra = very *ultra-rightwing, ultra-clean*
out = more/external *outgrow, outnumber, outdoors*

It is very useful for the students to realise that they can enlarge their vocabularies by learning how a word can be changed into a noun, adjective, verb or adverb. There are no rules as such which are easily accessible to students at this level (the suffix often depends on the root of the word – Latin/Anglo-Saxon/Greek, etc.) and therefore they just need to learn them.

Answers

3
a happiness **b** intelligence **c** approval **d** repetition
e information **f** popularity **g** friendship **h** socialism
i payment

4
a truth **b** success **c** death **d** height

5
a windy **b** attractive **c** hopeful/hopeless
d peaceful **e** edible/eatable

6
a widen **b** behave **c** sympathise **d** clarify

7
a hard **b** well **c** slowly **d** peacefully **e** fast
f truly/truthfully

8 Read through the Advice section and check that students have understood what they have to do. If time is short, then this exercise can be set for homework, otherwise it can be done in pairs or individually in the class. Tell students to always look carefully for prefixes, especially negative ones.

Answers
0 noun – publication **1** verb – produced
2 noun – youth **3** adverb – extremely
4 adjective – scientific **5** adjective – religious
6 noun – safety **7** adjective – successful
8 noun – variety **9** adjective – inaccurate
10 adjective – impossible

UNIT 4 Our four-legged friends

Unit topic	Animals
4.1	
Speaking	
Exam skills	Reading Paper 1 Part 4
Vocabulary	Word formation
4.2	
Grammar focus	*as* and *like*
	Compound adjectives
Exam skills	Listening Paper 4 Part 1
Vocabulary	Animals
	Expressions with *time*

Workbook contents

1, 2, 3, 4, 5, 6	Reading – comprehension, guessing unknown words
7, 8	Grammar – *as*, *like*, compound adjectives

4.1 SB pages 26–27

Lesson plan

Speaking	15–20'
Reading	40–50'
Vocabulary	15–20'

SV Omit the pet questionnaire and set 7 for homework.
LV See notes below for 3 and 7.

1 In pairs, students discuss how they feel about animals in general and having a pet in particular. This sets the scene for the reading which follows, which is about pets with problems. Students then do the questionnaire in pairs.

Answers
2 b 3 b

2 Ask students to look at the four photos and discuss which pet would be suitable for the people in them. There is no right answer as long as students can justify their choice.

3 The texts are about a cat, two dogs and a parrot, which all have behavioural problems. Students read the introduction.

Answer
an animal therapist/behaviourist (a kind of psychiatrist)

Extension activity

Have a quick class discussion about the sort of behavioural problems cats, dogs and parrots might have to try to predict the vocabulary that might come up in the texts. Students might have experience of problem animals. If not some ideas might be:
cats: scratching, biting, fussy eaters, killing small animals, etc.
dogs: barking all day and night, biting, running off, attacking people, etc.
parrots: squawking, talking, using rude words, pecking people, flying off, etc.

4 Refer students to the Exam spot. Students skim the texts to say where they come from. At this stage there might be some discussion about the different genres, i.e. what differences there are between a magazine article, an encyclopedia, a pet-care book and a novel.

Answer
a an article

5 Students now scan the texts to find the information. Tell them not to worry about individual words that they don't know. Don't let them use a translation dictionary during this exercise.

The example is underlined and it is a good idea if the students underline the part of the text where they find their answers to questions 1–11. When they finish, they should compare their answers with another student's.

Answers
1 B 2 D 3 A 4 D 5 A 6 B 7 C 8 A
9 B 10 D 11 C

6 Do a quick round-up discussion about behaviour therapy, if time.

7 Students have to make adjectives from these nouns. They will find the answers in the article they have just read.

> **Answers**
> a tricky b different c successful
> d aggressive e excessive f reputable

Extension activity

Put the following words on the board (they are all from the texts) and ask students to write down the form of the word asked for in the brackets. They should use a dictionary to help them find the answer as only the base word is in the texts.
organisation (verb), noise (adverb), neighbour (noun – place), arguments (adjective), forget (adjective), manage (noun), tempt (noun), anxiety (adjective)

> **Answers**
> organise, noisily, neighbourhood, argumentative, forgetful, manager/manageress/management, temptation, anxious

4.2 SB pages 28–29

> **Lesson plan**
>
> Grammar   30–40'
> Listening   10–15'
> Vocabulary   25–35'
>
> **SV** Set 5 and 6 for homework.
> **LV** See notes below for 3 and 5.

1 and 2 The aim of these exercises is to encourage students to use proofreading skills as well as to show them the main uses of *as* and *like*. Refer students to the Grammar folder, page 199.

> **Answers**
> a as b – c such as/like d as + like e – f like
> g – h As i – j as k – l like/such as

3 Compound adjectives are very useful when writing descriptions, both of people and things. It is also important that students learn to recognise them when they come across them in their reading.

Extension activity

Ask students to write a short piece describing two or three people in the class, using at least one compound adjective. All the students circulate reading out their descriptions to each other, trying to see if the other student can guess who the descriptions are of. It might be as well to make sure the descriptions are flattering.

> **Answers**
> a
> 1 animals in general
> 2 a tiger which eats people (not just men!)
> 3 a blue-eyed, long-haired, bad-tempered cat
> 4 a two-toed, scaly-backed animal
>
> c
> 1 You'd sit in a car.
> 2 You'd probably feel miserable because you'd be very poor.
> 3 You need to have a lot of money.
> 4 a phone-in programme, a pick-up truck, a standby flight, a takeaway meal
>
> d
> 1 a fifty-kilometre journey
> 2 a twelve-year-old girl
> 3 a seventy-five-minute film
> 4 a thirty-five-thousand-pound car
> 5 a ten-second pause

4 There are three short recordings, which are similar in type to the ones found in Paper 4 Part 1. The tape should be played twice, and then the students should not only give their answers, but also say why they chose that answer and not the other ones. The reasons are underlined in the tapescript. Ask students to read the questions before they listen.

> **Answers**
> 1 B 2 A 3 B

Tapescript

1

Man: Well, I've had him about six years now, and he's grown a bit in that time. He was only tiny when I first got him from the pet shop. People said I was mad keeping an animal like that in a small flat, but I haven't really had any problems. Cats are a bit of a problem sometimes, of course. They try to get in through an open window, but I haven't noticed him eat any. Then again I keep him well fed. Here, feel his skin – it's lovely and smooth, isn't it?

2

Woman 1: How are you getting on with that puppy you were given?

Woman 2: Oh, not too well I'm afraid. I have tried hard to be a good owner, taking it to the vet for injections and all the other things you need to see to regularly. The thing is that he's one of those types of dog that is always on the front page of the newspapers for attacking children. So even though he's as good as gold, I have to make the time to take him out for runs in the countryside, just to avoid people.

3

Man: We always seem to be taking the kids to zoos. It doesn't matter where we are on holiday we seem to end up there. They have a really great time – it doesn't seem to bother them that these poor creatures are miles away from their natural habitat. I guess nowadays zoos spend most of their time trying to breed endangered species, but I always feel uncomfortable somehow and have this urge to unlock the cages, even though the kids tell me zoos are doing a good job really.

5 If time is short, this exercise can be set for homework. It can also be used for dictionary work, using an English-English dictionary.

Answers
1 parrot – perch, squawk, claw, beak, feather, wing
2 cat – fur, paw, whiskers, claw, kitten, purr
3 dog – bark, paw, kennel, puppy
4 horse – hoof, stable, foal, mane, neigh

Extension activity

There are many expressions in English where comparisons are made with animals, e.g. *as quiet as a mouse*.
It is often a good idea to introduce these expressions by asking students what they think things are compared to in English. For example *as hot as? as cold as? as hungry as? as drunk as?* They will probably say a variety of things and be amused to find out some of the answers (*as hot as hell, as cold as ice, as hungry as a hunter, as drunk as a lord*). Students often find it interesting to compare what they would say in their own language, with English.

Examples with animals are:
as brave as a lion
as strong as an ox
as slippery as an eel
as stubborn as a mule
as poor as a church mouse

6 Go through the expressions, explaining what they mean and how you'd use them. Give some examples for each one. Try to make the examples relevant to the students. For example:
This morning I spent a long time in a traffic jam on my way to class. How much time do you spend doing homework? What do you do to pass the time when you are on holiday? etc.

This exercise can be set for homework, if time is short.

Answers
a behind the times b time for lunch c times as much as
d In time e have a good time f pass the time/kill time
g tell the time h wasting time

Writing folder 2

Paper 2 Part 1 (Question 1)

SB pages 30–31

In Paper 2 Writing Question 1, the transactional letter is compulsory. It may be either formal or informal depending on the reader and purpose specified so students need to be able to write in the correct register. They will also need to know how to use a range of functional language such as making suggestions and getting feedback, giving information, requesting information, making complaints and making corrections. They should also realise the importance of layout, using paragraphs and organising their work, and of using the appropriate opening and closing formulae.

Students should make sure that they cover all the points mentioned and they use a range of vocabulary and language.

1 Go through a–e with the students, asking them for some general examples of how to express the functions. For example, '*suggesting*':

What/How about …?
Why not …?
You should/ought to …
I suggest/propose that …

Allow students some time to read through extracts 1–3 and then ask them to tell you why they chose the answer they did. It is important to note that some answers may be used more than once and others not at all.

2   The aim of this exercise is to encourage students to think about what they have to do and not to start writing immediately. Put students in pairs and ask them to read through both the rubric and the task carefully. Go through any vocabulary that might be a problem.

3   Students then work together in pairs answering the questions about the task.

Answers
- You need to write a formal letter – it is to an airline rather than to someone you know.
- There is no name so you begin *Dear Sir* and end *Yours faithfully*. Always give your reason for writing at the beginning of the letter. It is important always to be polite. **You lose marks if you are rude in any way**.
- This kind of letter is usually broken up into 2–3 paragraphs. It is important to use a variety of linking words, not just *and* and *but*. Other words include *although, nevertheless, however, moreover, finally, in conclusion*, etc.
- There are five important points in this letter (the first one is in the instructions):
  - ask for some money back
  - late boarding
  - rude staff
  - no vegetarian
  - old movie
  Never leave out any points.
- You can add information about the seats if you have enough words left.

4   Ask students to read through the answer given and explain which of the mistakes a–j are present. For homework they could be asked to rewrite the letter with suitable corrections.

Answers
b paragraphing   g content points   i tone
j linking words

5   This exercise is to make students more aware of register in English. Students are often completely unaware of this and as a result their written work is a mixture of the formal and informal. Something that also will lead to lower marks is rudeness. Even if the letter is one complaining about something, the student should always complain politely.

Answers
Formal – b, d, e, f, h, k

6   Sometimes, abbreviations are used in this part of the Writing paper. This exercise contains some common ones that students should be aware of. This could be set for homework if time is short. Abbreviations are often followed by a full stop in English, but this practice is becoming less common. Where the abbreviation ends with the same letter as the word, no full stop is used (e.g. Doctor = Dr). Whichever style you use, it is important to be consistent.

Answers
a Please reply   b For example   c and so on
d Note well   e Telephone   f Square, Avenue, Street, Road   g Please turn over   h kilograms, kilometres
i numbers   j maximum, minimum   k Doctor
l Care of   m approximately   n continued   o minutes

7   This answer contains no mistakes and answers the question fully. It would receive full marks in the examination. Impress upon the students that they will NEVER need to write out postal addresses in their answer.

Sample answer

Dear Sir,

I am writing to correct the information in an article in your newspaper, dated 10 November, about foreign students working on a local farm. I worked at the farm all summer and I enjoyed myself very much and made many good friends.

There were only 15 of us, not 30 as you said, and we came from many different countries. I am from Italy and my friends were from Russia, Spain, Brazil and Germany – not just from France and Sweden. Moreover, we only worked in the mornings so we had plenty of time to go sightseeing and relax. In addition, we were paid adequately – not much but enough, considering that we had free food and accommodation.

Our living accommodation was excellent. The farmer, Mr Stevens, had built modern, wooden cabins with good washing facilities – there were enough showers for us all and everything was spotlessly clean. I should know, as I helped to clean them every day!

I would be happy to go back and work for them again, and I know my friends would as well.

Yours faithfully,

UNIT 5 Fear and loathing

Unit topic	Narration: frightening experiences
5.1	
Exam skills	Listening Paper 4 Part 1
Pronunciation	Past tense endings
Grammar extra	Irregular verbs
5.2	
Grammar focus	Review of past tenses
Exam skills	Use of English Paper 3 Part 2

Workbook contents	
1	Vocabulary
2, 3	Grammar – past tenses
4	Reading – Part 4 matching

5.1 SB pages 32–33

Lesson plan

Speaking	20–30'
Listening	30–40'
Pronunciation	10–10'
Grammar extra	5–10'

SV Shorten 1; omit 7; set Grammar extra table for homework.

LV Students write up one of the stories chosen in 3 in class.

1 Elicit reactions to the picture from the class and ask what else they find frightening. This can be omitted if time is short.

2 Ask students to work in pairs and allow them a couple of minutes first to think about ideas. Tell them to think of a suitable title for the story they hear. The title should be short, and should make use of some of the vocabulary given.

3 Tell students to come and write their titles on the board, or write them up yourself. Invite students to choose the three most frightening ones and then ask the listeners of these stories to narrate them to the class.

Teaching extra

To encourage students to write short pieces of narration on a regular basis, start a class ring-binder file called 'True stories'. Ask students to include funny, frightening or other unusual personal accounts, and suggest that others in the class read these. You could even state that the stories can be fact or fiction, with the class deciding whether the writer has made up the story or not.

4 Explain that students are going to hear some more frightening experiences. Play the tape once and check students are able to answer the two gist questions.

Answers
The man was in a lift.
He spent over four hours there.

Tapescript

1

I'd had this interview for a job, up on the twenty-seventh floor of a big office block. It was after six and a lot of people had already left. I got in the lift and pressed the button. At first, I noticed that it sort of shook but it started to go down. Then there was this horrible sound of twisting metal and it shuddered to a stop. I was stuck between the twelfth and thirteenth floors! To begin with, I was determined not to panic. There was an emergency button, which I pushed for ages. Next, I saw a phone, but when I lifted the receiver, it was dead. At this point, I completely went to pieces. I shouted and screamed, I hammered on the doors, but nobody helped. Eventually, I sank to the floor and wept like a child. In the end, it was a good four hours before the night porter realised what had happened and called the Fire Brigade. I've never been in one since.

Play the tape again and ask students to take it in turns to narrate what happened. The answers to the questions give the basic storyline.

Answers
1 to attend an interview for a job
2 early evening
3 from the 27th to between the 12th and 13th floors
4 He tried to press the emergency button and use the phone.
5 Most people had already left and it was four hours before the night porter realised he was there.

5 Refer students to the Exam spot and then look at the question for the extract they have heard. Play the tape again, asking students to note down sequence words and phrases.

Note that extracts 1–6 are slightly longer than typical Part 1 recordings in the exam. This is to give students more context for identifying their answers, and also to focus on narrative, the unit topic.

Answer
1 C (To begin with)

---

6 Ask students to read through questions 2–6, thinking about the words in bold. Then play the tape. Each recording will be heard twice, as in the exam. Remind students to check their answers at the second listening.

Answers
2 C 3 B 4 B 5 A 6 B

Tapescript

2

It was late at night and I was in the living room watching television on my own. Funnily enough I was watching a horror movie – it wasn't very spooky though! Well, I thought I heard footsteps upstairs. So I turned off the TV, held my breath and listened. Someone was definitely moving around up above me. My first thought was – it's a burglar. And then, there was this horrific crash. I was scared stiff but I knew I had to go up there. I remember I picked up an umbrella – goodness knows what I would have done with it! Anyway, I crept up the stairs and the first thing I saw was a bookcase on its side, with hundreds of books on the floor. Then I heard this whimpering sound, coming from underneath the pile of books. It was the next door neighbour's cat! It was her footsteps I had heard. While I was putting away the books, I found something else. A live frog! It sort of jumped out at me. I tell you, that was the really hair-raising part!

3

Somehow I have to sort out their problem, this fear they have of flying. First we talk as a group, and one by one they tell me about particular times when they've flown and what happened. Nine times out of ten they describe regular, problem-free flights, just like the hundreds I flew myself. You see, most of their worries are only in their imagination. I also use drama and role play, to teach them how to deal with other people's fears, because through that they sometimes forget their own problem, or take it less seriously than before. Finally, but only if I think it's still necessary, we go up in a plane. My passenger is accompanied by an actor, who plays the part of the nervous first-time traveller. I sit a few rows behind and it's wonderful to watch my 'student' staying calm, offering advice to this stranger. I've never failed yet.

4

We were all living in a small house in the countryside at the time. The house was in the middle of nowhere and it was quite a long journey back from the university each evening, so I'd bought myself a small motorbike. Anyway, on one particular evening I was on my way home when a really thick fog came down. I didn't know where I was and I became very uneasy. I went on – rather slowly – but couldn't see anything I recognised. At one point the road curved round, but because of the fog I didn't see this and carried straight on ... and hit a wall. The impact threw me off the bike and I ended up underneath it, with my leg trapped. I screamed for help but of course there was no one about. I realised that I had to get up and carry on – or stay there all night. So I pulled myself out from under the bike, got back on and somehow arrived home, where my friends all took one look at me and drove me off to casualty. I needed seven stitches and they kept me in for observation.

5

Int: Malcolm Jarvis, you have recently sailed single-handedly around the world. At one stage, you were shipwrecked all alone in the middle of the ocean, clinging on to your damaged yacht. Weren't you terrified?

MJ: Not at the time. I suppose I was too busy trying to survive.

Int: You mean finding things to eat?

MJ: More basic than hunger! First, I had to get myself out of the sea. Sharks had been a problem there. I managed to pull myself back into the yacht but it had taken in a lot of water. So I spent a bit of time sorting that out.

Int: And then were you able to keep yourself warm?

MJ: Only for a while. I wrapped myself in whatever I could find, including the sails, but by the second day I was in a really bad way because I couldn't feel my fingers and toes, they were completely numb. It was just as well they found me when they did.

6

We were all in the main room planning what to do that day. The others were looking at a map on the table, but I was standing by the back window. About six of them burst in, waving guns and shouting things in a dialect we didn't understand. I knew they hadn't seen me over by the open window. They grabbed John and Gary. Ruth rushed to the doorway but they got her too. In the meantime, I had managed to throw myself safely outside and had crawled underneath the house – because of the rainy season, all the houses there are raised above the ground on wooden stilts. I kept totally still. I remember watching a beetle on a leaf, staring at it and hoping that they wouldn't find me. Finally, when I realised that they'd gone, I ran inside and radioed for help. My friends weren't so lucky. They were held as hostages for over three months.

7 This recording contextualises the use of the past perfect. After getting students to note down the order of events, ask them to check their notes by listening to the recording, paying attention to when this tense is used.

8 Students listen again to the first extract and underline the verbs which contain the /ɪd/ sound.

> **Answers**
> started   lifted   shouted
> The /ɪd/ ending follows the consonants *t* and *d*.

Grammar extra

If this is set for homework, remind students to think about other verbs which have the same form throughout.

> **Answers**
> *Burst* has the same form. Other verbs like this are, e.g. cut, hit, set, put, bet.

5.2 SB pages 34–35

> **Lesson plan**
>
> Grammar focus   60–70'
> Use of English   10–20'
>
> **SV**   Set 4 as a written task for homework; shorten the work on parts of speech in 6.
> **LV**   Ask students to write up the skills descriptions in class.

1 Ask students to work through the examples on their own and then compare answers with a partner.

> **Answers**
> **a** PP   **b** PS; PS   **c** P   **d** PC   **e** PS; PP   **f** PC; PS
> **g** PC; PC   **h** PS; PP   **i** PS; PP; PS   **j** P

Elicit the reasons why two different tenses are used in *e*, *h* and *i*.

> **Answer**
> The past perfect denotes an action further back in the past.

Now ask students to think about the different tenses used in *f*. They should then read the explanation about the past simple and past continuous, which follows in the Student's Book.

2 Ask students to fill in the gaps, using either the past simple or past continuous. They can then compare their answers.

> **Answers**
> **1** was walking   **2** was blowing   **3** was pouring
> **4** was   **5** drove   **6** stopped   **7** curved   **8** decided
> **9** was feeling   **10** got   **11** drove   **12** happened
> **13** pulled up   **14** waited   **15** drew up   **16** pulled away
> **17** was   **18** stood   **19** was coming down
> **20** was shaking   **21** (was) wondering   **22** came
> **23** was pushing   **24** grabbed   **25** made   **26** went
> **27** was trying   **28** heard

3 Ask students to look at the information about the past simple and past perfect. They can then complete the sentences.

> **Answers**
> **a** had spent; decided
> **b** told; had happened; explained; had found
> **c** had kept; thought; was

Refer students to the Grammar folder, page 200.

4 Ask students to work in pairs, taking it in turns to describe each scene, starting with the fourth one and working backwards.

Useful vocabulary:
Picture 1: hold up a bank, hold-up/bank raid, masked robbers, balaclava, pointing a gun at/at gunpoint, cashier
Picture 2: make a getaway, drive off, bag/holdall
Picture 3: car chase, police siren, in hot pursuit, catch up with
Picture 4: force to stop, pull over, arrest, take off (the balaclavas)

> **B**ackground information
>
> Raymond Chandler, author of *The Big Sleep*, was born in Chicago, but went to school in London. For most of his life, he lived in Southern California, which is where most of his novels are set. His most famous character is the private detective Philip Marlowe, who has been played in films by Humphrey Bogart, Robert Mitchum and Elliot Gould.

5 Ask students to read the extract and decide why the narrator wasn't frightened. They should then check on page 45.

6 Explain that this task is an introduction to the 'open cloze', Paper 3 Part 2, which tests mainly grammar. Ask students to work through the gaps in pairs and then check their answers with another pair of students.

Write the following headings on the board and ask students to sort the words into these categories. Two words are left over (*not* and *when*).

ARTICLES   CONJUNCTIONS   PREPOSITIONS QUANTIFIERS   VERBS

Remind students that these types of words are commonly tested in this part of Paper 3.

Exam folder 3 on the following two pages of the Student's Book covers Paper 3 Part 2.

Exam folder 3

Paper 3 Part 2 Open cloze

SB pages 36–37

The open cloze consists of fifteen spaces and an example at the beginning. Each space can only be filled with one word – you can't use contractions. If students put in more than one word, they will be marked wrong. The spaces are mainly grammatical in focus, but there are sometimes some vocabulary items. The space must always be filled with one word and that word must be spelt correctly.

1   Students need to get used to using all the clues they are given. The title is obviously a good clue. Make sure they read the whole passage before they attempt to answer this question.

Answer
'Balancing the risks' is the best title, as it looks at both sides of the question.

2   Students can try to fill in the spaces with or without the clues which are given, depending on how confident they feel.

Answers
1 These 2 spend 3 unless 4 a 5 at 6 have 7 few
8 if, though 9 who 10 than 11 although 12 more
13 out 14 In 15 such

Teaching extra

If your students need to gain confidence, this type of gapped text can be introduced gradually, starting at sentence level. Give students sentences with words blanked out. Each block of sentences could deal with one grammatical area – articles, prepositions, relative pronouns, quantifiers, etc. When more confident, the students can work through a whole passage. The first passage could gap prepositions only. Continue in this way with articles, quantifiers, relative pronouns, connectors and so on, until the students know what to look for. Later they can move onto a mixed open cloze passage.

UNIT 6 What if?

Unit topic	Winning prizes (and daily life)
6.1	
Exam skills	Reading Paper 1 Part 3
Grammar extra	Adverbs of frequency
6.2	
Grammar focus	Review of conditionals with *if*
Vocabulary	Phrases with *in*
Exam skills	Use of English Paper 3 Part 1
Workbook contents	
1, 2	Reading – Part 3 gapped sentences
3, 4	Grammar – Conditionals; adverbs of frequency
5	Use of English – Part 3
6	Vocabulary

6.1 SB pages 38–39

Lesson plan

Reading	40–50'
Grammar extra	10–20'
Speaking	15–20'

SV Set Grammar extra exercise for homework.
LV Extend Speaking activity.

1 Ask students to read the quote only and to then speculate about the subject of the article. It is about winning the lottery and describes someone who visits winners the day after their win.

> **Answers**
> Key words: winner's home; draw

2 Point out that the article contains four gaps, with a sentence missing from each. This is an easy introduction to the gapped sentence task (Paper 1, Part 3); in the exam itself, seven or eight sentences will be missing from the text.

Encourage students to skim read the article quickly, spending about three minutes at most. When reading a text, they should always do a quick initial read-through, to get an idea of what the text is about.

3 Now ask students to spend a bit longer rereading the article, so that they can then talk to a partner about the man's job. Remind them to look out for time references, as some of these will be helpful in fitting the sentences into the gaps later (*The first thing I say; Then I leave them to it; On this second visit; The first important question*).

When students are ready, in pairs, one student should describe what the man does on Sunday and the other should add any points not covered by the partner. Go round the class listening to the pairs, checking whether they are naturally using adverbs of frequency in their discussion. This will affect your approach to the Grammar extra later.

> **Answer**
> He works for Camelot, the National Lottery in Britain and visits people who have won big prizes.

Background notes

The British lottery started in November 1994. There are now two draws per week, on Wednesdays and Saturdays. Jackpot wins have been as big as £13 million. The lottery is run by a private company, Camelot, with some of the profits being handed to the government for distribution to good causes.

4 Refer students to the Exam spot and elicit other words and phrases that are used as reference words, for example, other pronouns; sequence words such as *first, next*. Then get students to decide where sentences A–D fit.

> **Answers**
> C and D include a time reference (My initial visit; Then).
> 1C; 2A; 3B; 4D.
> B refers back to the previous paragraph.

5 Explain to students that they will now be scanning for specific information, guided to the correct part of the article by the time clues in the four questions. These are: *second visit; initially; first arrives; When … claim.*

> **Answers**
> a They have forgotten what he told them, usually because of shock.
> b They can't sleep or eat properly.
> c He asks to take his jacket off and is offered a cup of tea.
> d On the Monday morning following their win.

6 Suggest that students do this exercise in pairs, taking turns to find and explain the words or phrases.

> **Answers**
> **a** link **b** deal with a problem successfully
> **c** making the right decisions **d** say no
> **e** become public knowledge **f** afraid of other people.
> **g** is unable to trust **h** happening frequently
>
> **Words to do with emotion**: burst into tears; confusion; anxiety; behave.

7 Remind students that they can use a lot of vocabulary from the article. Divide students into small groups of three or four. Encourage them to discuss each question, but if time is short, allocate each group one question only. Be ready to supply any vocabulary needed, but do not stop the discussion. Refer them to the useful language for discussion.

Round off the discussion with a reporting-back stage, writing up any useful points or language on the board. The photo is an advert for the Spanish lottery, *Once*.

Grammar extra

If students used these adverbs in their discussion, no introduction will be necessary. If not, spend a couple of minutes looking at the first example (normally), making sure students understand what this type of word is. Then ask students in pairs to find the other adverbs of frequency, to note the word order where they occur, and to then complete the grammar statements.

> **Answers**
> usually   always   seldom   never   sometimes   often
>
> I usually arrive (line 1)   It's always a very crowded room (line 1)   ... they always say (line 3)
> They seldom bother to read it (line 6)
> I usually have to go over the same points (line 12)
> Winners often burst into tears (line 15)   I always go to the door (line 16)   They'll sometimes say (line 24)
> they never really expect to win (line 29)
> They're often surprised (line 34)
>
> before; be; after; after
>
> If time is short, the rest of the exercise can be done at home.
>
> **Suggested answers**
> **a** On Sundays, I always get up late, because I don't have to go to work.
> **b** I've never been frightened of spiders, which is why I don't mind picking them up.
> **c** When I was younger, I often enjoyed playing board games, but now, I never get the time.
> **d** I'm never good at remembering people's names and this is often embarrassing at parties.
> **e** I sometimes wish I could win a lot of money, because then I would be able to do exactly what I want.

6.2 SB pages 40–41

> **Lesson plan**
>
> | Listening | 10–20' |
> |---|---|
> | Grammar focus | 30–40' |
> | Vocabulary | 5–15' |
> | Exam skills | 15–15' |
>
> **SV** Set 5 and part of 6 for homework.
> **LV** See notes below for optional Extra activity in 1.

1 Explain that students are going to hear four British people talking for less than a minute each. As these are unscripted, authentic recordings, there will be some unfamiliar words and phrases, but encourage students not to be put off by this. For each speaker, they should concentrate on listening for the answer to the focus question (*How would their lives change if they won the lottery?*). Point out to students that each speaker will use the second conditional form, at least in part (*I'd ...*). This will cue the answers for them.

> **Answers**
> Speaker 1 would have more homes and would eat better.
> Speaker 2 would spend all his time on a yacht in the sun.
> Speaker 3 would no longer be in debt and would own a massive house in the country.
> Speaker 4 would live in a warm climate.

Tapescript

1
I'd buy a Seychelles blue Bentley convertible. I'd buy a nice, fat house in Holland Park. I'd get a lovely, big house in the countryside. I'd buy a beautiful house in Spain, with swimming pool, palm trees, that sort of thing. I'd get a flat in Manhattan probably. Um ... I'd also have a permanent chef ... top of the range chef who could cook all different types of food, so I could have whatever food I wanted whenever I wanted it. I'd have my own personal masseur ...

2
I don't believe it when people say that if they won the lottery it wouldn't change their lives, because it would certainly change mine. Um, and I think I would just alter my life entirely. I love the sun and I hate English winters so I think I'd buy a yacht. And as I don't know anything about um ... sailing, I'd have to buy a crew as well. So, um, I'd ... I'd get this luxurious yacht and a very skilled crew – and probably a ... a ... a skilled cook – who would just take me all around the world going from hot spot to hot spot, so I could have a really great time.

3

Well, I know I'd have a problem with having all that money. I'd … I think it is a problem really, in some ways, because you … you'd have a sort of social responsibility and there are all kinds of people who you need to help, which I would want to do very much. Um, so of course I'd sort out my debts, my family's, but in the end I think what I'd do is buy – depending on how much money I had – buy a huge house, a really massive house somewhere in the country and just surround myself by all the people I want to be with, um and people who perhaps never had a chance to get out into the country at all.

4

Again depending on how many millions I won, um it would change what I would or wouldn't do with it. Frankly, if it was a lot, I mean five million upwards … sort out my own debts, which God knows are bad enough, sort out the family's debts and then invest as much as possible and just try and live off the interest, keep it there, nice little nest egg, growing and growing and growing, developing, flowering bountifully, and holiday, get away, move, anywhere but cold Britain.

Photocopiable tapescript activity (P ···⟩ page 182)

Ask students to underline words and phrases connected with the following:

Speaker 1 – an exclusive lifestyle
Speaker 2 – sailing
Speaker 3 – problems
Speaker 4 – money

> **Answers**
> Speaker 1: Bentley convertible, top of the range, permanent chef, personal masseur
> Speaker 2: luxurious yacht, skilled crew, going from hot spot to hot spot
> Speaker 3: social responsibility, sort out debts, people who never had a chance
> Speaker 4: £5 million upwards, debts, invest, live off the interest, a nest egg

As a short follow-up writing task for homework, students could then use some of this language, writing a paragraph about one of the four speakers.

> **Suggested answer**
> If Speaker 4 won a large sum of money on the lottery, first of all, he would sort out his and his family's debts, then he would invest the rest of the money and live off the interest. He talks about having a nest egg, which would grow, and which he could use to travel.

2 Most students will already have been taught these conditional forms at an earlier stage, but may need to be reminded of the differences in use. Elicit from students what the 'd means in *a* and *b* (a: I'd go = I would go; b: I'd won = I had won, I'd have been = I would have been).

> **Answers**
> **a** 2 **b** 3 **c** 0 **d** 1

3 Students can complete the matching exercise in pairs.

> **Answers**
> 1 d 2 a 3 g 4 b 5 f 6 c 7 h 8 e

4 Point out that proofreading is an important activity, which also occurs as an exam task in Paper 3 Part 4. Here, students need to correct tenses, whereas in the exam, they would only have to find extra words in a text.

> **Answers**
> won't → wouldn't (line 4)
> I'll find → I find (line 6)
> couldn't → can't (line 9)
> would have → had (line 10)
> will → would (line 11)
> will really have it in for → really has it in for (line 12)
> will do → do (line 14)
> would pay → paid (line 16)

5 Ask students to spend a couple of minutes finishing the sentences in pairs. Then ask students to report back to the whole class. Correct any errors in conditional forms. Write up some examples on the board and at the end, ask students to identify them again.

6 Refer students to the Vocabulary spot. Check students know the meaning of all the phrases. The sentences can be set for homework if time is short.

Answers
a In fact   b in case   c in control   d in time

Suggested answers
e Jenny rang us from a phone box, in a real panic – she had lost both sets of keys.
f I couldn't take the news in – Jess had already left for New York and wouldn't be coming back.
g Mike really has it in for his secretary – she can't seem to do anything right, according to him!

7 First, refer students to the Exam spot on Paper 3 Part 1. Elicit other parts of speech, such as adjectives, pronouns, conjunctions. Then ask students in pairs to sort the words into the four categories. Remind them that some words may fit more than one category, so they will have to check that the meaning of each group of four words is similar.

Answers
Nouns: experiment, trial, try, attempt
Verbs: received, accepted, gathered, welcomed
Prepositions: on, by, in, to
Adjectives: tiny, light, delicate, gentle

Students complete the short article, using one option from each group of four words.

Answers
1 attempt   2 light   3 received   4 by

If there is enough time, ask students to discuss their views on the story. What is the 'fuss' that the elderly woman referred to? (publicity). Why did she not want to claim her jackpot prize? (the excitement might kill her).

Writing folder 3

Paper 2 Part 2 Stories 1

SB pages 42–43

Candidates have a choice of questions in Part 2 and one of these may be a story. Tell students that the sentence given must be included in their answer or they will be penalised.

1 Ask students to discuss the range of tenses needed in pairs. Remind them that the given sentence in *a* comes at the beginning, whereas the other one ends the story. This discussion picks up on the review of past tenses from Unit 5 and the work on conditional structures in Unit 6.

Answers
a There could possibly be some continuation of the third conditional structure (talking about what would have happened if he hadn't picked up the phone), but the story must focus on actual past events, mainly using the past simple.
b Because of this final sentence, the past perfect will be needed earlier in the narrative, along with past simple and possibly past continuous.

2 Explain that the sample answer contains both sentences. Ask students to read the answer and say which past tenses have been used.

Answers
past perfect, past continuous, past simple

Extension activity

Ask students to underline the examples of these tenses and explain why they have been used rather than the past simple.

Answers
past perfect: had lifted, had heard, had been taken (passive) – all three examples are used because they refer to earlier events in the narrative.
past continuous: were demanding, were waiting, was crying – used to reflect continuous states.
was pulling away – used to describe the bus in the act of pulling away. Point out to students that if the past simple was used here, he could not have jumped on the bus!

3 Explain to students that in the exam their range of language will be assessed. Encourage them to use a variety of words, as illustrated in 1 and 2. Explain that although 'went' is correct in both places in the sample answer, the narrative can be improved by using different verbs, which have more impact on the reader.

Ask students to decide which verb should be used in 1 and 2 instead of 'went'.

Answers
1 A   2 C

In pairs students look at spaces 3–5 in the sample answer and discuss which adverbs would work best.

Answers
3 suspiciously   4 nervously/anxiously OR desperately
5 wildly OR nervously/anxiously

4 Ask students to reorder the sentences to fit the picture sequence. Explain that using a variety of sentence openers in a story is another indication of good range of language, and shows that attention has been paid to the organisation of the story.

Answers
Order: g, e, b (Suddenly...), h (Without a second thought...), d, f, a (By now...), i (Eventually...), c (At first ...)

5 Try to allow time in class for paired discussion of content ideas and range of language to be used. The story can then be set for homework. Remind students that they must write within the word length (120–180 words) and include the sentence given.

Sample answer

As soon as he got out of the car, Martin felt uneasy. He was in the middle of nowhere, with only a few sheep for company. Why had he agreed to meet Martha and John so far away from the city? It had been Martha's idea to go for this picnic on a Scottish hillside. Now, in mid-November, the whole thing seemed completely crazy. To make matters worse, they were late. Or was he in the wrong place? Perhaps he had missed a turning, or misread their map. He felt more and more anxious, and sighed as he pictured his nice, warm flat in Edinburgh.

Just then, he heard the unmistakable noise of Martha's Vespa and saw them climbing slowly up the hill. He recognised the little scooter immediately, as Martha had painted it bright pink. He shouted and waved, and soon they were there beside him. John gave Martin a big bear hug. "Happy birthday, mate," he said, "we've brought your birthday cake!" Martha grinned at them both and at that moment the sun came out. It was a truly memorable afternoon.

ⓣeaching extra

Suggest that students have a file where they keep all their written work. They should date each piece so that they can review the whole file regularly and see how much progress they have made. If students are willing and it is appropriate, ask them to do a second draft, based on your comments and corrections. This is a very efficient way of improving writing skills, and allows students to learn from their mistakes.

Units 1–6 Revision

SB pages 44–45

Lesson plan

Topic review   15–20'
Grammar   10–15'
Phrasal verbs   10–15'
Tense revision   30–40'

SV Omit the Topic review; allow students to do phrasal verbs for homework, with an English-English dictionary.

LV Ask students to write short compositions, 60–80 words each, on two of the review topics.

The aim of this unit is to go over some of the main points covered in Units 1–6. With the exception of the Topic review, this unit can be done as a test or for homework.

Topic review

1 Ask students to work in pairs. They need to look at questions a–j and talk about whether the statements are true for them or not. Encourage them to go into detail, not just say 'yes' or 'no'. The point of this exercise is to get students to use some of the vocabulary and language they have studied, but in a personalised way. This part of the Revision unit is designed to be integrated with the other revision exercises if wanted, or to be done completely separately.

Grammar

2   This passage is about the sort of claims an insurance company receives from holidaymakers. The stories are all true. Students should read through the passage carefully and then fill in the spaces with ONE word only.

> **Answers**
> **1** of   **2** on   **3** the   **4** some   **5** has/have   **6** while/when
> **7** for   **8** was   **9** if   **10** enough   **11** because   **12** who
> **13** but   **14** his   **15** from

Phrasal verbs

3   This section is divided into three sections – phrasal verbs with '*up*', with '*out*', and then verbs/phrases that can be replaced with a phrasal verb. All the phrasal verbs tested here appear in Units 1–6. This exercise would make a good dictionary exercise – it is essential to get students used to using an English-English dictionary at an early stage. Translation dictionaries should be kept at home and used as a last resort.

If students are finding this exercise difficult, and most do, then give them some clues to help them. Tell them how many letters are in the word, maybe what the first letter is, etc. Encouragement should be the key here.

> **Answers**
> **a** save   **b** ring/call/phone   **c** dress   **d** end   **e** put
> **f** stand   **g** sort   **h** work   **i** go   **j** make   **k** to cut down
> **l** an upturn   **m** you take back   **n** to set off/out for
> **o** to get over

Revision of present and past tenses

4   Ask students to read through the passage carefully and then decide on the correct present or past tense for the verbs. Sometimes more than one answer is correct.

> **Answers**
> **1** are   **2** seems   **3** are   **4** sees   **5** has been trying
> **6** has done/been doing   **7** developed/has developed
> **8** is   **9** has put/puts   **10** has had   **11** came
> **12** had never flown   **13** had had   **14** took   **15** never worried
> **16** announced   **17** were going   **18** had/had had
> **19** had tried/tried   **20** overcame   **21** managed

5   This exercise is the type of question found in Paper 3 Part 3. Students should keep in mind that there is a maximum of five words only, and that contractions count as two words.

> **Answers**
> **1** wouldn't go dancing unless   **2** worst film I've ever
> **3** would have met you   **4** aren't allowed to
> **5** more frightened of ghosts than
> **6** shouldn't have bought you
> **7** had (already) started   **8** see to drive without

Paper 1 Part 3

You are going to read a magazine article about a safari guide. Eight sentences have been removed from the article. Choose the most suitable sentence from the list **A–I** for each part (**1–7**) of the article. There is one extra sentence which you do not need to use. There is an example at the beginning (**0**).

A hair-raising experience!

Safari guide Pete Johnson had found a good place to camp. But it turned out not to be quite as good as he first thought.

After three days of driving our truck through the heat and dust of northern Botswana, my assistant John and I were covered in sweat and mud and looking forward to cleaning ourselves up. **0 I** Our enquiries had led us to a disused and abandoned public campsite.

The cool shade of the thick bush and towering trees in this secluded clearing was a welcome change from the scorching heat. This deserted place, famous for lions and wild dogs, was perfect and far away from the main tourist areas. After dusting ourselves down, we gazed over the deserted site. **1** How would the film crew, several weeks behind us and hoping for some comfort, take to it? We began to investigate the area.

Nearby we found a large rusty reservoir tower. **2** With broken window frames, missing doors and a damaged roof, the washing block was a horrible eyesore in this otherwise beautiful area. For our purposes, however, it was ideal, and I was delighted to find that water still flowed through the showerheads. This would provide a week or two of relative luxury for the film crew, as they had had to make do with a bucket shower up to now.

Pleased with our find, yet too tired to move on that afternoon, John and I set up an overnight camp. Once it was established, I excitedly headed for the cool darkness of the shower block, armed with four-days-worth of dirty clothing and a bar of soap to begin my laundry. Just how did the windows, doors and roof of the building become so damaged, I wondered? **3**

While kneeling down at a shower basin, rinsing the last of the soapsuds out of my travel-stained clothes, I was startled by a loud slithering noise. It was the beginning of my nightmare. **4** I realised that it was not a large snake, but an elephant who had expertly inserted its trunk through the window and was now sucking up water.

Suddenly, another trunk coiled through the window right above me, sniffed the air and proceeded to suck up my laundry water. I was now absolutely petrified and began to nervously edge away on my knees, making slowly for the door. I knew that if any one of the elephants sensed me and panicked, they might easily injure or kill me. I had only moved a few inches, but before I reached the door yet another trunk burst in, this time through a hole in the corrugated roof, and found its way into one of the lidless water tanks. **5**

There was nothing I could do but stay perfectly still in the corner, listening to the sounds of bits of roofing being torn away and the deafening sucking up of water. **6** I remained frozen where I was for a few moments to make sure they had gone, then stood up and stumbled out into the welcoming sunlight.

7 The animals had disappeared into the bush as if they had never been there. Feeling dazed I bundled up my laundry and quickly boarded up the doorway to the shower block with pieces of roofing. The film crew would have to make do with bucket showers after all.

A I glanced over my shoulder towards the source of the noise, and my eyes immediately fixed on a huge grey serpent-like thing that was slithering through one of the high windows.

B This ugly construction provided essential dry-season water for the old washing block on the edge of the camp clearing.

C There was no sight nor sound of the herd.

D And beyond it, two more of them were swinging their way towards me.

E Though quiet, the campsite also looked completely run down.

F After several terrifyingly long minutes, the elephants stopped drinking as quickly as they had started and moved quietly away.

G I was about to find out.

H I was now surrounded.

I As professional safari guides we were looking for good base-camp locations in the Savuti National Park before our film crew arrived.

© Cambridge University Press, 2000

Paper 2 Part 1

1   You ordered three computer games from a mail-order company and you are disappointed with the company.

Read the original advertisement, on which you have made some notes. Then, using all the information, write a letter of complaint to the company, *GamesDirect*.

GAMESDIRECT

GamesDirect is a specialist company supplying computer games worldwide.
We offer:

◆ the friendliest service

*Phone our order hotline and you
will be pleasantly surprised.* — v. unhelpful – and rude

◆ the widest choice

*We stock almost every game
produced on this planet!* — disagree, e.g. …

◆ the fastest delivery times

All orders are sent out within 48 hours. — not true – first game, Quake = three weeks (still waiting for two more)

◆ the lowest prices

*If you find a game cheaper anywhere else,
we will refund the difference
between the two prices.* — Yes please: your price for Quake 49 Euros – local shop 45 Euros!

Order now on 07953 632100 – you won't be disappointed! — I am! Where is rest of order???

Write a **letter** of between **120** and **180** words in an appropriate style.
Do not include any postal addresses.

Paper 3 Part 3

For Questions **1–10**, complete the second sentence so that it has a similar meaning to the first sentence, using the word given. **Do not change the word given**. You must use between two and five words, including the word given.
Here is an example (**0**).

Example:

0   I have never been to Paris before.

     time

     This .... have been to Paris.

     The gap can be filled by the words 'is the first time I' so you write:

0	is the first time I

---

1   There's a possibility the plane will be delayed so take a book to read.
    case
    You should take a book to read .... delayed.

2   I will only feed your dog if it is friendly.
    not
    I will .... it is friendly.

3   I've never had such uncomfortable shoes.
    far
    These shoes are .... ones I've ever worn.

4   Winning the lottery is less probable than being hit by lightning.
    likely
    You are .... by lightning than win the lottery.

5   Fancy dress is optional at the party on Saturday night.
    have
    You .... fancy dress at the party on Saturday night.

6   Some people think Agatha Christie was the best crime writer ever.
    than
    Some people think no one has ever .... Agatha Christie.

7   It's not necessary for Pete to get a visa for Canada.
    need
    Pete .... a visa for Canada.

8   How long is it since you travelled abroad?
    last
    When .... abroad?

9   I haven't had a holiday for nearly a year.
    since
    It .... I had a holiday.

10 Smoking in the cinema is forbidden.
    permitted
    You .... in the cinema.

© Cambridge University Press, 2000

Paper 3 Part 5

For Questions **1–10**, read the text below. Use the word given in capitals at the end of each line to form a word that fits in the space in the same line. There is an example at the beginning (**0**).

Example: | 0 | beautiful |

THE HIDDEN FACE OF BEAUTY

Cleopatra was not (**0**) _beautiful_ , at least according to her portrait on	**BEAUTY**
coins. But she was loved by very (**1**) ..... men, like Caesar and	**POWER**
Anthony. The (**2**) ..... of beauty is similar everywhere. For	**APPRECIATE**
example, many people think Sharon Stone is an (**3**)	**ATTRACT**
woman. Males can (**4**) ..... handsome men, and females	**IDENTITY**
lovely women. We don't learn this (**5**) ..... , we're born with it.	**RESPOND**
We also believe that good-looking people are more (**6**) ..... ,	**LIKE**
competent and intelligent. It is an extremely (**7**) ..... form of	**PLEASANT**
stereotyping.	
However, in one (**8**) ..... experiment, researchers brought a	**REMARK**
group of (**9**) ..... together for an hour a day. Happily, after four	**STRANGE**
days, factors such as (**10**) ..... had become more important	**FRIEND**
than looks.	

Paper 4 Part 2

You will hear an interview with Steve Haynes, a man who loves going on rollercoaster rides. For Questions **1–10**, complete the sentences.

In order to travel cheaply, Steve worked for _____ **1**

He says he's ridden _____ **2** of the world's rollercoasters.

Members of his club include a _____ and some _____ **3**

The members of the club usually don't need to _____ **4** when they go to theme parks.

The club members prefer rides which have a _____ **5** construction.

One member is terrified of _____ **6**

Richard Dawes is spending _____ **7** on a rollercoaster trying to break a record.

The first ride was made out of a railway originally designed to carry _____ **8**

It took the rollercoaster at Coney Island three weeks to make a _____ **9**

Steve loves rollercoasters mainly because they remind him of _____ **10**

© Cambridge University Press, 2000

Paper 1 Part 3

1 E   2 B   3 G   4 A   5 H   6 F   7 C

Paper 2 Part 1

Sample answer

Dear Sirs

Last month, I ordered three computer games from your company, two of which have still not arrived. Your advertisement promised good service and value for money, but I have been seriously disappointed.

When I placed the order by phone, your sales staff were extremely unhelpful and even rude to me. As for your claim to have 'the fastest delivery times', it took three weeks for Quake to arrive, and as I said above, I am still waiting for Red Alert and Civilizations.

The advertisement also stated that GamesDirect have 'the widest choice' of any mail-order company, but this is just not true. I was told by your staff that both FIFA 99 and NHL 99 were unavailable, but have since purchased them at a local store without difficulty. To cap it all, in this same shop I found Quake on sale for 45 Euros, whereas your price was 49 Euros. I would be grateful if you could refund me the difference without delay.

I look forward to hearing from you, and to receiving the rest of my order.

Yours sincerely

Harry Howes

Paper 3 Part 3

1   in case the plane is
2   not feed your dog unless
3   by far the most uncomfortable
4   more likely to be hit
5   don't/do not have to wear / have the option to wear / have the choice of wearing
6   written crime stories/novels better than/written better crime stories than
7   doesn't/does not need to get
8   did you last travel
9   is nearly a year since
10 are not permitted to smoke

Paper 3 Part 5

1 powerful   2 appreciation   3 attractive   4 identify
5 response   6 likeable   7 unpleasant   8 remarkable
9 strangers   10 friendship

Paper 4 Part 2

1 an airline company   2 90%/ ninety per cent
3 pop star, film actors   4 queue   5 wooden   6 flying
7 a/one month/four/4 weeks   8 coal   9 profit
10 (his) childhood/youth

Tapescript

Presenter: Welcome to the programme, Steve. When did you first get into rollercoasters?

Steve: Well, I was six when I first realised what a great thing a rollercoaster was. I was on the Pleasure Beach at Blackpool in England – it was 1973. By the time I was a teenager, riding the rollercoasters had become my main aim in life. I left school as soon as I could, in order to earn enough money to rollercoaster my way around Europe. In my mid-twenties I got a job with an airline company. Using my staff discount on air travel, I went round the world looking for great rides.

Presenter: You're now the chairman of Britain's Rollercoaster Club. Have you ridden on every rollercoaster in the world?

Steve: I've ridden ninety per cent of them. My flat is full of models, badges, signs, T-shirts, baseball caps and other bits of rollercoaster stuff. When I'm not on a rollercoaster, I'm watching American movies about them.

Presenter: About how many rides do you take in a year?

Steve: Probably 1,000 in an average year.

Presenter: That's amazing! And is this passion of yours shared by many people?

Steve: Oh, yes, I'm not alone. I set up the Club ten years ago and I have 1,500 members from seventeen countries. They range in age from four to ninety. One of our members is a famous pop star and we've got a few film actors, too.

Presenter: So, what do you all do?

Steve: About once a month we try to meet up at some theme park in the UK to ride the rollercoaster. The parks usually set aside time especially for us so we can ride around in peace, free of queues. Last month we met at

Beechdale which has the best wooden rollercoaster in the world. These days, most rollercoasters are made of steel, but to us, nothing beats one made of wood. The steel ones might be faster and higher, but wooden ones are more beautiful.

Presenter: Do you see yourself as the keenest member of the Club?

Steve: No, not at all. One of the members has ridden the Beechdale ride more than 635 times. He lives near it and plans to ride it over a thousand times next season. The funny thing is that he'd like to go to the States to try some of the American rollercoasters – but he's scared stiff of flying.

Presenter: Your members are always trying to break records, aren't they?

Steve: Oh yes, at the moment we have Richard Dawes, an American who's trying to break his own record of riding a rollercoaster non-stop for a month. During the ride he will eat, drink and sleep on the ride. The main problem is being in the open air. Your face swells and you get windburns.

Presenter: Were the first rollercoasters from the USA?

Steve: Well, the Americans were the first to make them into a commercial success. The Russians were riding on ice-slides in the 15th century, and there were gravity rides in Paris in the early 19th century. The first gravity railway began in Pennsylvania, USA. It was built in 1827 to carry coal, but was then gradually turned over to tourism and became the second most popular attraction in North America, after Niagara Falls, in the mid-1870s. The first real rollercoaster was built at Coney Island in 1884 and went into profit in three weeks.

Presenter: So, what's the attraction for you? Is it the speed?

Steve: I do care about the height and the speed of course, but it's really the atmosphere – it's old-fashioned in many ways and takes me back to the time of my childhood. I don't think I'll ever grow out of it somehow.

Presenter: Well, thank you for …

© Cambridge University Press, 2000

UNIT 7 Life's too short

Unit topic	Sport
7.1	
Vocabulary	Sports equipment
Speaking	Discussion using gerunds for likes and dislikes
Grammar focus	Gerunds and infinitives I
7.2	
Speaking	Famous sports personalities
	Dangerous sports
Exam skills	Listening Paper 4 Part 3
Vocabulary	Where you do sport
Pronunciation	Question tags
Word formation	

Workbook contents

7.1 SB pages 46–47

Lesson plan

Speaking	25–30'
Grammar	50–60'

SV Set 8 for homework.
LV See notes below for 1.

1 In pairs, students look at the illustrations of the different sports equipment a–n. They write down what each is called. If time allows, this exercise can be done as a quiz in teams.

Answers
a swimming goggles and hat **b** ski sticks and skis
c football **d** rugby ball **e** table tennis bats and ball
f ice skates **g** golf clubs and ball **h** shuttlecocks – badminton **i** basket for basketball **j** squash racket and ball **k** baseball bat **l** tennis racket and ball
m oars – rowing **n** volleyball

Extension activity

Put students in teams and then ask one team to describe the rules of a game. The other team has to guess what the game is.

2 In pairs, students ask each other the questions a–f. Draw students' attention to the fact that some of the questions contain an -*ing* word.

Teaching extra

Point out that many verbs and phrases to do with liking and disliking are followed by -*ing*.

can't stand hate dislike loathe detest don't mind adore love be keen on feel like enjoy be interested in

3 Students will be familiar with the idea of the -*ing* form, but may not know exactly what it is. Explain that it is a verb which is used as a noun. It is important to point out that not all -*ing* forms are gerunds and the exercise is designed to make students aware of this.

Answers
a adjective (the kind of rope)
b participle (past continuous tense)
c gerund (gerund – subject of sentence)

4 Explain that students need to decide which of a–e goes with 1–5. The aim is to make them aware of the common uses of the gerund in English.

Answers
a 4 **b** 1 **c** 5 **d** 2 **e** 3

5 Some verbs and adjectives are followed by a preposition and we usually use a gerund after them. Students should watch out for verbs followed by *to* as a preposition. Common ones are *to look forward to doing* and *to object to doing*. They are frequently tested. There is a selection of common verbs which are followed by a gerund in the Grammar folder, page 201.

Answers
a in getting **b** of learning **c** on teaching
d for dropping **e** in doing **f** at swimming
g to playing

6 This exercise looks at the infinitive. Explain that an infinitive is usually, but not always, *to* plus the base verb, e.g. *to do*. Students need to match sentences a–f with the explanations 1–6. Before they start, check that they understand the terms in 1–6.

7 Students read through the letter before doing the exercise. They then have to decide whether to change the verb in brackets to a gerund or add *to* or a preposition, or leave the verb as it is.

Answers
1 climbing 2 tell 3 arriving 4 training 5 to assess
6 to make 7 to teach 8 mountaineering 9 to make
10 count 11 climbing 12 to sleep 13 reaching
14 jumping 15 to seeing 16 tell

8 Gerunds and infinitives are frequently tested in Part 3 of Paper 3. This exercise can be set for homework, if time is short.

Answers
1 accused him of pushing
2 is too wet to
3 had difficulty in learning
4 advised me not to go
5 would rather go on
6 insisted on our playing / insisted that we played

7.2 SB pages 48–49

Lesson plan

Speaking	10–15'
Listening	15–20'
Vocabulary	5–10'
Pronunciation	20–30'
Word formation	10–15'

SV Omit 1 and 5; set 10 for homework.
LV See notes below for 4 and 8.

1 In pairs students discuss the questions. Draw students' attention to the differences between *go*, *play* and *do* a sport. The photographs are of:

a – Nicholas Anelka (French footballer)
b – Marion Jones (US 100m sprinter)
c – Rubens Barichello (Brazilian racing driver)
d – Axel Merckx (Belgian cyclist)
e – Jelena Dokic (Australian tennis player)

Answers
I go swimming, windsurfing, abseiling, motor racing, powerboat racing, etc.
I play football, hockey, golf, tennis, etc.
I do aerobics, gymnastics, etc.

2 Refer students to the Exam spot. This part of the unit is looking at Paper 4 Part 3. The students hear five people speaking and have to match each speaker to one of six options. Play the first extract and ask students to name the sport. They may not know the name in English, but will be familiar with what it is.

Answers
bungee jumping (ground far away, jumps, attached to a rope)

3 Ask students to read through the options and check that they understand what they mean. Play the tape twice and ask students to mark down their answers.

Answers
1 E 2 A 3 D 4 C 5 F

Tapescript

Speaker 1: All of us in the office where I work love doing it, probably because we're all desperate to get out of that 9–5 routine. It's an expensive sport but we all joined a Dangerous Sports Club to help keep costs down. The first time I did it I really was frightened as the ground seemed so far away, but I said to myself that nothing would happen and I wasn't going to die. I did my first two jumps in Canada and then in London. Apparently, in Germany they're doing it without being attached to a rope but with just a net beneath. That could be pretty scary, couldn't it?

Speaker 2: About four years ago I was very ill and nearly died. Sometime later I was involved in a serious car crash. It made me realise how risky everyday life is, and it seemed to cure me of fear, so I said to myself why not push things to the limit? So, I had a go at white-water rafting in the States and then moved on to other things. It's been brilliant. I've done all sorts of things from abseiling down mountains to skydiving. The skydiving was the worst! Now I set myself challenges all the time, not that I've got anything to prove, it's just a personal thing really. I'm thinking of doing river sledging next.

Speaker 3: I took part in a trek to ski across the Arctic last year. It was probably the most dangerous thing I've ever done, but I'd do it again tomorrow. I was conscious all the time that death was very near and in a strange way that made it seem more fun. I cried in absolute terror sometimes, especially when the ice began to melt and great holes would suddenly appear just in front of me. It was the ultimate challenge for a skier like myself and I guess I'm not afraid of anything any more. In fact, I'm looking forward to skiing in the Antarctic next year!

Speaker 4: I've always enjoyed diving as it's quite an exciting sport, but last winter I had the ultimate experience of going shark-feeding in the Caribbean. The sharks were about three metres in length and obviously they are quite aggressive and can bite you, but if you put on the right protective clothing and take precautions it's no more of a risk than driving fast motor cars. I must say I had more accidents when I went horse riding. I did feel a bit nervous as I went over the side of the boat, after all, I've seen *Jaws* like everyone else! But I was never in any real danger.

Speaker 5: Some of my mates had started doing this free climbing – you know where you don't use ropes, only your hands and feet. I guess they needed to have a bit of excitement in their lives, didn't they? Me, I think I get enough from my job as a motorbike courier in London. Anyway, I went with them one weekend. It was terrifying and I was sure I'd end up lying in a hospital bed, but I felt I had to do it, especially with them looking on. There was no pressure from them, but you know how it is. Anyway, I did it and I have to say it gave me a real 'buzz'. I can understand why people go in for this type of thing now.

4   If time allows, follow this activity with a discussion on dangerous sports.

Answers
1   bungee jumping
2   white-water rafting, abseiling, skydiving, river sledging (going down rapids on a small sledge)
3   skiing
4   diving, driving fast cars, horse riding
5   free climbing (without a rope or harness)
---

5   This exercise checks students know the names of places where these sports take place.

Answers
a 2   b 4   c 1   d 3   e 6   f 5
---

6   Play the tape so that students can hear the two examples of question tags. Point out that question tags are very common in English, but that they are very difficult for students to do properly. There are two main aims to this part of the unit. One is to make students aware of the grammar involved and the type of exceptions there are, and the other is to make them aware of when a question tag is not a real question. There is some practice in intonation work, but students will find it quite difficult and there's little point spending too long on it at this level.

First check they understand the form of a question tag and they know which part of a verb is repeated. Play the tape so they hear the examples.

Tapescript

1

That could be pretty scary, couldn't it?
I guess they needed to have a bit of excitement in their lives, didn't they?

Then go through the sentences a–j with the class. These tags are ones which often give students problems.

Then play the next part of the tape and check that students can hear the difference in intonation between the two sentences. Tell them that, although *It's a nice day, isn't it?* has a question mark at the end, the voice doesn't go up; it is spoken as if it were a statement.

Tapescript

2

It's a nice day, isn't it?
You haven't got change for £5, have you?

7   This exercise gives practice in using questions tags. Ask students to form pairs, one of them being the editor of a local newspaper, the other a reporter who needs a job. Tell the editors that they need to imagine they have received a CV from the reporter and for the first six or seven questions they are just checking the answers, they are not real questions.

Then the editor must ask real questions using question tags. Students should, at this stage be able to distinguish the difference in intonation, even if they can't reproduce it perfectly.

To end the exercise, give students a test on whether they can spot a real question or not. Put up the two intonation patterns on the board and then read out eight sentences. Students have to decide which intonation pattern is being used, A or B.

8   The aim of this exercise is to check that students have grasped the grammar element of question tags.

Answers
a wouldn't you?   b aren't I?   c can you?   d won't you?
e don't they?   f won't there?   g will you?   h haven't you?
i don't you?
---

9 This exercise can be set for homework, if time is short. Students read through the article and decide what changes need to be made to the word in brackets, so that it makes sense in the sentence.

> **Answers**
> 1 famous   2 ensure   3 qualified   4 training
> 5 youth   6 demanding   7 movement   8 education
> 9 qualifications   10 freedom

10 These words are all adjectives.

> **Answers**
> a danger   b fear/fright   c risk   d aggression
> e protection   f nerve(s)/nervousness   g terror
> h excitement

Exam folder 4

Paper 3 Part 1
Multiple choice cloze

SB pages 50–51

Although this is the first part of Paper 3, students should realise that they can do the five parts of the paper in any order they want. Make sure students read through the advice which is given in this part of the Exam folder, especially about reading the passage from beginning to end before they start deciding on answers. They might easily get an answer wrong if they don't understand the meaning of the whole passage. There are fifteen spaces and four options for each space with an example at the beginning.

In this introduction there are five categories of words which are often tested on this part of the paper. They are:

Expressions
Verb/Adjective + preposition
Phrasal verbs
Linking words
Vocabulary

Ask students to read through the categories and look at the examples. These explain how to get the correct answer.

Students should then read through the passage on the history of football very carefully. Although they are not allowed to have a dictionary in the examination, it is good policy for them to use an English-English dictionary in class and at home.

Put students in pairs and ask them to decide on the correct option from A, B, C or D. They should also be able to give a reason for their choice.

> **Answers**
> 1 B   2 C   3 A   4 C   5 A   6 D   7 B   8 B   9 A
> 10 D   11 C   12 C   13 B   14 A   15 B

Make sure that students read through the information in the Vocabulary spot, and that they understand what it involves. Learning vocabulary in this way is the key to doing well in this examination.

UNIT 8 Downshifting

8.1 SB pages 52–53

Lesson plan

Speaking	15–20'
Reading	40–50'
Speaking	10–20'

SV Omit 6.
LV See notes below for 1.

1 Ask students to think about their own jobs or those of their parents. In pairs ask them to describe what they do or their parents do and how they feel about it. Then ask them to think back to their grandparents' day and discuss the differences that there were.

Extension activity

Students could talk about different periods in the past – Stone Age man, the Ancient Egyptians, etc. Divide the students into groups and ask them to choose a certain time period. Get them to write down five or six sentences about what people *used to do/would do* during that time, and then ask them to read them out to the class.

2 It is important that students compare and contrast the photos, not just describe them.

The first two are of commuters in New York and of people in a village all helping with the harvesting.

The second two are of an old woollen mill with a lot of workers and of a factory run by robots.

3 Explain that 'downsizing' is when a company decides to reduce the number of staff employed or to move offices somewhere cheaper. Ask students to skim the passage to find out what 'downshifting' is.

Background information

'Downshifting' is when people decide they don't want to carry on working in a large city or for a large company. Underlying is the idea that quality of life is more important than money or prestige. They usually move out to the countryside for a better life.

4 Refer students to the Exam spot. Ask them to read the passage more carefully and to find the answer for question 1. They should then look at the explanation to see if they were right.

Get students to do the rest of the questions, making sure that they are aware of the different types of question that they might meet on this paper. There are usually 7–9 questions and there could be reference, idiom, global as well as detail questions.

Answers
1 C 2 B 3 D 4 B 5 C 6 D 7 C

5 Finish the topic with a quick round-up discussion on the ideas in the text.

6 Allow students to remind themselves of the language of opinion, agreement and disagreement. Refer them to the expressions in the box. It is all too easy for students just to use *I think, No, you're wrong* and *Yes*. They need to practise using more varied language. Explain that a more varied vocabulary gains more marks in the speaking part of the examination.

Students can be given one of these topics for written homework. Ask them to choose the topic which interests them most and to write a short paragraph about it.

7

Answers
para 1 – volume, stuffed with, horrified   para 2 –
single-minded pursuit   para 3 – approach, radical
para 4 – swapping   para 5 – suburbs   para 6 – run

8.2 SB pages 54–55

Lesson plan

Grammar	30–35'
Listening	20–25'
Vocabulary	25–30'

SV Omit 4; set 5 for homework.
LV See notes below for 1 and 5.

1 and 2   The aim of this section is to clarify the differences between *would/used to do* and also between *used to do* and *be/get used to doing*. Students often confuse these structures and it is important they can differentiate between them as they are often tested.

would/used to
Students usually know *used to* at this level, but might not be familiar with *would* used in this way. If they find it a problem, give them some more examples.
When I lived in Paris I would take taxis everywhere, eat in restaurants and go out every night to nightclubs.
Point out that they can use *used to* when you use *would* but you can't use *would* for *used to*:
   You can say: *I used to have long hair.*
   You can't say: *I would have long hair.*
   You can say: *I used to go to town on the bus.*
   You can also say: *I would go to town on the bus.*

This is because we don't use *would* for past states or situations – only for past actions. Students might ask why they have to learn it and the simple answer is that it is a very common structure in narratives and also that it is tested at FCE. *Would* is more formal than *used to*.

Answers
1
a =1, b=3, c=2
2
a used to be   b correct   c used to have   d correct
e correct   f used to doing   g correct   h used to working
i are used to seeing   j correct   k correct   l correct

Extension activity

For more oral practice put students in pairs and ask them to talk about their relationship with their grandparents when they were younger, only using *would*. For example:
   My grandmother would let me help her do the baking.
   My grandfather would take me fishing. etc.

be/get used to doing and *used to do*
The problem that arises here is not usually in understanding the concept, more in getting the structure correct. Ask students in pairs to compare their past with their present. For example:
   I used to get up at seven o'clock when I was at school. Now I have a job I've had to get used to getting up earlier – at six thirty.
Point out that *be/get used to doing* can be used with all tenses. Refer students to the Grammar folder, page 201.

3   Check that students understand what all the jobs involve. Ask them to talk about how they feel about each job – whether they would be interested in doing this kind of job and why.

Play the tape and ask them to decide which jobs the speakers do. Clues to the answers are in bold in the tapescript.

Background information

A *gig* is a performance somewhere – at a club or a stadium.

Answers
Speaker 1: window cleaner
Speaker 2: dentist
Speaker 3: pop singer
Speaker 4: plumber/heating engineer
Speaker 5: chef

Tapescript

Speaker 1: It was quite a good job, but I never got used to working at the top of a **ladder**. I've got **no head for heights** at all. **Cleaning** the ones in those large tower blocks was the worst. You also have to be careful not to look too closely as well. I often used to see things I shouldn't have done. People would forget I was outside and they would be inside having a big argument or having a bath.

Speaker 2: Well, life's much better now I don't spend my time listening to that **drill** going all day. It really got me down when people would arrive shaking with fear – I used to take it personally. The **anaesthetic** is so good these days that they really had nothing to be worried about. I'm running a bed and breakfast place in the country now. Much nicer, though not as well paid of course.

Speaker 3: Yeah, well it was great while it lasted. But look at me now – I look about twenty years older than I really am. We used to have to travel overnight to a different **gig** each evening. They used to put us up in good hotels but there were always one or two **fans** who managed to get through security and come looking for a souvenir. It wears you out after a while, you know.

Speaker 4: The best thing about it used to be people I'd meet. They would always be so pleased to see me. Well, wouldn't you be if you were **freezing** to death in the middle of winter? They'd be making me cups of coffee and offering me biscuits all day. They weren't so pleased when they got **the bill** though.

Speaker 5: It was the recession really that closed us down. We had a great **business** going and we used to be full every time we opened. There were great **reviews** in all the best newspapers and people would be queuing at the door. I suppose it couldn't last, though. I had a **team of six under** me, so all I had to do was be **creative** all day – great.

4   To follow on from the listening, ask students to work in pairs. They both think of a job they used to do, but don't tell their partner what it is. They then take it in turns to talk about it and their partner has to guess what the job was.

5   Students have to think of all the people who work in the places listed. Try to get them to think around the subject, not just coming up with the obvious people.

Answers
1   captain, purser, steward, mate, chef, waiter
2   headmistress/headmaster/principal, teacher, caretaker, secretary
3   matron, surgeon, doctor, nurse, porter, staff nurse, sister, consultant, specialist
4   manager/manageress, buyer, assistant, window dresser, accountant
5   manager, coach/trainer, cleaner, receptionist

Extension activity

This task can be expanded to include other places of work, e. g. a police station, a university.
You can also take a different approach and ask students to think about jobs connected with the production of a product. This exercise could then bring in the names of places where you buy a product. For example:
   fish – fisherman, fishmonger (sells fish)
   sheep – shepherd, farmer, butcher, chef
   milk – farmer, dairyman, shop assistant
   coal – miner, coal man (delivers coal)

6   Students are often confused by all the uses of *get* in English. In this exercise they have to replace *get* with another verb which means the same.

Answers
a must   b take/eat/have   c being/going to be/will be
d fetch/make   e received   f arrives/comes   g have
h persuade/ask/find/hire

7   There are two tasks which students need to do in this exercise. First of all, they must complete the sentences with one of the phrases in the box. Ask them to think about another way of saying the same sentence before they look at the next exercise.

Answers
a his guards   b my new boss   c your exams
d being made redundant   e his new job   f much money

Students now need to choose one of the verbs or phrases to replace the phrasal verb.

Answers
a escaped   b like   c pass   d recovered from
e making a success of   f manage

8   Ask students to find four examples of compound adjectives in the article.

Answers
single-minded, long-hours, time-consuming, better-balanced

9   Students can use a dictionary to help them make the changes asked for. This exercise could be set for homework.

Answers
a to horrify, horror
b to succeed, unsuccessful
c energetic, energetically
d nation/nationality, nationalise
e unemployed, employ
f responsible, irresponsible
g decisive, to decide
h commuter, commuting

Writing folder 4

Compositions 1

SB pages 56–57

Compositions are usually written for a teacher, usually as a follow-up to some class activity, such as a project or discussion. They include giving opinions and making suggestions on a given subject. They should be well-organised and students should always be encouraged to make a plan before they start writing. Students should bear in mind that an introduction and conclusion and good use of paragraphing will lead to better marks.

1   In this exercise students are given an example question and are asked to put sentences from a model composition in the right order. The aim of this exercise is to make students aware of linking words and their use. One problem at this level is that students too often use *and* and *but* in their writing. In the examination they will be assessed on how well they use linking words and how well they organise their work.

Putting sentences in order is a task which requires a certain amount of concentration. Give students a time limit, which you can extend by five minutes if they haven't finished, so that they don't feel the task is never-ending.

As well as making them aware of linking words, this exercise also uses a reference word *this*.

> **Answers**
> 1 F   2 A   3 E   4 G   5 B   6 D   7 C

2   Paragraphing is a very important part of the FCE writing paper. Work which isn't paragraphed has a very poor effect on the target reader. Students should try to use a minimum of two and a maximum of four paragraphs in their compositions. They should avoid writing one-sentence paragraphs or listing.

> **Answers**
> paragraph 1 – F, A   paragraph 2 – E, G, B   paragraph 3 – D, C

3   In this model letter the student has used only *And*, *But* and *So*. The aim of this exercise is to try to get them to use one of the other words in the box. However, it is important they realise that not all these words are interchangeable. Sometimes the structure needs to change as well.

> **Answers**
> **And** – *in addition, moreover, furthermore*
> You can't use *as well as* in place of the first *And* because you're not joining two ideas which are the same. The subjects of the sentence are different.
>
> **And** – *in addition, moreover, furthermore, as well as*
> You can use *as well as* in place of the second *And* but you would need to change the structure so that it reads:
> *As well as working about 35 hours a week, they have 4 weeks' holiday a year.*
> The subject in both is *people in my country*.
>
> **But** – *However,*
> Notice that after *However* you need to use a comma.
>
> **But** – *However, Nevertheless*
> In place of the second *But* you can't use *in contrast* or *on the other hand*. This is because no contrast is being offered in that sentence – just a comment on what is happening.
>
> **So** – *As a result*
> **So** – *Therefore*
> In place of the second *so* you can't use *as a result*. You are not giving a result, just concluding your ideas, whereas in the first sentence with *so* there is a result.

4   There are a few places where this expression could be put. Students need to practise using this linker, as it is very useful. They need to be aware of the inversion after *not only*. This is not to form a question, even though it looks like one. The subject and verb are inverted because they follow a negative adverb.

> **Answers**
> Not only is there very little heavy industry, but most manufacturing is fully automated.
> Not only do they usually work about 35 hours a week, but they also have four weeks' holiday a year.
> Not only are there fewer jobs, but more people are also out of work.

5   This provides more practice in dividing work into paragraphs.

> **Answers**
> Paragraph one: First of all – holiday a year.
> Paragraph two: But in some countries – up until now.
> Paragraph three: But things – too hard.

6   Check that students understand both the useful expressions and the advice. Students should discuss the topic in class and then write the composition for homework.

UNIT 9 The hard sell

Unit topic	Advertising
9.1	
Grammar	Modals 2: Speculation and deduction
Vocabulary	Adjective-noun collocations
9.2	
Exam skills	Listening Paper 4 Part 2
	Speaking Paper 5 Part 3
Pronunciation	Sentence stress
Grammar extra	Order of adjectives
Workbook contents	
1, 2, 3	Reading – Part 3 gapped sentences
4	Grammar – modals
5	Use of English – Part 2
6, 7	Vocabulary – collocations, topic words

9.1 SB pages 58–59

Lesson plan

Grammar	50–65'
Vocabulary	5–10'
Speaking	15–15'

SV Set 6 as homework.
LV See notes below for 4 and 7.

1   Allow students around three minutes to speculate about the advert in pairs. Encourage them to use the sentence openers given, which exemplify the target structures for this lesson. Students can then look at the slogan on page 83. The advert is for the Renault Espace.

2   Ask students to read the information given in pairs and then discuss the second pair of examples.

Answer
No, in these examples, the speaker is certain (*must be*; *can't be*).

Now ask students to look at the final example given and try saying the statement to each other with and without the question mark.

Answer
When the sentence is read as a statement, the speaker is certain (the use of *possibly* reinforces this certainty). However, when a question mark is added, the utterance becomes a speculation (and the use of *possibly* becomes a 'hedging' device). As a question the words *could it* would sound better at the end.

Refer students to the Grammar folder, page 201 and ask them to read the first four points. Note the use of the question tag in the first example of the fourth point (question tags were covered in the last unit).

3   First, ask students to skim the text to find out what type of product the advert is for.

Answer
a hand cream

Background information

The Cannes Film Festival is held every May–June in the south of France, where a parallel Advertising Film Festival is also held.

Now ask students to read the text again more carefully, underlining all the examples of modal verbs. Don't draw attention to the example of a past action (*must have won*), as this is the focus of 5.

Answers
3rd paragraph: can't be; Might it be; Could it be
4th paragraph: must have won; couldn't

4   Ask students to work through a–f in pairs.

Answers
a spoken commentary played over a film
b a short, memorable tune, often with words, used to advertise a product
c someone famous
d decision
e one particular make of product
f clever

Check understanding of *brand non-attributes*, pointing out that the text goes on to explain this in the rest of the third paragraph. Remind students not to panic if they don't understand every word when they are reading; as this text shows, they will probably be able to deduce the meaning from the surrounding information.

Ask students to explain why the title is appropriate.

> **Answer**
> The expression *missed the boat* is an appropriate one, as it refers to the failure of Delvico Bates to meet the deadline for the festival.

ⓔxtension activity

Ask students whether they can suggest another exploitation of 'brand non-attributes', for example showing people who *wouldn't* use the product to reinforce the target users. Ask them to discuss in pairs why this approach might be effective in selling a product.

5 Remind students of the example of a past action in the text and then ask them to discuss examples a–c in pairs.

> **Answers**
> a sure b sure c unsure

Refer students to the explanation and examples in the Grammar folder, page 201.

6 If this is being done in class, suggest students work through the transformations on their own and then compare their answers in pairs.

> **Answers**
> 1 can't/couldn't (possibly) be 2 it must be
> 3 might be sung 4 must have had 5 must have been paid 6 couldn't/can't have been

7 Ask students to work in pairs, listing the possible phrases. Allow them five minutes for this.

> **Answers**
> huge: variety, budget, market, picture
> high: budget, voice
> low: budget, voice
> deep: message, character, voice
> shallow: message, idea, character,
> narrow: variety, market, picture, view (+ narrow ideas)
> wide: variety, market, picture

Refer students to the Vocabulary spot. Give them a few more examples of adjective-noun collocations, taking adjectives from previous units, such as:
initial (visit, reaction, impression) – Unit 6
aggressive (behaviour, attitude, play) – Units 2 and 7
pressured (lifestyle, job, career) – Unit 8

8 Put students into small groups of three or four. Those on the left side of the room follow instructions for Group A, while the others follow Group B's instructions, which are on page 83.

Allow students adequate time to prepare for the role play (at least five minutes). Recommend that they decide on their individual roles within the group, as well as discussing who will say what.

Move round the room to check on progress and supply any vocabulary needed. Try to make sure that dictionaries are available.

Match each Group A with a Group B and ask the Group B students to move, in order to join their Group A. Tell students that they will have five minutes for the face-to-face discussion, asking them to try to reach an agreement within this time. Then elicit the outcome of each meeting to find out what was agreed.

ⓣeaching extra

Role play can be an effective way of getting students to express themselves more fluently, particularly when opposing ideas are involved, as these often provoke extreme reactions! Encourage students to use their imagination to the full, giving them some initial suggestions if necessary.

9.2 SB pages 60–61

> **Lesson plan**
>
> | | |
> |---|---|
> | Listening (Part 1) | 10–10' |
> | Grammar extra | 5–15' |
> | Pronunciation | 10–10' |
> | Listening (Part 2) | 10–25' |
> | Speaking | 30–30' |
>
> **SV** Set Grammar extra exercise for homework.
> **LV** See Extension activities in 4 and 6.

1 Use the board to summarise vocabulary that comes up during this discussion. Start by reminding students of relevant vocabulary from 9.1: special effects, voice-over, jingle, brand, etc.

Students discuss their favourite/least-favourite commercials in pairs for about three minutes. Remind them that they should explain why they like or loathe them.

2 Allow students a minute to look through the phrases in a–h. Then play the tape, asking them to tick the phrases as they listen. Explain that this is to help them to listen out for key information.

> **Answers**
> a, d, f and h are mentioned.

Tapescript

Part 1

Man: There's one car advert that opens with part of a song by Bjork – it must have cost a <u>fortune</u> to make, and it looks tremendous …

Woman: I've seen that one. You're not sure what it's advertising to begin with, are you? A graceful silver vehicle moving through an unusual landscape … it could be a spacecraft of the future. All very stylish. The trouble is, it's a bit of a let-down when you realise it's just another <u>car</u> advert!

Man: Yes, the beginning <u>is</u> a bit misleading … It's funny, isn't it, sometimes the most effective ads are the really simple ones – you know, like a football manager sitting down at the breakfast table with his family, enjoying a particular cereal …

Woman: … he eats it so it <u>must</u> be good. And that actress from *Friends* advertising shampoo – Jennifer Aniston, wasn't it? You know, seeing famous people on screen can be a huge influence on us, we see them as … well, as role models.

Man: Definitely. … The ads they put on TV before the World Cup or the Olympics always use mega stars, don't they?

Woman: Yeah, remember the one that had a <u>whole team</u> of top footballers from around the world! The special effects were incredible – the budget must have been <u>huge</u> … all for <u>one</u> advert!

Man: But the company probably earned <u>millions</u> of dollars in increased sales, so for them it was worth it.

Check understanding and explain that students will hear the recording again later in the lesson.

Grammar extra

Ask students to identify the opinion adjective and discuss the order of adjectives in the example.

> **Answer**
> The order cannot be changed because an opinion adjective (*graceful*) always comes first.

Ask students to work through the slogans in pairs, identifying the types of adjective used.

> **Answers**
> Opinion adjectives: classic, sensational, popular, delicious
> Size: full-length, bite-sized
> Age: new
> Colour: navy
> Nationality: British
> Material: cotton, creamy

Students can either do this exercise in pairs in class, or for homework. Refer them to the Grammar folder, page 202 for further explanation.

> **Answers**
> a a huge black dog b ✓ c the famous Italian singer
> d a large red apple e an elaborate square wooden box
> f a sophisticated new novel by a tremendous Scottish author

3 Look at sentence *a* and ask if students can remember how the sentence was stressed. Then play the tape and ask students to underline the stressed word in each example as they listen. (See the tapescript.)

> **Answers**
> a fortune b car c is d must e whole team
> f huge … one g millions

4 Explain that students will hear the same speakers talking about one specific advertisement, which is for Bacardi rum. Ask students to read through statements 1–5 before they listen. This is an introduction to the 'Who says what?' task in Part 4 of the Listening paper. Students need to write M for the man, W for the woman, or B if the question applies to both speakers.

> **Answers**
> 1 M 2 W 3 B 4 M 5 W

Tapescript

Part 2

Woman: There's one advert I really like, partly because it's brilliantly put together …

Man: And it's for?

Woman: Bacardi – it's set on a tropical island somewhere in the Caribbean. And there's this radio DJ who's broadcasting in a studio and …

Man: Oh, not Ray on Reef Radio?

Woman: You've seen it too!

Man: Yep. Detest it, actually. All about some friend of Ray's who's leaving for the mainland and how he's going to miss his wonderful life on the island …

Woman: And you see what he's been up to – I adore the way the DJ, Ray, tells the storyline on air and you see flashbacks of the other guy … Like 'I know you're going to miss the way they serve Bacardi around here' – and you see a girl throw a glassful in the friend's face! Such a striking image and totally unexpected.

Man: Mmm, I suppose ads do work well when they contain something out of the ordinary – I guess they stick in your mind that way.

Woman: Right … and of course, the ending itself is unforgettable – quite spectacular, isn't it? Seeing the friend sailing away on the boat, listening to all this on his radio – and then, what does he do …

Man: He dives off the deck and swims back to the island.

Woman: For another night on the town and a glass of …

Man: Yes, yes … You know, I must admit that although I personally loathe the ad, it sells the product pretty well. It's got the right ingredients – you know, exotic location, powerful images …

Woman: So what <u>didn't</u> you like about it?

Man: The characters themselves, I think … especially Ray!

Woman: But come on, the very fact that you remember him now means he made an impact on you … which must mean that the ad has worked.

Man: True enough … And what about you? You said it makes you laugh, is that why you like it so much?

Woman: That … and the way it succeeds in telling a story in such a short time, I think that's quite clever, getting the message across like that. The music's great, too.

Man: But was it <u>truly</u> successful? I mean, did you dig into your pocket and buy a bottle?

Woman: Well, no … I don't drink spirits! I bet plenty of people were persuaded to rush out and buy some, though …

Extension activity

Ask if any students have seen the advertisement referred to on the tape. If so, elicit their opinions about it. If not, ask them to decide whether it sounds an effective way of selling an alcoholic drink, eliciting reasons why (not).

5   Play the tape again and then ask students to explain the phrases.

Answers
a   very well made/edited
b   an unusual and memorable sight
c   you remember something and think about it again
d   the essential parts
e   interesting (and faraway) place
f   had an effect on
g   communicating
h   buy

Photocopiable tapescript activity (⋯⟩ page 183)

Give out the tapescript as support for exercise 5. Then ask students to find the following vocabulary in the tapescript:

1   a verb meaning 'like a lot'
2   two verbs meaning 'hate'
3   three or more phrasal verbs
4   four or more ways of agreeing with someone

Answers
1   adore
2   detest; loathe
3   put together; be up to; sailing away; rush out
4   Yep; Mmm; Right … ;Yes, yes; True enough

You could also ask students to listen again and underline the stressed words in the discussion.

6   Have a brief class discussion on the important factors. This will consolidate new topic vocabulary, which is needed for the exam speaking task which follows.

Possible answers
high-quality production, striking images, memorable in some way, uses famous people, catchy jingle

Extension activity

Ask students to vote for the best commercial currently showing on television or at the cinema. Select a shortlist of four commercials and ask students to award each one 1 (good), 2 (very good) or 3 (excellent), for each of the following categories. They can do this in groups or as a whole class.

Storyline / images   Actors / voice-over
Music / jingle   Slogan / message

Add up the marks awarded and announce the winning commercial.

7   Refer students to the Exam spot and stress the fact that this is a 'shared' task, where the two candidates need to be sensitive to each other's opinions, and take turns to speak. Then ask students to read the task description. Check that they fully understand what they have to do.

8   Allow students five minutes to prepare their ideas and list useful vocabulary. They should do this on their own and then compare notes with another student.

Here is some information about each billboard, which contains relevant vocabulary.
a   Volkswagen Bora: the ad suggests that owners of the car will want to think up further reasons for taking long, time-consuming drives to inaccessible places, as driving the Bora is such a pleasurable experience.

b Vodafone: traffic cones on motorways and other busy roads are a major source of irritation to drivers. The ad shows a solution, by using the mobile phone to get advance warning.

c Electricity: the basset hound usually has a sad facial expression, with droopy ears and doleful eyes, and this is certainly the case in the left-hand image; however, the dog sitting in front of the loudspeaker on the right is animated, with ears raised.

d Dolphin: this ad for another mobile phone company suggests the many contexts where a mobile phone is useful or essential, and the slogan stresses the improved communication that results.

e Cable film: the ad is launching two new film channels on a cable TV company. The double clipper board image reinforces this.

f Daily Telegraph: because this is a serious newspaper, the ad sticks to text rather than visual images, playing on the common saying 'It's easy to be wise after the event'.

9 Ask students to discuss in pairs how they could approach the task. For example, they could take it in turns to deal with each photograph, or one student could identify all six products and the other evaluate the advertisements. Remind them about the need for equal talking time!

10 Tell students that they have three minutes to do the whole task. Remind them to use some of the phrases from 9.

11 Elicit which adverts are seen as the most effective.

Exam folder 5

Paper 3 Part 4 Error correction

SB pages 62–63

1 Stress that this part of the paper is testing grammar. This exercise raises awareness of the types of error that regularly come up in the exam. If done in class, students can work in threes, taking it in turns to find the error in each sentence.

> **Answers**
> A pronouns: 1 them 2 it 3 herself
> B articles: 4 a 5 the 6 the
> C modal verbs: 7 do 8 to 9 have
> D quantifiers: 10 some 11 of 12 much
> E prepositions: 13 to 14 of 15 for
> F phrasal verbs: 16 with 17 over 18 out

2 Refer students to the advice section. The text is a letter to a magazine.

3 Explain that the reason for reading the text through in complete sentences is that sentences usually stretch over more than one line, and the error can only be decided on by understanding the complete meaning of the sentence.

4 Checking in this way will eliminate any wrongly chosen errors.

> **Answers**
> 1 they 2 ✓ 3 that 4 being 5 ✓ 6 an 7 for
> 8 up 9 too 10 of 11 ✓ 12 so 13 him 14 the
> 15 than

5 Underline the importance of completing the answer sheet correctly and legibly, following the numbering of the task. If possible, take in a complete example of a Paper 3 answer sheet to show students.

UNIT 10 | The final frontier

Unit topic	Space
10.1	
Reading	Paper 1 Part 3 (gapped paragraphs)
Vocabulary	Signposting words in texts
Speaking	Discussion
10.2	
Grammar	Review of future tenses
Listening	Global meaning
Vocabulary	Phrases with *at*
Workbook contents	
1	Use of English – Part 1
2	Phrasal verbs
3, 4	Grammar – future tenses

10.1 SB pages 64–65

Lesson plan

Reading	50–60'
Vocabulary	10–15'
Speaking	10–15'

SV Keep discussion in 2 brief; set 8 as homework.
LV See notes below for 8 and 10.

1 Allow five minutes for this paired discussion. If necessary, put up the following vocabulary to help students. The two pictures show an artist's impression of astronauts working on the surface of another planet, with a landing craft and a science fiction still of people in stasis (deep sleep) during space travel.
Useful vocabulary:
astronauts: helmet, gravity, breathing apparatus, artificial light
stasis: suspended animation, timescale, solar system, intergalactic, light speed

Teaching extra

If you have access to the Internet, it is possible to research a topic area further. For example, the Space Frontier Foundation has its own Web site, and through a search engine such as Yahoo or Alta Vista, you will probably find many other relevant sites. Encourage students to do this for themselves as they will be using their English in a very practical way.

2 For a briefer activity, the three discussion topics could be given to groups in different parts of the room, with an optional reporting back phase on all three at the end.

3 Refer students to the Exam spot and remind them that Part 3 can either be a gapped sentence or a gapped paragraph task. The gapped sentence version was covered in Unit 6.

Ask students to read the title and opening paragraph. Explain that this part of a newspaper or magazine article often holds many clues to the overall content of the piece. Ask students to discuss its possible content in pairs.

4 Ask students to look at the two paragraphs and explain how the underlined words link back to the beginning of the article.

Answers
'Cheap' – title; 'more economical'
re-usable rockets – 'able to go into space again and again'
such a rocket – as above
different technology – the opposite of the rockets already mentioned

5 Ask students to skim the skeleton article first and then read it again, together with the handwritten notes. Allow them up to ten minutes to do this, as they have to think carefully about the relationship between the notes and the key words in the article.

Answers
1 above: Rick Tumlinson, Space Frontier Foundation, businesses; below: Tumlinson, in business, *Space: Open for Business*
2 above: conference in Los Angeles; below: Another company, Kistler Aerospace
3 no links with paragraph above; below: Their own view, NASA, SFF
4 above: opportunities for everyone, new choices; below: *ex*-astronaut, businessman, affordable, everybody can go enjoy
5 above: space hotel; below: If he, 2010, space tourism

6 Ask students which paragraph fits the first gap, and why.

Answer
Paragraph B. The beginning of paragraph A talks about companies, so does link to the end of the previous paragraph, but there is no mention of an individual person (*Tumlinson/he*). This means that paragraph A cannot fit above the sentence: *So Tumlinson is also in business to prove a point.*

7 Ask students to read the remaining paragraphs C–F and decide where they fit in the article. Point out that in the exam there is one extra paragraph, which is not used.

Answers
2 E   3 C   4 F   5 D

Refer students to the Vocabulary spot. Give them a few more examples of adjective-noun collocations, taking adjectives from previous units, such as:

initial (visit, reaction, impression) – Unit 6
aggressive (behaviour, attitude, play) – Units 2 and 7
pressured (lifestyle, job, career) – Unit 8

8 This exercise is to draw attention to the kinds of words which can act as signposts in the gapped paragraph task. It can be read at home if time is short.

Extension activity

Ask students to identify the part of speech in each example and to suggest similar words or opposites that might also behave as signposts.

Answers
a determiner *A second* ; adjective *different* (opposite)
b adjective   c verb *disagrees* (opposite), *supports*
d adverb *too*   e pronoun *many*   f verb *included*

9 Move round the room monitoring the discussion. Be ready to help students to explain the words and phrases, if they are struggling! They will find the words in the skeleton text as well as in paragraphs A–F. Some of the phrases are explained in the answer box.

Answers
doing business   businessman   company
economical, cheap   economics   budgets, schedules
profit, investors, commercial, taxpayers
controlling costs – keeping costs down
viable industry – an industry that is feasible to set up and will make money
billion dollar market – market worth a billion dollars
free enterprise – competing businesses, which can act without much government control
private sector – companies not controlled by the government

10 Suggest that students spend some time planning what they are going to say. They can time themselves on each point.

10.2 SB pages 66–67

Lesson plan

Grammar	30–40'
Use of English Part 4	0–10'
Listening	10–20'
Vocabulary	20–20'

SV Set 6 for homework; omit discussion in 7.
LV See notes below for 8.

1 Explain that this lesson reviews several ways of referring to the future, all of which students should already know. Suggest students work in pairs.

Answers
a future simple   b 'going to'   c present continuous
d future continuous   e (simple present – *plan to ...*)
f future perfect   g (simple present – *is due to ...*)
h future simple (passive)

2 Now ask students to match the five categories to the examples a–h.

Answers
1 (prediction): a, h   2 (planned event): c, e, g
3 (event that has not yet happened): f
4 (certain to remain true): d   5 (intention): b

3 Both examples use modals to talk about future predictions. Elicit the other modal that is used in this way: *might*.

4 This sentence contains reported speech with backshift (*once said ... would begin; says ... will begin*). Explain that students will be reviewing reported speech in Unit 13.

5 Allow students up to five minutes to complete the exercise and then check answers, eliciting reasons.

Answers
a will fall (not a continuous state)
b won't be (prediction rather than definite truth)
c may (prediction)
d will carry (future event + verb not tied to an end date)
e am going to (definite plan in the near future; intention)
f would (reported speech)
g will be living (future truth)
h will have been (anniversary has not yet happened)

6 Refer students to the advice given in Exam folder 5 on page 63. If doing the task in class, ask students to work through it on their own and then compare answers in pairs.

Answers
1 one 2 for 3 they 4 the 5 there 6 ✓ 7 who
8 most 9 did 10 ✓ 11 and 12 a 13 ✓ 14 more
15 to

Ⓔxtension activity

Ask students to look closely at the picture in pairs and speculate about which 'people' could be aliens, giving their reasons why. For example, one of the 'humans' has yellow eyes!

7 Students should listen for gist and global meaning, in order to decide whether the speakers express positive or negative views. Play the tape a second time so that students can confirm their answers.

Answers
Speakers 1 and 2 express negative views; Speaker 3 is positive.

Tapescript

Speaker 1: I find it quite scary actually. Films like *Bladerunner* could really come true. Imagine a city like Los Angeles in twenty years' time. I mean it's dangerous now, isn't it – remember the riots? People will be living in run-down buildings, too frightened to come out. Oil supplies will have run out, so there won't be any cars. And with global warming and El Niño, the climate is changing, so the lack of sunlight and pouring rain in the film may well be accurate … what LA weather will be like.

Speaker 2: I'm reading one of his sci-fi ones at the moment. It all happens way off in the future, thousands of years from now. There are human-<u>like</u> characters, but they're a very sophisticated race – we'll never be as clever as them! They live for at least three hundred years and after that, they can choose to live on in a different state. And there's no poverty, no war … For the human race, this seems completely unattainable – there will always be some country at war with another. I don't see a long-term future for the human race … even if our planet survives in one piece, we'll have wiped each other out or something.

Speaker 3: Things may be different, but they won't necessarily be any worse. We'll just enter a new phase of our culture, our existence. We've always adapted … I mean, think of the huge changes with the Industrial Revolution … why should this be any different? And as for the eco-threat, we're going to have to deal with it somehow, aren't we? I think we will. I can't accept that the human race will cease to be. Call me an optimist, but that's what I feel …

8 Explain to students that the preposition *at*, like *in* and *on*, commonly occurs in fixed phrases (examples *a–c*) and patterns (example *d*). Ask students to complete the exercise and then list all the options, with their meanings or an example sentence, in their vocabulary notebooks.

Answers
a B b C c A d B

Ⓔxtension activity

Write some adjectives on the board and ask students to come up with more examples of the pronoun and superlative pattern. For example:
silly: The children were at their silliest towards the end of the party.
mean: The tatty present showed my uncle at his meanest!
strong: With three players back from injury, Norwich City will be at their strongest tomorrow.
high: The dollar was at its highest in several months.
interesting: Live coverage is news at its most interesting.

Writing folder 5

Paper 2 Part 2   Articles 1

SB pages 68–69

1   Elicit why people read articles in magazines and newspapers: usually for pleasure or for information. Explain to students that it is important for an article to engage or entertain the reader, and that a suitable title will help to do this. Ask students to decide in pairs which title most appeals to them.

2   Ask students to match the titles to the paragraphs. Point out that the opening paragraph for B does not pick up on the idea of a lifelong ambition. The other three titles are intriguing and the reader would probably want to continue reading.

> **Answers**
> A 3-2-1 Lift off!   **B** A lifelong ambition
> **C** Aliens are coming ...   **D** Is anybody there?

3   Encourage students to use a variety of vocabulary in their writing. This exercise raises awareness of this and shows them the importance of improving a first draft.

> **Sample answer**
> (D, first stage)
> On some nights, I open my window and gaze at the stars. It's a wonderful thing to do. Sometimes I stay there for ages, wondering what the universe holds. It makes me feel humble. Space is a vast place. There are so many galaxies apart from our own – so there must be other life?

> **Answers**
> **a** adjectives   **b** noun phrase   **c** quantifiers   **d** adverbs

> **Sample answer**
> (D, second stage)
> On some beautiful, cloudless nights, I open my window and gaze at the twinkling stars. It's such a wonderful thing to do so I sometimes stay there for ages, wondering what the universe holds. It makes me feel very humble as space is a truly vast place. There are so many galaxies apart from our own – so there must surely be other forms of life?

The photograph shows distant galaxies observed by the Hubble Space Telescope.

4

> **Sample answer**
> (B)
> It has always been my dream to step on board a shiny, silver rocket and be launched into space. An article which I read recently said space travel may be possible for ordinary people soon. Wouldn't it be wonderful to be one of the first to go? I really hope that I am lucky enough to experience this.

5   Refer students to the Exam spot and stress the importance of writing in a suitable style for an article. Then ask them to read through the exam task carefully. As they read, they should think about the magazine the article will appear in and its likely readers.

6   Students can discuss a–d in pairs.

> **Answers**
> **a** Future forms of transport; destinations for holidays
> **b** More than one kind of transport should be mentioned
> **c** Given the type of magazine, it should be fairly lively and 'easy to read'
> **d** Probably four: an opening paragraph; one on transport; one on holidays; a final paragraph

7   Tell students to use their imagination to the full when thinking of ideas. Suggest that they write a first draft, and then try to make improvements to it.

> **Sample answer**
>
> TRAVEL TO THE STARS
>
> You are probably reading this on board a jumbo jet, but imagine how you could be travelling and where you might be able to get to on holiday in fifty years' time!
>
> By then, planes could be seen as old-fashioned, with re-usable space rockets being used for holiday destinations instead. Or perhaps someone will have invented a completely new form of transport, capable of travelling faster than the speed of light?
>
> If that ever happens, we will be able to go wherever we want to on holiday – not just within our own solar system, but out to other parts of our galaxy, or even to another galaxy further away. A cheap weekend break might consist of a couple of nights on an orbiting space station, watching the world below.
>
> Just sit back in your seat, close your eyes, and dream of your future. Isn't it exciting!

UNIT 11 Like mother, like daughter

Unit topic	Families/Relationships
11.1	
Exam skills	Speaking Paper 5 Part 1
	Listening Paper 4 Part 4
Grammar extra	*like*
Speaking	Characteristics
11.2	
Vocabulary	Describing personality
	Mixed phrasal verbs
Grammar focus	Adverbs and adjectives
	Past and present participles

Workbook contents

1, 2, 3, 4	Vocabulary – word formation, word groups, American English
5, 6	Writing – error correction, informal letter

11.1 SB pages 70–71

Lesson plan

Speaking	10–20'
Listening	30–40'
Speaking	20–30'

SV Omit 7 and 8.
LV See notes below for 2.

1 The photos (left to right) are of:

Cher and her daughter Chastity
Jerry Hall and her daughter Elizabeth Jagger
Prince Charles and his son Prince Harry
Bill Clinton and his daughter Chelsea Clinton

Ask students to look at the photos. They should think about the similarities and differences in the photos. The aim of this is to get students thinking and talking about themselves and their families.

Refer students to the Exam spot. At the beginning of the Speaking part of the examination, the interviewer will chat to the two candidates about everyday things. They'll

ask for personal information, about their studies or job, about their hobbies and future plans. This is mainly to settle the candidates down and get them talking. It also gets them used to the sound of the interviewer's voice and whether everyone is speaking loudly and clearly enough.

2 Students should talk to each other in pairs about themselves and their families. They need to answer questions on facial and body features, personality and sound. If they know each other very well then you should ask them to find out three things about each other or their families that they didn't know before.

Ⓔxtension activity

If you have time, then you can play the game of 20 questions. Think of a famous person but keep it to yourself. Then students find out the identity. It must be someone they would have heard of but don't make it too easy. When they get the idea, put them in pairs to practise. Try to get them to use: *sound like; take after; look like.*

3 Refer students to the Exam spot. The aim of this exercise is to show students how to deal with a multiple choice listening task. Ask students to look at question 1 and the 'things to think about' which follow. Play the tape until … *some of the kids I knew did.*

Ask them which is the correct answer and why.

Answers
- Did she go to the cinema? How do we know? No. Because she went to a film set, which is a place where a film is made.
- Did she meet Harrison Ford? We don't know.
- How did her parents treat her? Well, but they didn't spoil her.
- Did she have any brothers and sisters? No.

4

Answer
1B – 'my mother arranged for me and a few friends to go to the film set to see him working on his latest film, as a birthday treat.'

Tapescript

Presenter: So, Hannah, what was it like growing up in Hollywood as an only child, and having such a famous mother?

Hannah: Well, I guess I was pretty privileged as I had things most other kids only dream about. For instance, when I was 14 I just loved Harrison Ford films, and my mother arranged for me and a few friends to go to the film set to see him working on his latest film, as a treat for my birthday. I don't think I was particularly spoilt though, even though I was an only child, and I didn't get into trouble like some of the kids I knew did.

Presenter: You, yourself, are an actress now. Did she ever try to put you off acting?

Hannah: Not at all. Just the opposite. She felt I should follow my feelings, I guess in the same way she had done when she was younger. My grandparents hadn't wanted her to take up acting you know, especially as she had to move from Europe to Hollywood. I don't think her family took her seriously at first and I think she was quite homesick and felt she could have done with a little more family support.

Presenter: Now, you look very like your mother, don't you?

Hannah: Oh, yes. My mouth, the shape of my face, my jaw line is my mother's. My nose too, but only the tip of it, not the bridge – that is unique, like no one else's in the family. My eyes, my forehead, my colouring, my height are different from my mother's but everyone tells me I look like her. When I say everybody, I mean everybody. People stop me in shops, on the subway, in the street.

Presenter: What does your mother say about this?

Hannah: Well, we both looked in the mirror one day and came to the same conclusion – people exaggerate. Then one day I went into a dress shop. I was alone except for another customer. I thought to myself, 'She looks like my mother.' Then I walked too close to her and crashed into a mirror – the lady was me! I hadn't recognised myself!

Presenter: What qualities do you think your mother possesses?

Hannah: Great physical energy. She used to walk fast, and when she wasn't acting she cleaned and organised the house perfectly. She loved acting more than cleaning; she loved acting most and above all. It took me some time not to feel hurt by this. I wanted to come first. When asked what was the most important thing in her life, she got real embarrassed and nervous, but my mother couldn't lie; she had to say 'acting'; though I know for our sake she wished she could say 'family'. She is terribly practical, and I am too. We consider it one of the greatest qualities in people. We give it the same status as intelligence. Practicality is what made my mother advise me to learn to be an accountant. 'If you know how to do it, you know you'll never be cheated out of any money,' she says. I didn't finish the course as I decided I wanted to act.

Presenter: Did she have any personal experience of being cheated out of money?

Hannah: Well, my mother has always been a very generous person to people she likes. I think another actor who she fell out with started the rumour that she is a bit stingy. She does say that I'm a bit extravagant.

Presenter: Now, you don't sound like your mother, do you?

Hannah: Oh no. She still has a bit of an accent. But her voice is definitely an actress's voice – the clearest speech, the most commanding delivery, and loud. The family used to tell her that she didn't need a phone, she could have just talked to us on the other side of town and we would have heard her. She justifies it with 'I picked it up in the theatre. My voice has to reach all the way to the last row.'

Presenter: Thank you for coming in today to talk to us Hannah and good luck in your new film, which I believe, is released on Tuesday?

Hannah: Yes, that's right. Thank you.

5   The students need to know that sometimes one of the options in a multiple choice question may be factually correct, but doesn't actually answer the question. They should also be aware of just choosing an answer because they heard one of the words on the tape.

Ask students to look at the rest of the questions and play the tape twice.

> **Answers**
> **2** B   **3** C   **4** B   **5** A   **6** C   **7** B

Photocopiable tapescript activity (**P** ⋯⟩ page 184)

Give out the tapescript after you have played the tape twice, to help students locate the answers if needed.

6   Ask students if they can answer the questions without listening to the tape again.

> **Answers**
> **a** privileged   **b** homesick   **c** unique
> **d** embarrassed and nervous   **e** being practical
> **f** generous/stingy   **g** loud/commanding

Grammar extra

Students often confuse these two uses of like:
> What's she like?
> What does she like?
This is just a short awareness exercise.

> **Answers**
> **A** tall, friendly, amusing
> **B** swimming, hamburgers, watching TV, photography

7 This exercise is to get the class talking but possibly in a way that they haven't thought about before. It means they have to move round the room and form new groups, depending on their place in their own family – oldest child, middle child, youngest, only, one of twins, etc. If there is a student who has no-one in their group, ask him/her to go to each group in turn to talk about his/her experience. Care should be taken if you know there are people in the class who have family problems.

8 The aim of this exercise is to broaden students' vocabulary. They are often very unimaginative when it comes to descriptions of people and they need to be directed into other ways of looking at people/families.

11.2 SB pages 72–73

Lesson plan

Vocabulary	30–45'
Grammar	20–25'
Speaking	15–20'

SV Set 3 for homework.
LV See notes below for 2.

1 This exercise can be done using an English-English dictionary. Ask students to work in pairs.

Answers
a conceited **b** cheerful **c** optimistic **d** generous
e sensible **f** considerate **g** unreliable **h** self-conscious
i bad-tempered **j** amusing **k** aggressive **l** lazy
m loyal **n** sociable

2 Refer students to the Vocabulary spot. Students have to think about the positive or negative meaning of the words in exercise 1, and then their opposites. Sometimes an opposite can be formed by adding a negative prefix, sometimes another word is required.

Ask students to talk about their families if time, using some of these adjectives. Alternatively, they could write a short piece for homework on this subject.

Answers
positive = cheerful, optimistic, generous, sensible, considerate, amusing, loyal, sociable
negative = conceited, unreliable, self-conscious, bad-tempered, aggressive, lazy

Opposites
a modest **b** miserable **c** pessimistic **d** mean/stingy
e irresponsible **f** inconsiderate **g** reliable/dependable
h unselfconscious **i** good-tempered/easy-going
j serious **k** peaceful/cowardly **l** energetic **m** disloyal
n shy/introverted

Extension activity

You should discuss the use of the words 'funny' and 'nice' in English. 'Funny' can mean 'funny odd' or 'funny amusing' and therefore should be avoided by students. Tell them always to use 'amusing'. Also point out the use of 'fun' rather than 'funny' in the sentence: 'I went to the beach and it was great fun.' 'Nice' is overused in both spoken and written English. Point out that there are many adjectives that can be used instead to describe a person, object or place. An awareness exercise could be done at this point.

Replace 'nice' in these descriptions:
A nice vase: beautiful, old, antique, expensive, valuable
A nice old grandmother: kind, friendly, loving, dependable
Nice weather: lovely, beautiful, sunny
A nice meal: delicious, tasty, well-cooked
A nice film star: handsome, good-looking, pretty, talented
A nice TV programme: interesting, absorbing, intriguing, exciting

3 These phrasal verbs were all in the listening passage. Ask students to replace the ordinary verb with one of the phrasal verbs in the box.

Answers
a picked up **b** grew up **c** put them off **d** turns up
e stood by **f** look on

4 This section looks at a certain type of verb, usually connected with our senses. They are called 'copular verbs' and after them we use adjectives, not adverbs.

Suggested answers
a It sounds romantic/revolting, etc.
b It smells salty.
c It feels scary/quiet.
d It tastes great/delicious. It looks difficult/messy. It smells lovely.
e It looks interesting/honest/tempting.
f It feels good. It looks expensive. It smells expensive.

5 The students need to compare A and B.

In A *looked* means 'seem' or 'appear', whereas in B *look* means 'direct her eyes *towards*' – it is an action.

In A *feel* means 'have the sensation of', whereas in B *felt* means '*touch*' – it is an action.

> **Answers**
> **a** adjective – delicious   **b** adverb – gently
> **c** adjective – happy   **d** adverb – carefully
> **e** adjective –loud/scary/terrifying
> **f** adjective – expensive   **g** adverb – meaningfully
> **h** adverb – suddenly

6   Students often confuse the use of past and present participles. This exercise is to sort out any problems differentiating between the use of *-ed* and *-ing*.

> **Answers**
> It would mean she was embarrassed by her mother.
> **1** -ed
> **2** -ing
>
> **a** interested   **b** bored   **c** exhausting   **d** exciting
> **e** worrying

7   This provides more practice in using *-ed* and *-ing*. Ask students to give real answers to the types of entertainment in a–g. Make sure they know the meaning of all the adjectives.

Exam folder 6

Paper 4 Part 1 Short extracts

SB pages 74–75

Refer students to the description on page 74 and discuss the content of Part 1, in relation to the pictures. It is important for students to understand that the questions test a variety of situations, functions, and types of spoken material.

1   Ask students to underline key words on their own and then compare with another student. They should underline words both in the question and in the options.

> **Sample answers**
> 1   You hear this advertisement on the radio for a new <u>magazine</u>.
>   <u>Who is the magazine aimed at</u>?
> **A** <u>gardeners</u>   **B** <u>cooks</u>   **C** <u>climbers</u>
>
> 2   As you leave the cinema, you overhear this conversation.
>   What is the man's <u>opinion</u> of the <u>film</u>?
> **A** It is <u>longer</u> than necessary.   **B** It <u>has</u> a <u>weak storyline</u>.
> **C** Its <u>actors</u> are <u>disappointing</u>.

2   Play the tape and check answers at the end. Each recording is repeated on the tape, with the appropriate pauses.

> **Answers**
> 1 A   2 C   3 C   4 B   5 C   6 A   7 B   8 A

Tapescript

You will hear people talking in eight different situations. For Questions, 1–8, choose the best answer A, B or C.

1   You hear this advertisement on the radio for a new magazine.
    Who is the magazine aimed at?
    A gardeners
    B cooks
    C climbers
    If you enjoy spending time in the kitchen, you'll already know about our successful magazine *Taste!* In answer to readers' requests, we've introduced a sister magazine called *Dig!*, for everyone who enjoys being outdoors whatever the weather. It's full of tips to keep things looking at their best throughout the year and includes a free packet of seeds every month. Available now!

2   As you leave the cinema, you overhear this conversation.
    What is the man's opinion of the film?
    A It is longer than necessary.
    B It has a weak storyline.
    C Its actors are disappointing.
    Woman: Well that was a long one, wasn't it?
    Man: Was it? Seemed normal …
    Woman: No, no. That scene at the end should have been cut, if you ask me. I thought Jim Franklin was really good though.
    Man: Hmm, I've seen him do better … and that co-star was a weak character, wasn't she? What a shame – the book was absolutely gripping and they haven't changed anything, so you can't criticise the story.

3 You overhear a woman talking on the phone.
What sort of person is she?

A unhappy

B impractical

C disloyal

Hello, is that the news desk of the *Daily Times*? Yes, I'm ringing with some information … you see, I'm a close friend of Heather Woods … last week's jackpot winner, that's right. I know she doesn't want any publicity but if the price is right, I'm willing to give you a story. I mean it's ridiculous, all that money and she's sitting there miserably! I could visit your office tomorrow … or fax you something if you prefer. … Okay, that sounds interesting, my number's 0181 …

4 You hear this interview on the radio.
Why did the man give up his job?

A to recover from stress

B to reduce his expenses

C to move somewhere quiet

Int: So, Duncan, you left a well-paid job in Glasgow to move to this beautiful island off the west coast of Scotland. Was it to escape the pressures of city life?

Duncan: Not really. I grew up in the countryside and I know only too well how quiet it can be – I go back to Glasgow regularly, in fact, to enjoy the fast pace again! The point is, I was trying to write a novel while I was working – you know, weekends, evenings – and I realised I couldn't do both. So I quit and came here to cut costs … at the time I didn't even have a publisher's contract, so it was a risky move.

5 You overhear this conversation in a hotel.
Why has the woman come down to reception?

A to ask for another room

B to order some food

C to complain about the service

Receptionist: How may I help you, madam?

Woman: I was on the phone to you from my room just now and …

Receptionist: Oh yes. There was something wrong with the phone … Is there a problem with the room? You're in 203, aren't you?

Woman: Yes I am … it's fine. I was actually ringing about room service – it's taken over forty minutes for them to bring me a simple sandwich and a cup of coffee. Well, I was so appalled, I decided to come down here, to have a word with you …

6 You hear this radio report about a football match.
What happened at the match?

A Some fans ran onto the pitch.

B A player was badly injured.

C The referee stopped the match.

Well, Grangewood – Trent United has finished one nil, after a match that was full of excitement. Grangewood took the lead with Bellamy's early goal, a wonderful return for him after his long absence with that broken leg. A crowd of supporters rushed across to Bellamy when the game was over, glad to see their hero back. The referee tried to stop them but in the end, it was the whole Grangewood team who walked off the pitch with their delighted fans.

7 You hear this interview on the radio.
Where is it taking place?

A in a clothes shop

B at an exhibition

C on a beach

Int: I'm with Liam O'Neill, and we're surrounded by his latest range of swimwear that's caused a real sensation here at the Clothes Show. Liam, why do you think you've done so well this year?

Liam: It's unbelievable, isn't it? … I dunno, it's kind of strange. The new stores have created a lot of interest throughout the country and I guess people wanted to come and see for themselves.

Int: Liam, your display is most impressive – how did you move all that sand?

Liam: We had three lorries driving through the night to get here – it just wouldn't be right to launch swimwear without the beach!

8 You overhear this woman talking about an evening course.
What does she enjoy most?

A doing maths

B watching videos

C having coffee

I've started this astronomy course – two hours a week on a Monday evening. Every week the lecturer shows a short film … we've seen one on the Hubble Space Telescope and another about the sun. It's useful, although I can't help thinking we could take the tapes away and do that bit at home. We have to work out lots of calculations in class and I must say that it's terrific! I thought it would be really hard work, but the time goes by really fast and there's always a break – not that the coffee is anything special! I can't wait to get back to my sums!

3 Suggest students use a pencil to shade in the answer sheet extract. Remind them that they will have an extra five minutes in the exam to do this.

UNIT 12 | A great idea

Unit topic	Technology and inventions
12.1	
Speaking	Questionnaire on technology
Reading	Guessing unknown words
Exam skills	Reading Paper 1 Part 1
	(summary sentences)
12.2	
Grammar focus	The Passive
Exam skills	Use of English
	Paper 3 Part 3
Listening	Inventions
Vocabulary	Collocations

Workbook contents

1	Reading – Part 2 multiple choice
2	Use of English – Part 4
3	Use of English – Part 1
4	Phrasal verbs with *come* and *take*

12.1 SB pages 76–77

Lesson plan

Questionnaire	20–30'
Reading	50–60'

SV Omit 1.
LV See notes below for 1 and 5.

1 Ask students to look at the illustration of a gadget called an 'office on your arm'. Have a short discussion on what it is, have they heard of it, would they want one, etc. It is a phone, computer, e-mail facility which can be used anywhere.

Ask them to read through the questionnaire by themselves or go through it with them if you feel there may be vocabulary they are unfamiliar with. The following is some vocabulary they might not know:

to plug in; to fuse; to put on a plug; vending machine; viciously; resignedly.

Ask students to discuss their scores in pairs.

Extension activity

The words *technophobe* and *technophile* are introduced here. This could be used for vocabulary expansion, depending on the level and interest of the students. The use of *phobia* for 'fear of' is very common in English.
positive words: anglophile, bibliophile, etc.
negative words: arachnophobia, claustrophobia, agoraphobia, hydrophobia, etc.

2 Refer students to the Vocabulary spot. No dictionaries are allowed in the examination and students need to feel confident they can cope with a text without immediately reaching for their dictionary. This exercise picks out various words from the text that they might not know and asks them to work out the meaning from the context. It doesn't matter if they can't come up with an exact synonym – it's the fact that they've understood what it means that counts.

Answers
a wooden/metal closures that cover something – in this case a window
b something that came before
c something over his face which disguises him
d small
e place everyone recognises
f whole/complete
g reasons

3 Refer students to the exam spot. In this exercise students have practice in matching summary sentences to parts of a text. They should read through the paragraphs to get an idea of the subject matter before they look at the summary sentences.

4 In pairs, or alone if they prefer, ask them to underline what they think is the key idea in each paragraph.

5 Students should then look at the summary sentences and try to match them to the paragraphs.

Answers
o H
1 C   with great care
2 B   the forerunner of today's point and shoot cameras
3 D   poor definition
4 A   not particularly revolutionary
5 G   Previously, photographers had had no choice
6 E   within reach of practically everybody

Extension activities

A
Ask students to find words in the text which mean the same as a–f.
a a mixture b to let go c round d only
e a product which makes life easier
f money earned in a week

Answers
a a combination b to release c circular d solely
e a convenience f a wage

B
Ask students to form groups to discuss which modern conveniences they couldn't live without, for example, a TV, a washing machine, a PC, central heating, lifts, a fridge, a car, aeroplanes, motorways.

Background information

Some inventions and the dates they were invented:

1902 – teddy bear
1910 – washing machine
1914 – bra
1928 – peanut butter
1935 – colour film
1947 – microwave oven
1951 – home computer
1959 – Barbie doll
1964 – fax machine
1970 – snowboard
1980 – inline skates

12.2 SB pages 78–79

Lesson plan

Grammar	20–25'
Exam skills	10–15'
Listening	10–15'
Vocabulary	20–25'

SV Omit 9; set 12 for homework.
LV See notes below for 6, 9 and 12.

1 In this exercise students have to recognise the form of the passive. They often confuse the tenses of the verb *to be* with the passive.

Answers
a past simple passive b past simple
c passive infinitive
d past perfect passive/ past simple passive
e past perfect of verb *to be*
f modal passive/passive infinitive

2 Try to elicit the answers to these questions from the students. For the formation of the passive ask students to look in their Grammar folder, page 202. If they are still unclear, then give them a table of the tense changes. *Get* can be used informally instead of *be*.

Teaching extra

Students often worry about the formation of the passive. If they are unclear about this, put the following table on the board for them to copy down. It is important in Part 3 of Paper 3 that they keep in the same tense as the prompt sentence, so they need to be able to manipulate active to passive and passive to active easily. Note that *get* can be used informally instead of *be*.

Simple present	am/are/is + past participle
Present continuous	am/are/is being + pp
Simple past	was/were + pp
Past continuous	was/were being + pp
Present perfect	have/has been + pp
Past perfect	had been + pp
Will	will be + pp
Future perfect	will have been + pp
Going to	am/are/is going to be + pp
Passive infinitive	(to) be done; (to) have been done

3 The passive is often used in newspaper reports and also to talk about processes. This is because the action is more important than the person who is doing the action.

Answers
1 could be persuaded/encouraged
2 were encouraged/persuaded; have been encouraged/persuaded
3 were used
4 are (often) filled
5 can be talked into
6 are (being) supplied
7 are dissolved
8 can be dispersed/are dispersed
9 (can be) stored
10 will be issued/are going to be issued
11 is hoped
12 can be made up
13 are constantly being asked

4 This short exercise shows students the difference between *by* and *with*. We use *by* when a person or animal is involved; *with* is used for objects.

Answers
a The kitchen floor was covered with mud.
b He was scratched by a cat.
c He was run over by a car. (someone was driving the car)
d The old house was smashed down by bulldozers. (someone was driving the bulldozer)
e The school is being rebuilt with a new type of brick.

5 Students often feel they need to use *by* every time they use the passive. However, it is often not needed – it can be understood.

Answers
a by Spielberg. (It's important to know who the person was.)
b – (obviously by builders)
c –/by her uncle (usually you'd say who by, unless she'd been out of work for a while and actually getting the job was the important point)
d –/by his wife/by the Mafia
e – (unless a famous surgeon)
f deliberately/by children

6 The passive is used in newspaper headlines, but as words are missed out, this can be very confusing to non-native speakers. Ask students to form pairs and discuss these headlines.

Answers
a A man has been rescued by a dog.
b Lost treasure was found in a garden yesterday.
c A man is being held in the police station for questioning.
d The championships are going to be/will be held in Japan.
e People who use chewing gum will be faced with a campaign to clean up the streets.

Teaching extra

The passive is used a great deal in news items – both spoken and written. Encourage students to put together articles for a class newspaper or radio programme so that they can practise using the passive in a realistic way.

7 Students look at these notices and decide where they would see them.

Answers
a In a canteen.
b Same or in any building or on public transport.
c Parking spaces or seats at a club. Somewhere where membership is important.
d On a parcel or packet of biscuits, etc.
e In a book or magazine.

8 Students should try to use the passive in their answers.

In *e* students can answer in two ways:

I was given or *… was given to me*. The first way is neater.

9 The two pieces of information are linked in some way. Ask students what the link is. If they have problems, then give them the first one as an example.

Answers
a John Lennon was killed in New York.
b Gunpowder was invented in China.
c The telephone is used by half a billion people.
d The tomb of Tutankhamun was discovered by Lord Caernarfon.
e Satellites were first sent into space in 1957.
f The Olympic Games were first held in Athens.
g India was made independent in 1947.
h Leather is made from cows.

Extension activity

This exercise can be extended into a game. Each team thinks of two ideas and the other team has to guess what the link is.

10 Refer students to the Exam spot. This exercise is exam practice using the passive in key word transformations. This exercise can be set for homework if time is short.

Answers
1 object to their ideas
2 were those chemicals being mixed
3 was made to hand over
4 is supposed to be
5 was informed of his
6 has been a decrease in

11 Play the tape and ask students to try and decide what invention is being talked about in each case.

Answers
a the printing press   b penicillin (antibiotics)   c plastic
d the wheel

Tapescript

1 Around 1450 a man in Germany created a means of mass-production. In doing so, he gave the world a way of getting knowledge, and therefore power, out of the hands of the few and into the hands of the many. No other invention has done as much to make knowledge available. By 1500, nine million were in circulation – at least a thousand times more than there had been before when things had been done by hand.

2 This key breakthrough in medical history might never have happened had a scientist in London been more particular about keeping his laboratory clean. By leaving a glass plate coated with bacteria lying around, the scientist discovered something that has saved millions of lives round the world.

3 This cheap, light material was invented in the nineteenth century. It was first used to make cutlery handles – which unfortunately went up in flames rather easily. Not until 1910, with the advent of a tough, non-inflammable kind did this invention really take off. Now we throw away around 45 kg of this material each year in Britain alone, and the product has a bad image as a pollutant. The truth is, however, that in terms of total energy and resources they use, this product often turns out to be 'greener' than glass or paper.

4 Well, this invention is probably the most important ever invented. No one knows for certain where or when it came about, but it is perfectly designed for what it has to do. It is the mathematically optimal shape for minimising the amount of contact with other surfaces – leading to minimal friction and energy loss. Plus its surface has no edges, so it's good for smooth, repetitive motion.

12 In pairs students match the verbs with the words or phrases in the box.

Answers
come – to a conclusion, into money, to a decision, apart
take – a seat, advantage of, offence, turns, notice of, apart, an interest
tell – a story, a lie, the difference, the time, apart, the truth
fall – asleep, in love, ill, apart

Extension activity

Ask students to fill in the gaps in the columns, where possible.

Noun	Person	Adjective	Verb
science			
invention			
technology			
discovery			

Answers

Person	Adjective	Verb
scientist	scientific	–
inventor	inventive	invent
technologist/technician	technological	–
discoverer	–	discover

Writing folder 6

Paper 2 Part 2 Reports 1

SB pages 80–81

In Paper 2 Writing, one of the tasks in Part 2 could be writing a report. A report could be written for an employer or a teacher or for colleagues or club members. Using both paragraphing and headings are very important when writing a report. Students achieve higher marks if the layout is correct. Without a correct layout, it is impossible to achieve top marks.

1 Ask students to read through the five paragraphs and then decide which order they should be in. They should then choose the right heading.

Answers
Paragraphs   Headings
4, 1, 5, 3, 2   4A, 1B, 5C, 3D, 2E

---

2 The passive is often used in a report. This makes the report seem more formal and impersonal. Ask students to rewrite the five sentences in the passive.

Answers
1 It is said that the museum charges too much to get in. It is said that people are charged too much to get in the museum.
2 The exhibits are never dusted.
3 A café and a gift shop should be opened.
4 The displays will be made to look more interesting.
5 More people should be employed to explain things to the visitors.

---

3 Ask students to look back at the report on Wademouth Museum. They need to see how the words and phrases in bold are used.

Answers
a To sum up **b** I would recommend that
c Most people mentioned **d** Generally

---

4   Students then have to decide which function each
    phrase is expressing.

2

Answers
Introducing – The aim of this report (The purpose of
this report)
Reporting an impression – Most people mentioned
(According to most of the people I spoke to, In the opinion
of most people)
Generalising – Generally (Overall, On the whole,
In general)
Making a recommendation or suggestion – I would
recommend that (I would suggest that, In my opinion)
Concluding – To sum up (In conclusion, To conclude)

Other ways of expressing these functions are shown
in brackets.

5   Two questions, which require students to write in report
    format, are given. They can be discussed in class first
    and then set for homework.

T eaching extra

The students should always keep in mind the target reader –
that is the person who will receive the report. They should ask
themselves whether their report is clearly paragraphed and
organised with headings and that it answers the question
completely.

Sample answers
1

Newbridge cinema
Introduction
The aim of this report is to discuss the facilities offered at
Newbridge cinema and to make recommendations, based
on interviews with students at Newbridge College.

Recommendations
Most of the students I spoke to think that it would be
good if a new heating system were installed in the
building. In addition, they would like films to be shown
twice in an evening – once at 6.30 and also later at 10.30.
This would allow them to do some work before going out
to relax. Generally, most students wanted to see films
with sub-titles. Their feeling was that there are too many
cinemas showing the latest Hollywood movies and they
wanted somewhere they could see important foreign
language films.

Conclusion
To sum up, overall most students would be very happy to
use the cinema more if some of the ideas above could be
implemented by the cinema owners. They would be sorry
to see the cinema closed and many students would be
willing to work some evenings at the cinema for free if
help were needed.

Newbridge College Science Club
The club
The college science club has been open for ten years now.
It is held every Wednesday evening in term time from
6.00–9.00pm. There are sixty-eight members.
Membership costs £15 a year and for that members
receive a newsletter and free entrance to the weekly
events. We need an increase in our grant so that a larger
hall can be hired.

Recent activities
This term the club has held some very interesting
meetings. We were lucky enough to get Professor Tom
Baker of Oxford University to talk to us about the history
of space exploration. This attracted a lot of people to the
club who would not normally attend our meetings. Also
this term we had a visit to the police forensic science
laboratories.

Recommendations
The club has a good reputation within the college for
trying to promote an interest in science. It is lively and
well attended and we have a great deal of support from
staff as well as students. In conclusion, we feel that a
larger grant would enable us to contribute even more
to student interest in science.

UNITS 7–12 Revision

SB pages 82–83

Lesson plan

Grammar	15-15'
Topic review	15-35'
Vocabulary	15-15'
Phrasal verbs	0–10'
Writing	15–15'

SV Set Phrasal verbs as homework.
LV Extend Topic review (see 2).

Grammar

1   This picture shows the poster for the film LA Confidential.

> **Answers**
> **1** so **2** too **3** ✓ **4** were **5** while **6** who **7** of **8** in
> **9** as **10** the **11** into **12** ✓ **13** ✓ **14** been **15** to

Topic review

2   Follow the procedure given for Units 1–6 (see page 36).

> **E**xtension activity
>
> Ask students to write one or two sentences each, based on some of the six topics. They should then discuss them in groups.

Vocabulary

3   The verbs are *get* and *take*.

> **Answers**
> **a** getting **b** gets **c** take **d** get **e** take **f** got
> **g** take **h** took

4   Stress that students must explain why each word they choose is the odd one out. Give them an example if necessary:

   a I think 'cunning' is the odd one out because it means clever. The other three words all refer to something bad, like a frightening experience.

> **Answers**
> **a** cunning **b** campaign **c** plumber **d** fancy
> **e** shallow **f** rink **g** pretend **h** extravagant

Phrasal verbs

5   If this is done in class, suggest that students complete the sentences on their own and then compare their answers in pairs.

> **Answers**
> ON
> **a** looked **b** get **c** insist
> OFF
> **d** take **e** work **f** put

Writing

6   Give students time to read through the paragraphs and then suggest that they work in groups, discussing the different styles for 1–4.

> **Answers**
> **A** 4 **B** 2 (conclusion) **C** 3 (opening)

Paper 1 Part 1

You are going to read a magazine article about getting into film and television. Choose from the list **A–H** the sentence which best summarises each part (**1–6**) of the article. There is one extra sentence which you do not need to use. There is an example at the beginning (**0**).

A Demands on actors vary according to the type of work.

B It is preferable to seek the help of experts.

C Sometimes, experience from real life can be useful.

D Film producers are cautious for a reason.

E There is an accepted code of behaviour on a film shoot.

F Most actors have to learn to handle disappointment.

G Chances exist to break into films in a small way.

H It is possible to find screen work as an actor.

The Big Break

0   **H**

Have you ever wondered about getting a role in a television programme, or a film? Forget it, some people will tell you, arguing that it's much too difficult. However, you can make it, if you go about things in the right way.

1

First, let's look at why there are so many theatre actors who have not been successful in films or on TV, and why we see the same people on our screens over and over again. Of course, films and TV programmes are very expensive to make. A typical four-hour costume drama could cost around £4 million at least. Now, imagine yourself as a producer: you get halfway through and some actors go missing or let you down in some way. You have already spent £2 million and you have to start again. It is largely because of this that the tendency is to employ actors who have proved reliable in the past.

2

It has to be said that TV and theatre acting are totally different. Actors in the theatre have to make grand gestures and project their voices, so that those sitting right at the back can hear and understand. On TV, on the other hand, we see everything up close. We notice the smallest changes in facial expressions. Movement is often limited, as otherwise, the actor would disappear off the edge of the screen.

3

Let us assume that you want to take part in a major TV drama series, not as a star yet, but as an 'extra', principally for fun and pocket money. Most dramas and all films use extras: the people who are in the background in restaurants, hospital waiting areas, at weddings, or in a street scene. You will also have seen 'supporting actors', for example, nurses in a hospital ward, a taxi driver, or whatever. In any one film there may be hundreds of extras and supporting actors.

4

Although you can chase after acting assignments on your own, life for extras, supporting actors and producers is made far simpler by specialist casting agencies. These range from little local agencies that keep a list of available people and wait for someone to knock on their door to fully professional agencies with complex databases, listing each client's skills and preferences. The best agencies keep in constant touch with producers and are therefore very knowledgeable about current and forthcoming opportunities. Once they find you work, an agency will take between fifteen and twenty per cent of your earnings on that assignment.

5

So let us now imagine that you have landed your first acting assignment. If you have had any training whatsoever, you will of course know what to do – and more importantly, what not to do! For example, it is not a good idea to take a photo of the leading lady without her wig on, or to turn up late on the set. If you haven't had any training, you can always get a book on film-making, or just follow what everybody else does.

6

Having been an extra, how do you move on to a supporting role and then eventually to a speaking one? The most common route is to identify or acquire special skills so that you can be considered as a supporting actor. A person who has actually been a nurse, for example, can play a nurse far better than someone fresh out of drama school can. And once you have achieved that first supporting role, your chances of fame will be infinitely greater.

© Cambridge University Press, 2000

Paper 2 Part 2

Write an answer to one of the Questions **1–3** in this part. Write your answer in **120–180** words in an appropriate style.

1   Your English pen friend is doing a school project on TV advertising around the world and has asked you for some information. Write a letter to your pen friend, saying what products are commonly advertised on TV in your country and whether you think they are effective or not.

Write your **letter**.

2   You have had a class discussion on space. Your teacher has asked you to write a composition giving your opinions on the following statement:

Governments should spend money on problems on Earth, not on exploring space.

Write your **composition**.

3   You have seen the following advertisement.

```
┌─────────────────────────────────────────────┐
│                                               │
│             NEW IDEAS                         │
│          MONTHLY MAGAZINE                     │
│                                               │
│   ▶ What do you think has been the most       │
│     important invention ever?                 │
│                                               │
│   ▶ Why has it been so important?             │
│                                               │
│   We are looking for short articles answering │
│   these questions and we will publish some    │
│   of the best articles next month.            │
│                                               │
└─────────────────────────────────────────────┘
```

Write your **article**.

Paper 3 Part 2

For Questions **1–15**, read the text below and think of the word which best fits each space. Use only **one** word in each space. There is an example at the beginning (**0**).

Example: | 0 | in |

LOOKING FOR ADVENTURE

Insurance companies specialising (**0**) ....in............ insurance policies for dangerous activities (**1**) .... reporting a dramatic increase in (**2**) .... number of British holidaymakers choosing thrills and danger for (**3**) .... holiday fortnight. It seems that risky activities (**4**) .... white-water rafting, freefall parachuting and bobsleighing appeal in particular (**5**) .... high-earning young men.

Two years (**6**) ...., Andrew Blowers, a keen parachutist, set (**7**) .... his own travel insurance company. He did this because he had had such difficulty finding insurance cover for (**8**) .... In the past year, he (**9**) .... seen a huge increase in demand. Most other insurance companies (**10**) .... from his own exclude dangerous activities from their policies, whereas Mr Blowers insists that there are very (**11**) .... things that his company would not cover. Big game hunting, go karting, white-water rafting and scuba diving are all included in the standard rate of insurance (**12**) .... offer.

People (**13**) .... read the small print of their insurance policies (**14**) .... setting off on holiday, but they really should, especially (**15**) .... adventure sports are concerned. Otherwise, the consequences could be extremely costly.

© Cambridge University Press, 2000

Paper 3 Part 3

For Questions **1–10**, complete the second sentence so that it has a similar meaning to the first sentence, using the word given. **Do not change the word given**. You must use between two and five words, including the word given. Here is an example (**0**).

Example:

0   I have never been to Paris before.

         time

         This .... have been to Paris.

         The gap can be filled by the words 'is the first time I' so you write:

0	is the first time I

---

1   Many useful things have been invented because of the microchip.
    led
    The microchip .... of many useful things.

2   As a young child, Harry would visit his grandmother regularly.
    to
    As a young child, Harry .... regular visits to his grandmother.

3   I really hate the endless showing of car commercials on TV.
    stand
    I really .... that car commercials are endlessly shown on TV.

4   Giulia has a beautiful voice although she's never had any coaching.
    despite
    Giulia sings .... of coaching.

5   The hotel is offering you a good price on the room – I would accept.
    take
    Why don't you .... offer on their room price?

6   The city is cleaning up many of its ancient monuments at present.
    being
    Many of the ancient monuments in the city
    .... at present.

7   You must book for the sailing course immediately, as it is nearly full.
    at
    Sailing course bookings must ...., as it is nearly full.

8   Richard is away, so it is impossible that you saw him at the nightclub.
    been
    It .... you saw at the nightclub, as he's away.

9   Did your parents let you stay up when you were young?
    allowed
    Were you .... your parents when you were young?

10 Titan, one of Saturn's moons, will be visited by the American space probe in six years' time.
    belonging
    Titan, ..., will be visited by the American space probe in six years' time.

© Cambridge University Press, 2000

Paper 4 Part 3

You will hear five people giving their views on their families. For Questions **1–5**, choose which of **A–F** they state. Use the letters only once. There is one extra letter which you do not need to use.

A My family have never been close.

Speaker 1 | 1

B I got on best with my grandparents.

Speaker 2 | 2

C My father understood me best.

Speaker 3 | 3

D Children get on best when there's a small age gap.

Speaker 4 | 4

E Children can be thoughtless.

Speaker 5 | 5

F It's difficult being the youngest child.

© Cambridge University Press, 2000

Paper 1 Part 1

1 D 2 A 3 G 4 B 5 E 6 C

Paper 2 Part 2

Sample answers

1

Dear Anna,

Thank you for your letter. Your project sounds really interesting. There is a great deal of advertising on the TV in my country so I can probably help you quite a bit.

Generally, different products are advertised at different times of the day. For example, adverts for toys and sweets are advertised from 3.30 until 5.30, when children are watching the TV after school. These adverts are very effective and parents get quite annoyed when their children demand the toys they've seen.

Some of our ads have a storyline – like Nicole in the Renault Clio advert – she has a new haircut, buys a dress, meets a man and gets married. We also have a very effective coffee advert. This also has a storyline and people were often more interested in what was going to happen in this ad than in some of the popular soap operas.

Some of our ads have famous film stars in them – one is an American ad for shampoo. I expect a lot of people will buy the product because they want to look like the star.

Hope I've been of some help.

Best wishes,

2

There are so many problems on Earth that many people believe that more time and money should be spent trying to solve them, than on exploring the solar system. In many ways I would agree with them. It's sad that the richer nations show no interest in the poverty and need of the less developed ones. Even a small percentage of the Western World's defence budget would make an enormous difference to the lives of people in poorer countries.

However, it is an interesting, but little known fact, that many scientific advances have been the result of research into space. Although the scientists were not looking specifically for new inventions, they have come across some very useful ideas – the non-stick pan is an example of this.

In conclusion, I think that governments should do more to help people in less well-off countries, but that they should cut their budgets for defence rather than for the advancement of science. Although it sounds silly to spend money looking for other planets, it might turn out to be money well spent.

3

The Printing Press

I believe that the printing press, invented by Gutenberg in the fifteenth century, is the most important invention ever. Before this invention, every book had to be written by hand and very few people were able to ever see, let alone read, a book. After the invention of the printing press, books became more widespread, and nowadays books are widely available.

Having books and newspapers gave the ordinary man and woman access to information and education. Without them people had to depend on word of mouth, which as we are all aware, is not very reliable. Everyone knows that facts can change many times as they are passed from person to person. Having the information written down gives it authority and it doesn't change.

Besides giving us information, books can also give us a great deal of pleasure. There's nothing nicer than settling down to a good book when you have the time. Although people say that computers will take over from books in the near future, I believe there will always be a place for the book.

Paper 3 Part 2

1 are 2 the 3 their/a 4 like 5 to 6 ago 7 up
8 himself 9 has 10 apart 11 few 12 on
13 seldom/rarely/never 14 before 15 where/when

Paper 3 Part 3

1 has led to the invention 2 used to pay/make/go on
3 can't stand the way/how 4 beautifully despite her/the lack 5 take advantage of the hotel's/take up the hotel's
6 are being cleaned up 7 must be made/placed at once
8 can't/couldn't have been Richard 9 allowed to stay up by
10 a moon belonging to Saturn

Paper 4 Part 3

1 E 2 A 3 C 4 F 5 D

Tapescript

Speaker 1: There are six of us in our family, my parents, me, the twins and my older brother, Ted. Ted's a good ten years older than me and the twins – they're girls – are two years younger than me. We had a good childhood out in the countryside. My parents were always busy with the farm and so we didn't get the help with school work and things like that that children get today. They were very loving, though, especially my father. I regret not helping more around the farm – I realise now that it must've been very hard for my parents, especially as my grandparents lived so far away.

Speaker 2: Both my parents were in the theatre and they'd made quite a name for themselves on the stage. As a child I remember our house being constantly full of famous people, laughing and talking. My sisters and me would be brought down by our nanny to kiss my parents goodnight and then we'd be packed off to the nursery. That's as much as we ever really saw of them at that time. It's better now, but it's left its mark on all of us – we ring each other now and again, but that's about all. I think my father understands this, but I'm not sure my mother does.

Speaker 3: I left home when I was sixteen to live with my grandparents in Sydney. My parents had a farm in the outback and I needed to go to college. It was quite difficult for me to leave my younger brothers and sisters behind as we were quite a tight knit group, even though the age gap was fairly wide – as you can imagine there was no one else to play with out in the middle of nowhere! When I got fed up I'd give them all a ring and my dad would always put me right – a tower of strength he was! My grandparents were great too – helped me with my homework, took me on trips, things like that. I'll never forget that.

Speaker 4: There are quite a few of us in our family; mom and dad and my grandmother, and my older brother, who's married with three kids and lastly my sister, who lives in New York City. I can't wait until I'm in a place of my own too. My parents are great but there comes a time for everyone to move on and I can't keep on being the baby in the family. My sister thinks I'm being a bit selfish, and I keep having to remind her that she couldn't wait to leave home. Anyway, my brother will still be fairly close to my parents, even if we're some distance away.

Speaker 5: I'm always telling my kids – your family's always there for you, whatever happens. You might think we don't understand you and all that rubbish, but no one else will look out for you the way the family will. It's important to me, my family. You see, when I was young I didn't have much of a family life. Us kids were quite close in ages so that helped enormously, but we didn't see much of our parents – in fact we saw more of granny and grandpa, but they were a bit strict. We all got on and that, and we knew our parents cared for us, but there wasn't much in the way of trips, treats, things that nowadays people take for granted.

© Cambridge University Press, 2000

UNIT 13 Education for life

Unit topic	Education
13.1	
Speaking	Paper 5 Part 2
Listening	Paper 4 Part 4
Vocabulary	Phrases with *make*
Reading	First jobs of the famous
13.2	
Grammar	Reporting verbs
Listening	Radio call-in
Grammar extra	Reported questions
Exam skills	Use of English Paper 3 Part 3

Workbook contents

Note: this Workbook unit has a single focus, the true story of the sacking of a teacher of English in London in the 1970s, and the subsequent student protest.

1, 2	Reading – Part 3 gapped paragraphs
3	Vocabulary – Phrases with *make*
4	Grammar – reported speech

13.1 SB pages 84–85

Lesson plan

Speaking	20–30'
Listening	20–20'
Vocabulary	10–15'
Reading	20–25'

SV Set 3 and 7 for homework.
LV See notes below for discussion in 5.

This lesson gives plenty of opportunities for students to use reported speech, which will be familiar to most of them. Although they should be aware of the tenses they are using, don't introduce any grammatical explanation in this lesson; 13.2 will focus on this.

1 Allow students about five minutes to compare the photographs and make a brief reference to their own experience.

Background note

It is compulsory for children to attend school in Britain between the ages of 5 and 16. There are both state and private schools. State nursery education is offered to younger children and the government has promised more money for this; there is a growing private nursery sector.

2 Allow students around 6–8 minutes for this paired discussion, reminding them to listen carefully and take notes if necessary, so that they can report later. Be ready to help with vocabulary.

In the report stage, ask different pairs to report the information in a–d. Encourage students to vary the reporting verbs they use and write some of their sentences on the board. Underline the tenses used and elicit what they are.

3 If this is to be done in class, ask students to first read David's confession on their own. Then they can rewrite it on their own or in pairs, taking it in turns to do a sentence each. Check the finished piece of writing by asking a student to read it aloud, or take all copies in for marking.

Answer

David said that he wanted to describe what had really happened. He had been inside the classroom during break and he had seen a group of his friends outside. He had gone over to the window and had tried to get their attention. He had waved at them but they hadn't seen him, so he had hammered on the window. He said he knew glass was/is* breakable but he hadn't thought. When his hand had gone through he had panicked. He hadn't been hurt and he had wanted to avoid getting into trouble, so he had put Simon's bag over the hole and had left the room. He said he was sorry he hadn't told anyone the truth until that moment.

* because it is a fact that glass is breakable, the present tense can also be used here.

4 Refer students to the Exam spot and remind them that Part 4 of the Listening paper can be one of a number of formats (they have already practised multiple choice in Unit 12 and a short 'who says what' in Unit 9).

Ask students to read the seven statements. Elicit key words in each statement and check understanding, for example, *deliberately* in 2 and *irritating* in 3. Explain that the recording is full-length and may contain some difficult words, as in the exam. Play it straight through the first time. If students have problems when they compare answers, split the piece up the second time and reinforce where each answer comes (see underlinings in tapescript).

Tapescript

Int: With me now are Sandra Wilson and Mike Tripp. Mike is owner of a successful new travel company *Just Trips* and Sandra works for him as Publicity Manager. They were actually in the same class at school, though at that time, they did *not* get on with each other! They met again by chance last year, when Sandra went for an interview at *Just Trips* and was surprised to find Mike across the table, asking *her* the questions. Sandra, when you were at school, did you think Mike would become successful like this?

Sandra: To be honest, no one thought Mike would get anywhere – he was the original under-achiever! That's why we didn't get on. My group of friends were quite hard-working, you know, we did all the homework, made an effort in class, but Mike was the complete opposite. He was bad news, actually.

Int: Is this true Mike?

Mike: I'm afraid so. I wasn't the only one though. It was … uncool for boys to work, a whole group of us were like that. I don't remember being especially horrible to Sandra …

Sandra: Talk about a selective memory!

Int: Why?

Sandra: Well, he would regularly do annoying things like stealing my ruler or hiding my books. You saw it as a big joke, I suppose, Mike?

Mike: Never thought about it. I can see now that I might have been a … a bit of a nuisance.

Sandra: I've forgiven you though!

Int: And you've done very well since, Mike …

Mike: Yeah. I got on with my life. Um … I don't really regret my behaviour back then – obviously I shouldn't have made trouble for you, Sandra – but for myself, it didn't matter … I've done okay in spite of school.

Sandra: You have Mike, but there are lots of others in your gang who didn't make it.

Mike: Mmm … I can think of one or two … But I still think, if you know what you want out of life, you'll get there. I mean, look at me, I didn't pass many exams … I even walked out of some, like science … wrote my name at the top of the paper and thought, I can't do this … oh, what the heck, the sun's shining, I'm off.

Sandra: Incredible. I was totally stressed out during exams, spent hours revising, and Mike managed to fail virtually everything and still be successful.

Int: Should you have been more relaxed at school, Sandra?

Sandra: That's easy to say now. I had a lot of pressure on me to do well. My parents, my brothers … all my family expected … the best.

Mike: Same here. But my dad sort of looked beyond school. He knew I'd be okay – he'd left school himself at 14 and he always felt that I'd sort things out for myself, somehow.

Int: And how *did* you get the company started? No careers advice from school, I imagine?

Mike: Careers teachers? They didn't have a clue! I got things started in a small way while I was still at school, actually – I used to help out in a local travel agency, buying and selling cheap tickets on the phone. In my final year, I sometimes spent my lunchtimes checking the Internet on the school computer. I found some good deals for flights, that I managed to sell on. Then, when I left school, my dad gave me a bit of money and I set up an office … and it all … like … took off.

Int: So school did help you a little …or its facilities did?

Mike: Yeah …

Int: Okay, well we'll have to leave it there. One final thing, Mike. Why did Sandra get the job?

Mike: Oh, university education, languages, a good communicator – she's great, just what the company needed.

Sandra: All thanks to school, Mike.

Photocopiable tapescript activity (**⋯ page 185)**

Suggest students underline where each answer comes.

5 Play the extract where Sandra refers to others in Mike's gang *who didn't make it* again if necessary. Elicit the meaning and other situations.

Answers

succeed; do well – often used in connection with fame.

Another related meaning of this expression is:
manage to attend something, e.g. *The plane was late but I made it to the wedding on time.*
Often used in the negative, e.g. *I'm sorry, I won't be able to make it to the party on Saturday.*

Ask students to complete the exercise.

Answers

a made a start b made use of c made a profit
d made a success of e made an impression

xtension activity

To round off the topic of the recording, ask students whether they think that people who have underperformed at school find it more difficult to achieve success. Why?/ Why not? Then mention some famous examples of academic underachievers, such as the millionaire owner of *Virgin*, Richard Branson.

6 Ask students to look at the photos before they read the six texts. The photos show (top to bottom) Madonna, Agatha Christie, Tom Cruise, Annie Lennox, Paul Gauguin and Socrates. Explain that some answers are easier to work out than others and suggest that students look for clues in the texts.

Answers
A Tom Cruise **B** Socrates **C** Annie Lennox
D Paul Gauguin **E** Madonna **F** Agatha Christie

7 If done in class, try to have some English-English dictionaries on hand. The next Writing folder is after Unit 14, on pages 94–95. Useful words and phrases include:

gain experience, spend x years …, full-time career (A)
have (a) talent for, determination (B)
On leaving school …, find employment (C)
earn/make in a day (D)
work long hours (E)
take a position, unpaid assistant, qualify in, a sound knowledge of, extremely relevant (F)

13.2 SB pages 86–87

Lesson plan

Grammar	20–30'
Listening	25–35'
Grammar extra	5–10'
Use of English	15–15'

SV Set exercise in Grammar extra and Grammar folder for homework; keep 7 brief.
LV See notes below for 2 and 7.

1 Ask students to look at the three quotes in pairs and discuss the tenses used. They should then look at the Grammar folder, page 203.

Answers
In *a*, there is 'backshift' in the reported statement. Greg's actual statement contained a present and a future tense; in reported speech, the present tense *can't* has become a past tense *couldn't* and *will* has become *would*.

In *b*, there is similar backshift from the simple past to the past perfect in the reported statement.

In *c*, the reported statement uses the present because the situation reported continues to be true.

2 Impress on students the importance of using a good variety of words in their written work. Reporting verbs is a particularly rich area of alternatives, the most common of which are listed. Many of these and their accompanying structures are also tested in Paper 3.

Further useful verbs which could be given to students are:
encourage: encourage + someone + to + infinitive
threaten: threaten + someone + with + something; threaten + to + infinitive; threaten + that (optional)

Answers
apologise + for + -ing
argue + for + -ing; argue + that
claim + that (optional)
deny + that (optional); deny + -ing
explain + that (optional)
insist + on + -ing; insist + that (optional)
promise + that (optional); promise + to + infinitive
refuse + to + infinitive
say + that (optional); in passive, 'is said' + to + infinitive
suggest + that (optional); suggest + -ing
urge + someone + to + infinitive; urge + that
warn + that (optional); + to + infinitive

Extension activity

Develop this work into a dictionary session, where students find examples to illustrate each of the structures.

3 Ask students to do the exercise on their own and then compare their answers.

Answers
a 4 **b** 5 **c** 1 **d** 2 **e** 3

4 Elicit reactions to the picture, which shows some of the issues in the recordings students are about to hear.

Play the first extract and ask students to complete the statements. Check their answers.

Answers
a wanted **b** are; need **c** are affected

Note: present tenses are more appropriate in **b** and **c** because the reported situation is a general truth. However, past tenses would not be incorrect.

Tapescript

Caller 1: I'm a retired head teacher and I want to make two points. First, I know from my own experience that teachers tend to be female … and I believe we need to get more men into all our schools – boys need men around as role models, from an early age. My second point is linked to this. There is a growing problem of broken marriages and one-parent families, which affects all children but especially boys, because they usually end up living with their mothers and having less contact with their fathers. Men are so important to boys' development.

5   Continue the tape. Afterwards, students can compare the notes they have made and then write the statements together.

Suggested answers

Caller 2
She said that when boys and girls start school, they are both keen to learn.
She complained that parents don't help boys at home.
She insisted that basic skills have to be introduced in the home.

Caller 3
He suggested discussing society rather than just schools.
He explained that as society has changed so much, boys don't have clear goals any more.
He claimed that girls, in contrast, have a lot to aim for.

Caller 4
She explained that girls' brains develop differently to boys' at a young age.
She warned that in Britain, education is too formal at the beginning.
She urged that nursery education should be extended to the age of six in Britain.

Caller 5
He insisted on the recent achievement by girls being a good thing.
He argued that this was not true ten years ago.
He suggested that this is part of more equal opportunities nowadays.

Tapescript

Caller 2: Well, I'm an infant teacher and I work with children from the age of four. Both boys and girls arrive at school interested and excited on day one. But I find during that first year that I can't get the parents of boys to help their children at home. They expect their boys to be out playing football after school, not sitting at home reading a book. Basic skills have to be introduced in the home and because the girls' parents do this, the girls race ahead. Then the boys feel they're failing, so they start mucking about, and things go from bad to worse.

Caller 3: Can I widen the topic beyond schools? Society has changed radically in the last twenty years and fathers are no longer the bread-winners, necessarily. Indeed, the average boy growing up now may see a lot of men on the dole … and of course he's going to look at that and say, 'What's the point? There's no future for me.' Girls, on the other hand, now see lots of opportunities and they want to get out there and compete, get to the top. We haven't faced up to this, and yet it was obviously going to happen.

Caller 4: Picking up on what the infant teacher said, I've always understood the brain develops differently in boys and girls, so girls aged four develop quickly, whereas boys take longer to get going. For boys especially, I think we formalise education too soon in Britain. I can find no other examples in the world where formal teaching starts so early. I believe we should extend nursery education to the age of six, so that there is more time for play, for discovery … and above all, language. Then by the age of six, boys would be ready for formal learning.

Caller 5: I think we should give credit to what has happened … I mean, it's a success story for girls, isn't it? Okay, so girls are now achieving better results at school than boys … well, that's great. It was not the case twenty years ago … even ten years ago. For the last three years, more girls have gained university places than boys … good for them. I think this is all part of the wider picture of equal opportunities and we should view it positively.

6   Play the tape again and ask students to note down the relevant words and phrases.

Answers
a tend (to be)   b race ahead   c mucking about
d bread-winners   e faced up to   f picking up on
g extend   h give credit to

---

7   This discussion can be done in groups of three or four students. To keep it brief, allocate each half of the room one question. For a more extended discussion, ask students to prepare a brief presentation in their group, where they write some key points on a flip chart or an overhead transparency and report these ideas to the class.

Grammar extra

Draw attention to the changes in word order in the examples. The exercise can be done in class or for homework.

Answers
a why girls are/were gaining more university places.
b in what ways the situation had been different twenty years ago.
c if/whether things would get better in the future.
d if/whether British children should spend more time at nursery.
e why we hadn't faced up to this problem.

---

8 It is best to do this exercise in class, as it acts as a summary of the reporting structures that have been dealt with in the unit. Students can refer to the Grammar folder, page 203 if they are unsure.

Exam folder 7

Paper 4 Part 2
Sentence completion/note-taking

SB pages 88–89

Explain that in this part of the Listening paper students will hear a monologue or a conversation which lasts approximately three minutes. They will hear the piece twice. There are ten questions in which students have to complete either notes or sentences, and sometimes there is a mixture of the two. This part tests understanding gist, main points, detailed or specific information, or deducing meaning.

It is important that students realise that they don't have to write a full answer to any of the questions. One to three words is usually the number required.

Spelling need not be totally correct, but whatever has been written needs to be easily recognisable! If a word has been spelt out letter for letter on the recording, then that word must be spelt properly. There is one mark for each answer.

Ask students to read through the section on Advice and make sure that they understand it.

Students should then read through the question paper and try to predict what answers are required. At the end of the lesson they can then go back and see if they were correct.

There are some clues to help students. There are no clues in the examination! You can either let them read the clues before the first listening or after it.

Play the tape twice. In the exam, students should write their answers on the question paper the first time they hear the passage, and then, when they are sure of their answers, transfer them to the answer sheet at the end of the Listening test. Tell them not to worry too much about one question. They should go on to the next one if the previous one is too difficult for them. Tell students that they should never leave a blank but always write something.

Teaching extra

Students usually need a lot of practice in note-taking. They often panic when they have to write things down and worry over-long about their answer. Give them a lot of practice by reading out newspaper stories and asking them to take notes. You could concentrate on numbers one week, places the next, etc. Playing a pop song and giving them a worksheet with gaps in the lyrics is a very good way to keep their interest in this sort of exercise.

Tapescript

Interviewer: Good morning and welcome to the *Food and Drink Show*. In the studio today we have Christine Whitelaw who works as a Personal Assistant to the world famous chef Patrick Millar. Christine has worked for him for the past 18 months and has loved every minute of it. Her boss has many interests ranging from a cookery school for professionals and amateurs, to a catering service and a range of luxury food items. Christine's organisational skills have to be faultless as a result. She also considers a good memory, confident phone manner and fast typing speeds to be vital to her job. So Christine, how did you become PA to such an important figure in the food and drink industry?

Christine: Well, I always wanted to work in catering, so after leaving school I completed a year on a cookery course before spending another year at secretarial college. My first job came about following a visit to London. I went to lunch at the Palace Hotel and thought, 'I would really like to work here', so I wrote to see if they had any positions, and it just so happened they did.

Interviewer: That was a lucky break, wasn't it?

Christine: It certainly was. I worked as a PA to the executive director of the hotel group for more than three years before hearing that Patrick Millar was advertising for a new PA. I applied, had to go to two interviews, and got the job.

Interviewer: How does an ordinary day go?

Christine: I usually meet Patrick first of all to run through his diary and letters. If clients are expected for lunch, I may take them on a pre-lunch tour of the cookery school. It has a collection of 6,000 cookery books, which many people are keen to see. Then I take them to the restaurant. In the afternoons I usually do letters and make phone calls. I have an assistant to help me. Each day is fairly different, however. If Patrick is busy in the morning we sometimes have a working lunch together in the chef's office, never in the restaurant or kitchen.

Interviewer: Did you find your previous experience in the hotel business useful?

Christine: Yes, especially in learning how to deal with the public, both face to face and over the phone. One thing it didn't prepare me for was the long hours, as, nowadays, I often have to work until 7pm and then go on to a reception or function.

Interviewer: You often hear about how difficult these top chefs are to work for. Is Patrick very moody or do you get along well?

Christine: Oh, he's terrific and he involves me in most of the decision-making. The worst part of working for him is that I'm surrounded by delicious food all day. I try not to be tempted!

Interviewer: Can you cook yourself?

Christine: Well, I do enjoy cooking and I have tried a few things from his recipe books. However, I have no plans to work as a cook. The job I have combines everything I love: food, meeting people and being at someone's right hand.

Interviewer: Thank you, Christine for coming in to talk to us today. Next week we'll be interviewing …

Photocopiable tapescript activity (P ⋯⟩ page 186)

Ask students to take turns at choosing an utterance and putting it into reported speech.

UNIT 14 Career moves

Unit topic	Working life
14.1	
Exam skills	Reading Paper 1 Part 4
Vocabulary	Negative prefixes
Grammar extra	*all / the whole*
14.2	
Grammar focus	Perfect tenses
Role play	Job interviews

Workbook contents

1	Use of English – Part 2
2, 3	Writing – Story
4	Use of English – Part 5
5	Expressions with *all*
6	Vocabulary – money

14.1 SB pages 90–91

Lesson plan

Speaking	15–25'
Reading	25–25'
Vocabulary	20–20'
Grammar extra	10–20'

SV Keep 3 brief; set part of Grammar extra for homework.
LV See notes below for 3.

1 Allow about five minutes for this activity. Suggest that students work in pairs, each talking about one of the jobs shown. These are: a member of a Formula One technical support team and a restorer of ancient pottery. Skills needed include quick-thinking, physical strength, ability to work under pressure, team player (Formula One); precision, patience, specialised knowledge of archaeology, steady hands, good eyesight, self-motivation (restorer).

Elicit opinions from the class on the final question: Which job would you prefer and why? This is an example of what happens at the end of a 'long turn' in Paper 5 Part 2, where the candidate who has been listening makes a brief comment. Students will be introduced to a full Paper 5 Part 2 in Unit 17.

2 These words come up in the article which follows. Ask students to complete the quotes and then elicit the meaning of the other words.

Answers
a insecure   **b** flexible   **c** concerned

3 Run this as a class discussion, summarising views on the board.

Extension activity

If more time is available, divide the class into four teams and allocate one of the changes below to each team, asking them to discuss the advantages and disadvantages of the change. They should prepare their ideas on a flip chart or overhead transparency, to present to the class.

Other changes in the job market include:
- growing computerisation and automation, causing job losses
- outsourcing of work to other parts of the world where labour costs are lower, leading to downsizing of the original staff
- increasing numbers of freelance workers
- more employees working from home, with modem link-ups.

4 Refer students to the Exam spot and stress that because of the number of items and the length of the text, they must scan for the information rather than read word by word. Then ask them to look at the example (0) and find the part of the article which gives the answer: *the company passed to me.*

Ask students to read through the questions and think about key words to look out for in the article. They should then complete the task within ten minutes, and compare answers. Remind students that where there are two answers, for example in 1 and 2, they can be written in any order.

Answers
1, 2 A, C   **3** B   **4** A   **5** D   **6** A   **7, 8** B, E   **9** D
10 C   **11, 12** B, D   **13** D   **14, 15** B, E

5 These questions are to raise awareness of negative prefixes. Ask students to work through them in pairs and then elicit their ideas.

Answers
a *Possible answers*: she had been doing the job for too long; her life felt empty outside work; she was getting fed up with the travelling.
b *Possible answer*: if she doesn't earn enough!
c When she was a salon apprentice.
d It lacks a set routine and she has no regular income.
e She might be seen as unable to work in a team.
f Because a registrar has to deal sensitively with people and needs experience of life.

6

Answers
impractical, incapable, disorganised/unorganised, independent, unsuccessful, dishonest, disloyal, impatient

Grammar extra

Explain that *all* is a very common word in English and is used in many useful expressions. Ask students to look at a–h in pairs and elicit answers.

Answers
a had everything   b one bit
c used with a superlative to emphasise
d doing your very best, making the most effort possible
e used to emphasise   f despite
g on the whole; used to summarise
h every type of person

Refer students to the example and its use of *whole*. Explain that sometimes it is possible to use both, although usually other words have to be added to *all* to make the expression fit grammatically: *all of the class came; the whole class came.*

Set the sentences a–f for homework if necessary.

Answers
a all (of the)   b the whole (of the)   c the whole (of the)
d all   e all/the whole; all of   f all (of the)

Encourage students to work out the rules, suggesting they think about the words which follow *all* and *whole*:
- Are the nouns singular or plural?
- What other words have they used? (*of the*)
- What words can come before *whole*? Remind them of the example: *my whole life.*
- Elicit also the meaning of *On the whole …*

Refer them to the Grammar folder, page 203 afterwards.

Teaching extra

For some areas of common error, like *all / the whole*, students need to be reminded of the correct form or usage more than once. In a spare five minutes at the end of a lesson, try giving students a set of sentences which pick up on a previous grammar point. The sentences should be a mix of correct and incorrect ones, with students being asked to make the necessary corrections. Below is an example for *all / the whole*, which you could use in a fortnight's time.

1 Jack's whole life has been spent worrying about money.
2 All you must listen to what I'm saying.
3 My all plan for the future has gone wrong.
4 The police have warned the company to check all postal packages.
5 The whole drinks should be kept cool.

Answers
1 ✓   2 All of you …   3 My whole plan …   4 ✓
5 All (of the) drinks

14.2 SB pages 92–93

Lesson plan

Grammar focus	20–20'
Listening	15–15'
Role play	20–30'
Text	15–25'

SV Limit role play to one turn – see 5.
LV See notes below for 6.

1 Ask students to discuss the differences and identify the tenses used in pairs. Elicit responses.

Answers
Sentence *a* says that the person has sent no e-mails (neither in the past nor in the present). Sentence *b* only refers to the past and doesn't tell us whether the situation is still true. Sentence *c* tells us that the person started to send e-mails at some point in the past but before that time had never sent any. Sentence *d* forecasts a future situation at a certain time.

a present perfect   b simple past
c past perfect; simple past   d future perfect

2 Allow students around six minutes on this task. All the examples came from the article in 14.1. If they need extra context, they can look back at this.

Answers
1 b,h   2 f,j   3 i   4 c,e   5 a   6 g   7 d

Future perfect continuous tense has not been exemplified. Example: *John will have been driving a taxi for thirteen years next April.*

3 Refer students to the Grammar folder, page 203 before they do this exercise.

> **Answers**
> **a** have been showing **b** has been voted
> **c** has been studying **d** will have been working
> **e** had feared **f** will have been launched **g** has made
> **h** had been waiting

4 Ask students to note down the relevant words and phrases for skills and qualities in each extract. Pause after each one to review answers.

> **Answers**
> Speaker 1 (office administrator): flexible; (have) commitment; working long hours
> Speaker 2 (interpreter): keen on languages; fluent; dealing with people face to face; a talent for communication; think really fast; confidence; positive
> Speaker 3 (shop assistant): dress well; know a lot about ...; handle pressure
> Speaker 4 (first-aid worker): (have) lots of energy; extremely fit; specialise in
> Speaker 5 (cook): cope with working at speed; being better organised; staying in control

Tapescript

Speaker 1: There's a big music festival in my town every summer. For the last three years, I've worked in the festival office, doing a whole range of things, from putting leaflets in envelopes to arranging hotel bookings for the various performers. I know I'm flexible – I've had to be – and I've definitely got commitment – I don't mind working long hours as long as there's an end in sight! I really enjoy big events, too – the more people there are, the more enjoyable it is!

Speaker 2: I've always been keen on languages. My mother's from Quebec in Canada, so we speak both German and French at home. I've been learning English since I was twelve. By next summer, I'll have been learning it for over ten years, so I'm sure I'll be really fluent. I like dealing with people face to face and people say I've got quite a lot of talent for communication. I can think really fast which gives me a lot of confidence. Oh, and I'm a very positive person too!

Speaker 3: I've been working in *The Gap* since I left college last year. I think I dress well myself – that's important when you're in this sort of job. I know a lot about sports and leisure clothing, and I often get asked for advice when people are choosing what to buy. Once you've worked in a busy clothing store you can handle anything – I don't mind pressure, in fact it's usually a good thing – makes the day go more quickly.

Speaker 4: I'm having a year off between school and medical school. I've been doing part-time voluntary work in a hospital and I'm also going to evening classes to get a first-aid qualification. I've got lots of energy and I like to think I'm extremely fit. My boyfriend thinks I'm obsessed with sport, actually – I swim for a club and I play tennis or basketball whenever I get the chance. I'd like to specialise in sports medicine when I'm older.

Speaker 5: I did a one-year course in catering after leaving school, and since then I've been working alongside one of Edinburgh's top chefs. She's taught me so much – not just recipes and techniques, either. The most important thing I've learned is how to cope with working at speed. It can get very busy some evenings, but through her, I've developed ways of being better organised ... er ... staying in control when it gets really hot in the kitchen.

Now write the five jobs as headings on the board and elicit other useful skills and qualifications for each one, in preparation for the role play.

5 Explain that the role play involves attending an interview for one of the five jobs. Student A is the interviewee and Student B is the interviewer. A variation on this would be to set up groups of four, consisting of a panel of interviewers and one interviewee, but this may be too daunting for some students!

Allow students about four minutes to read their instructions and prepare what they are going to say. Student B should decide which job is on offer and think of questions to ask.

Allow students about five minutes for the first turn and then suggest they swap roles (<u>not</u> SV).

At the end ask some of the interviewers to report their views to the class, based on the criteria and scale of 0–5. Tell students that the language they have used will be extremely useful in Writing folder 7, which is on applications.

6 Ask students to skim the article and decide who it is written for (office workers). Then ask students to work through the article on their own, filling in spaces 1–15 with the correct perfect tense.

Writing folder 7

Letters of application appear in Paper 2 Part 2. They are usually presented in the form of an advertisement for a job. Writing folder 14 Applications 2 deals with other types of application.

1 Many of these words have come up already in Units 13 and 14. Ask students to write the adjectives related to these nouns.

Answers
motivated   committed   determined   cheerful
enthusiastic   energetic   organised   talented
skilled/skilful   confident

2 In pairs, ask students to discuss the qualities and skills needed. Remind them to think about the whole content of the advert, that is, the introductory text and all three bulleted points. They should put themselves in the position of the target reader (ZY Cruises) and decide what information the company would need in order to make a decision about an applicant.

3 Ask students to discuss the two letters and decide whether both have covered everything.

Answers
Letter A has covered all the points.
Letter B has omitted to talk about his knowledge of English. The letter is thin on relevant experience and on the reason why he would like the job. It is also thin on personal qualities and what is said would probably irritate the reader.

4 Suggest students rewrite the letter in pairs, discussing their improvements. Refer them to the Exam spot.

5 Ask students to read the task and underline the key points.

Answer
They should answer all three bulleted questions, including some reference to the qualities needed (*energetic* and *cheerful*). For a high mark, there should also be a mention of where they saw the advertisement.

Encourage students to make a paragraph plan and remind them not to include postal addresses in their answers.

Sample answer

Dear Sir or Madam

I am writing to apply for the job of tour guide with Europewide Coach Tours, which was advertised in The Times last Saturday. I am just the person you are looking for.

I have been studying English for twelve years, so I am fluent. I recently spent three months in London, as part of my studies. I also speak French and a little German.

Although I know many parts of Europe well, I am always keen to visit new places and find out more about them. It would be good to share this knowledge with others.

People say I am a good communicator and I enjoy being with other people. I have a good sense of humour and plenty of energy.

In terms of relevant experience, I have spent the last two summers working as a guide, taking groups of foreign tourists on walking tours around our city. I therefore have a good understanding of the needs of visitors from other countries.

I hope you will consider my application favourably.

Yours sincerely

UNIT 15 Too many people

Unit topic	The environment
15.1	
Exam skills	Speaking
	Listening Paper 4 Part 2
Vocabulary	Environment vocabulary
Exam skills	Use of English Paper 3 Part 5
Pronunciation	Numbers and letters
15.2	
Grammar	Countable and uncountable nouns
	Some, any, no
	Expressions with uncountable nouns
Exam skills	Use of English Paper 3 Part 2
Workbook contents	
1, 2	Vocabulary – Use of English Part 1, environment
3, 4	Writing – linkers, informal letter
5	Grammar – *some, any, no, every*

15.1 SB pages 96–97

Lesson plan

Speaking	5–10'
Listening	15–20'
Vocabulary	5–10'
Speaking	5–10'
Word formation	10–15'
Pronunciation	20–25'

SV Omit 2 and 4; set 5 for homework.
LV See notes below for 8.

1 The photos are of:
A: One of the Pyramids and the outskirts of the city of Cairo
B: The Colosseum in Rome, surrounded by traffic
C: The Grand Canyon and a group of tourists

Ask students to look at the photos of famous places, then discuss the questions either in groups or pairs. Some ideas of the problems caused by too many tourists are:
    erosion of paths, buildings
    litter, air pollution from traffic

wildlife disturbed by noise
wildlife die – broken bottles, being fed the wrong food, etc.

2 A woman is talking about the problems faced by the Grand Canyon National Park Service. Students have to take notes from what she is saying.

Answers
1 northwestern   2 1.6 kms / kilometres   3 1919
4 5m / million   5 people   6 air pollution   7 water
8 all year   9 rapids   10 (seven/7 natural) wonders

Tapescript

Presenter: Situated in the northwestern part of Arizona, the Grand Canyon is one of the natural wonders of the world. Contrary to popular belief, the Grand Canyon is not the longest, deepest, or widest canyon in the world. But it is accessible, and with little vegetation to hide it, it feels big. Nothing prepares you for that first sight of it. From the top it drops 1.6 kilometres to the desert floor below. But however vast it seems, it is not big enough to support the millions of people who visit it every year.

When one section of the Grand Canyon was declared a national park in 1919, three years after the creation of the National Park Service, visitor numbers were 44,000. Today, with five million visitors a year, the Park Service is finding it difficult to keep the Canyon accessible to the public and to safeguard it for future generations.

The pressures on the Grand Canyon National Park have forced the Park Service to draw up a management plan. One of the first problems it has tackled is that of the large number of visitors' cars. Options included the introduction of an electric bus service and a light railway system in and around Grand Canyon village.

Some of the other problems faced by the park are the result of things happening outside its boundaries. Take air pollution. On summer days, when there are southwesterly winds, the pollution blown in from Southern California can restrict the views over the Canyon.

Then, another of the big problems is the availability of water resources in the park, as, at present, there is a drought. The Park cannot draw water from the river but only from a spring on the north side of the canyon, using a pipeline. If this pipeline is damaged, then water has to be brought in by truck. This last happened in 1995 when floods caused a landslide, which destroyed the pipeline.

The Colorado River, which created the Canyon, looks wild but in fact, is managed intensely. Twenty-four kilometres upstream is the Glen Canyon Dam which has had a profound impact on the river. Now the river flow is about a tenth of what it was previously.

The Colorado used to reach temperatures of twenty-four degrees in summer. Today, it is a cold seven degrees all year as water release comes from deep within the reservoir. As a result, some species of fish have become extinct. In addition, the rapids are getting bigger, as the river is too weak to move the boulders washed out of the canyons downstream.

Visitors are proving to be powerful allies of the park. Those who once thought that the Grand Canyon was just an awesome hole in the ground soon learn that however big it is, its popularity is in danger of destroying the very qualities that made it one of the seven natural wonders in the world.

Photocopiable tapescript activity (P ⋯⟶ page 187)

Ask students to compare what is actually said with their notes.

3   Refer students to the Vocabulary spot. Ask students to explain/draw what the meaning of the water words are: floods, dam, reservoir, rapids, drought and river.

They should then sort the next list of words into two parts: words to do with throwing away and words to do with using again.

> **Answers**
> a   throw away: rubbish, junk, litter
> b   use again: recycle, bottle bank, second-hand

4   If time, students should talk about how they feel about being 'green', and how they see problems connected to the environment.

eaching extra

> Highlight the difference in meaning between:
> *economic* to do with the economy – *a country's economic policy*
> *economical* saving something – *I am as economical as possible with water/money.*

Following this exercise is some exam practice in word formation. Students need to make another word from

> **Answers**
>
> | adjective | noun | adverb | verb |
> |---|---|---|---|
> | longest | length | lengthily | lengthen |
> | deepest | depth | deeply | deepen |
> | widest | width | widely | widen |
> | weak | weakness | weakly | weaken |
> | strong | strength | strongly | strengthen |
> | short | shortness | shortly | shorten |

the word in capitals so that the text makes sense. Encourage them to read through the whole text first. They <u>must</u> spell the words correctly.

6   Play the tape about the Grand Canyon again and ask

> **Answers**
> 1 products   2 surroundings   3 chemical   4 unwanted
> 5 poisonous   6 unfortunately   7 scientists   8 eventually
> 9 disappear

students to write down all the numbers that the woman mentions.

> **Answers**
> 1.6kms   millions   1919   three years   44,000   5 million
> 1995   24 kms   a tenth   24 degrees   7 degrees   7

7   Now put students in pairs and ask them to read the numbers, letters and words in this exercise aloud. They should note the pronunciation of '0'.

Play the tape so they can check their pronunciation.

Tapescript

Measurement
thirteen kilometres
thirty centimetres
nought point five kilometres
two point five metres
one hundred and fifty-three kilos
one metre, fifty-three centimetres
a half
a quarter
two thirds

Dates

the first of May, eighteen ninety-nine
the third of August, two thousand
the twelfth of February, two thousand and four
the twenty-fifth of December, nineteen ninety
the fifteenth century
the fourth of the fifth, forty-five

Money

ten p or ten pence
one pound forty-five
fifty dollars

'0'

012-323-66778
three nil
forty love
zero or nought degrees Celsius

Telephone numbers

01256-311399
00-44-324-667012

Maths

two plus six equals eight
three minus two equals one
four times four equals sixteen
ten divided by two equals five
twenty per cent
three degrees
the square root of sixteen

8 In pairs students ask and answer the questions a–i.

Extension activity

This can be expanded into a team game between students. Ask them to think up some more questions which require a number as an answer. For example:
maths questions, questions about 'firsts', dates of battles, etc.

15.2 SB pages 98–99

Lesson plan

Grammar   50–60'
Vocabulary   20–30'

SV Set 5, which summarises the grammar in this unit, for homework.

LV See notes below for 1.

1 Students make many mistakes with countable and uncountable nouns. It is something that needs to be constantly worked at. The columns contain a mixture of countable and uncountable nouns. Students need to decide which word is countable.

Answers
Countable – country, meal, recommendation, journey, job, coin, storm, temperature, verb, vehicle, seat, hairstyle, suitcase, mountain, note.
Four words can be countable and uncountable.
lands e.g. tribal lands rather than the idea of ground/soil
works e.g. the works of Shakespeare rather than something you are employed to do
hairs e.g. hairs on the body rather than hair on the head
travels e.g. The Travels of Marco Polo rather than the concept of movement

Draw students' attention to the Vocabulary spot after they have finished the exercise.

Extension activity

Ask students to explain the use of the following with the differences in meaning.
paper/a paper – paper you write on and a newspaper
coffee/a coffee – coffee the product and a cup of coffee
experience/an experience – how much time you have spent doing something and one thing that happened to you.
damage/damages – damage to an object and the money you receive in compensation.

2 Students should look at the information about determiners before they do the next exercise.

Teaching extra

Note that *a lot of* is more informal than *a great deal/good deal of* or *large number/amount of*. In a formal letter, for example, it is better to avoid *a lot of.*

Answers
a How many of the tourists actually realise the problems they cause?
b Little of the soil can be used for cultivation now the trees have been cut down.
c A large amount of equipment is needed to camp at the bottom of the Canyon.
d Little luggage can be carried on the back of a donkey down the dirt tracks.
e A large number of rainforests are being cut down every year.
f The amount of traffic is causing too much congestion in major cities.
g Many governments believe that nuclear power is the key to future energy problems.
h The Park Ranger gave me a lot of/a great deal of good advice about camping in the national park.
i Few people nowadays wear fur coats.

3 Students often confuse *few* and *a few* and *little* and *a little*. *Few* and *little* are positive in tone. *A few* and *a little* are more negative.

> **Answers**
> few mistakes – I'm good at English.
> a few mistakes – I'm quite good at English, but not perfect.
>
> little time – I'm really too busy.
> a little time – I do have some time but it's not very much.

Grammar extra

When students first study English they learn the general rules about some and any. However, these rules don't always reflect the real use of some and any. Students should look at the sentences a–f and try to work out the rules.

> **Answers**
> *Some* is used with an affirmative verb, for offers and if the answer to a question is going to be 'yes'.
> *No* is used with an affirmative verb to give a negative meaning.
> *Any* is used with a negative verb and in questions. Also when the answer to a question maybe 'no'.

4 Students need to know the correct expression for limiting an uncountable noun. They can use *a piece of* or *a bit of* but these words are not precise enough.

> **Answers**
> a shower of rain   a slice of cake   an item of clothing
> a glass of water   a clap of thunder   a pane of glass
> a ball of string   a flash of lightning   a crowd of people
> a bar of chocolate

5 This exercise summarises the grammar work done in this unit. It can be set for homework if time is short.

> **Answers**
> **a** some; bars   **b** any/some; flashes
> **c** Many/Most/Lots; panes
> **d** hair   **e** some advice/information   **f** any coins
> **g** most/some; traffic

6

> **Answers**
> **1** some   **2** few   **3** ago   **4** into   **5** in   **6** deal/amount
> **7** Although/Though   **8** and   **9** than   **10** of/from
> **11** which/that   **12** one   **13** used   **14** had   **15** is

Exam folder 8

Paper 4 Part 3 Multiple matching

SB pages 100–101

Ask students to read through the introduction and the Advice. Each extract they hear lasts about thirty seconds.

1 Students need to look at the questions A–F very carefully. One wrong answer could affect two answers.

Let them have a good look at the questions and check they understand any vocabulary. Ask them to cover up the extract from the tapescript and the analysis, which follows. Play the tape until 'classes to get better qualifications'. Stop the tape and check they have B as the answer.

They should then read through the tapescript and look at the analysis of the questions.

Tapescript

Speaker 1: When I started my last year at school, I didn't take it seriously enough. I should've chosen subjects which were useful rather than ones I liked or that sounded easy. By the time the exams came I'd given up and I did very badly. I knew I'd have to work hard but I wasn't able to catch up with my friends. Because I failed at science I can't be a teacher, which is what I really want to do. I'm doing a part-time job in order to make ends meet and next year I'll be starting evening classes to get better qualifications.

2 Play the rest of the tape for questions 2–5. Ask the students to cover the tapescript.

> **Answers**
> **2** E   **3** C   **4** F   **5** A

Tapescript

Speaker 2: I left school and moved to a college to take my final exams. It was the best decision I could have made. At the college nobody seemed to care about homework and this really motivated me. I had to plan my work myself – there was no one to make you do it and no one to check up on what you'd done. I was still dependent on my parents for money – but that was OK. I learned a lot about real life there – things like getting on with people and organising your time, which has been really useful now I'm working.

Speaker 3: When I left school I didn't have a particular career in mind so I decided to do Environmental Studies at university, mainly because I'd enjoyed geography at school. I didn't really like the course at university and I did think about leaving but instead I changed courses, which was easier than I expected. I think university was useful in that I learnt how to live alone and how to budget, and as I'm an underpaid teacher now that really helps.

Speaker 4: I had no difficulty choosing what I was going to do – my parents are both doctors and ever since I was small I also wanted to do that. They really encouraged me and I did well at school and got into a good medical school fairly easily. It was surprisingly tough at medical school, but I had some good friends and we pulled through together. I think the doubts only began to set in when I graduated and got my first job in a hospital. I began to wonder if I'd missed out because I'd been so focused on becoming a doctor. So now I'm doing some voluntary work in Africa which I'm really enjoying.

Speaker 5: I decided to take a year off after doing my last year at school. I'd had enough of revising and sitting in a library so I decided to go off to Australia for nine months and earn a bit of money. I've got relatives there who put me up when I first arrived and found me a job. It wasn't doing anything particularly interesting, but the great part was that I was getting to know people who were completely different to the ones I'd known back home. I really recommend taking a year out, but you need to have a firm plan or it could end up a waste of time.

3   Students should now look at the tapescript and underline the parts which gave them the answer.

UNIT 16 Good, plain cooking

Unit topic	Food
16.1	
Exam skills	Listening Paper 4 Part 2
	Reading Paper 1 Part 3
Vocabulary	Expressions with *off*
Speaking	Food
16.2	
Grammar focus	Nouns
	Articles
	Expressions
	Possession
	Prepositions of time
Listening	A recipe
Workbook contents	
1	Reading – Part 4 matching
2	Vocabulary – expressions with *out of*
3, 4	Grammar – Use of English Part 4, articles

16.1 SB pages 102–103

Lesson plan	
Speaking	5–10'
Listening	10–15'
Reading	30–40'
Vocabulary	5–10'
Speaking	10–15'

SV Set 5 for homework; omit 6.
LV See notes below for 3 and 5.

1   Ask students to make a list of what they normally eat in a day and then discuss what they've written with a partner. This exercise could be quite sensitive if there are students in the class who are overweight or underweight. It can be easily omitted.

2   Ask students to speculate on what people in Japan, Alaska and the USA eat. If the students are Japanese then they could say what the stereotype of what they eat is and say whether it is true or not.

ⓑ ackground information

The Inuit is the proper name for what used to be called the Eskimo people who live within the Arctic Circle.

3   On the tape are three women talking about what they normally eat. Students should take notes of what is said. Play the tape as often as needed. Round up this exercise by asking students which diet they would prefer and why.

Answers	
Akiko	
Breakfast	soup, rice, fish,
Lunch	noodles, hamburgers
Dinner	pasta, soup
Kunu	
Breakfast	cheese sandwich, orange juice
Lunch	raw fish
Supper	reindeer, fish
Gayle	
Breakfast	omelette
Lunch	sandwich –tuna, tomato paste, non-fat bread
Dinner	grilled fish, chicken

ⓔ xtension activity

To give students more practice in note-taking, you could do a jig-saw listening. Divide the class into groups of three (Group A, B and C) and get them to take extensive notes about one person (not just about what they eat). Rearrange the groups into a mixed group with an A, B and a C member and ask them to discuss what they found out.

Tapescript

Speaker 1: My name is Akiko and I was born in Hiroshima in Japan. I moved to England with my family when I was three but my mother always makes us traditional Japanese food. For breakfast we have soup, rice and fish. For lunch I eat noodles, but I also love hamburgers. It's very common for Japanese people to mix traditional and Western food. I'm conscious of healthy eating and I eat a lot of vegetables, but I don't worry about my weight! In the evening I'll have pasta or some more soup.

Speaker 2: My name is Kunu, and I grew up in Alaska, where meals are central to Inuit life. I moved to Seattle when I was seventeen, and became physically ill because my body rejected Western foods. I do eat some Western food though. For breakfast I always have a cheese sandwich with orange juice. Lunch is usually raw fish, and for supper I have reindeer or fish. I hardly eat any sweet foods and I exercise five times a week.

Speaker 3: Everyone calls me Gayle. I exercise for about half an hour before breakfast, which is usually an omelette. For lunch I'll have a sandwich – a mixture of tuna and tomato paste on non-fat bread. I eat a lot but I never eat fat. If I go out to eat I always ask the waiter to miss out the cream or cheese or oil. People are used to it in LA. I keep a journal every day to say what exercise I've done and exactly what I've eaten. In the evening I'll have grilled fish or chicken.

4   Students should skim the text, that is, read it very quickly to get an idea of what it is about. They shouldn't worry too much about vocabulary. They should then look at the sentences A–H and decide which one should go in gaps 1–6. H is the example.

Background information

Students may not be familiar with the information that children in the UK often refuse to eat vegetables. They also prefer fish in fish fingers and meat as hamburgers and sausages. Pasta and pizza are also favourites with British children.

Answers
1 B   2 G   3 A   4 F   5 E   1 C

5   This exercise can be set for homework if time is short. Students must read through the passage again to find words with the same meaning.

Answers
a flavoured   b diet   c additives   d portions   e coating

Off is often used in English in connection with food. It can have various meanings.

Answers
a not available   b bad   c rude
d not keen on/not having

Extension activity

In the article there was the expression *in fact*. Here are some more expressions with *in*. Ask students to match the expression on the left with the explanation on the right. For example:

in fact ———— owing money
in common ———— actually

in debt	using a pen
in the end	finally
in particular	crying
in public	divided in half
in ink	some fact which is similar
in tears	a different way of saying something
in other words	especially
in two	so everyone can see, know

Answers
in common – some fact which is similar
in debt – owing money
in the end – finally
in particular – especially
in public – so everyone can see, know
in ink – using a pen
in tears – crying
in other words – a different way of saying something
in two – divided in half

6   Ask students to form groups to discuss the questions a–g.

16.2 SB pages 104–105

Lesson plan

Grammar	40–50'
Prepositions	10–15'
Speaking and listening	20–30'

SV Set 4 for homework; omit 6.
LV See notes below for 6.

1   The aim of this part of Unit 16 is to look at nouns. This first exercise revises and extends the work done on countable and uncountable nouns in Unit 15.

Answers
singular countable = waiter, lunch (a, the)
Normally , we talk about 'a' or 'the' waiter. However, we also use the word without an article when we are attracting attention: 'Waiter!' We can use lunch with 'a' or 'the', but when we are talking about it in general terms, we don't use an article: What time are we having lunch? (This is the same for all meals.)
plural countable = noodles (nothing, the)
uncountable = fish, cheese (nothing, the)

2   In this exercise students need to match the rule with an example sentence.

Answers
1 d   2 f   3 g   4 c   5 b,h   6 a   7 e,a   8 i
9 j,k   10 e

3 The gaps in the article can have more than one answer. Check students understand the possible differences.

Background information

In Japan, and in many other countries, customers can get an idea of what to order from looking at plastic replicas of the food available. This article is about fake food in Japanese restaurants. These plastic replicas are called *sanpuru*.

Answers
1 nothing/the 2 nothing/the 3 a 4 the 5 nothing
6 nothing 7 a 8 a/the 9 The 10 nothing 11 a
12 the 13 the 14 nothing 15 nothing 16 a

4 Using an article or not can change the meaning of some English expressions. For example:
I went to the hospital to see a sick friend.
I went to hospital because I was sick.
The same rule applies to *church* and to *prison*.
Also you *play football*, but *play the violin*.

Answers
a the b – c the d – e the/– f – g – h –
i – j a k – l – m the n the o the

5 Students are often confused about how to indicate possession in English. They have a tendency to only use *of*.

Ask students to read through the information about possession. This is a simplified list of rules about possession, suitable for intermediate students. They should then read the sentences and correct them, if necessary, giving reasons for their choice of answer.

Answers
a My husband's father (person)
b restaurant window (kind) c OK (position)
d a cooking magazine (kind) e OK (kind) f OK (time)
g a cup of coffee (container) h OK (position)

Grammar extra

Students fill in the gaps using one of the prepositions in the box. This exercise should be fairly straightforward and is mainly just to check there are no problems with the use of these prepositions. *Till* means the same as *until*.

Answers
a on, in, at, in b at/over c at, in/during d until/from/till
e on/for f on, at/from g from, to/until/till h since
i during/in j for k by

6 This is an unscripted recording between a man and a woman. The man is describing how to cook his favourite dish. Play the tape and ask students to write down the ingredients they hear. Then play it again and ask them to write down the method of making the dish. The name of the dish is Boeuf Bourguignonne. It is a French dish.

Students can then use the basic vocabulary from the listening to talk about their favourite dish. They should remember to use the imperative for giving instructions.

Answers
Ingredients – beef, red wine, bacon, small onions (shallots), seasoned flour, and mushrooms.
Serve with mashed potatoes, green vegetables or salad.
Method
Fry the bacon.
Add some onions and brown them.
Chop the beef into cubes.
Coat the beef in seasoned flour.
Fry the beef with the bacon and the onions.
Add the red wine.
Cook slowly in an oven for about two and a half hours.
Add mushrooms.
Cook twenty minutes more.

Extension activity

Ask students to write out their favourite recipe missing out the verbs (fry, add, chop, mix, stir, bake, boil, etc.). Ask them to swap their recipe with another student who has to see if they can fill in the gaps correctly.

Tapescript

Woman: Tell me about your favourite dish.
Man: Right, well, it's something I tasted when I was in France, called Boeuf Bourguignonne, and it's basically a stew of beef cooked in red wine. It takes quite a long time to prepare, and indeed, quite a long time to cook. You need some bacon, which you fry, then you add some very small onions, shallots, and you brown them. And then you coat the beef, which you've chopped up into small cubes in seasoned flour, flour with salt and pepper. And then you fry that, along with the bacon and the onions and then you add red wine – that's the nice bit 'cos you can usually take a sip while …
Woman: Of course, …
Man: … while you're doing that, and the better the wine, the better the dish.
Woman: Oh really? You can't use a cheap bit that's left over from the day before?
Man: It's better if you use burgundy, which, of course, is quite an expensive wine, but it does make the best boeuf bourguignonne …

Woman: Oh, right.

Man: … and then you put that in the oven and you need to cook it for quite a long time on a low heat …

Woman: … slowly …

Man: … so that all the juices meld, and then about, I suppose, a quarter of an hour before …

Woman: So when you say quite a long time, how many hours?

Man: Well, I think between two and two and a half on …

Woman: Yes.

Man: … on a lowish heat. Then about 20 minutes before you're going to serve it you put some small mushrooms in it and then ...

Woman: cut up?

Man: Yes, unless they're those small button mushrooms, or you can slice them up 'cos they make the liquid a little thinner, so with that you serve mashed potatoes maybe, and a green vegetable or a salad. It's absolutely delicious.

Woman: Sounds lovely.

Writing folder 8

Paper 2 Part 1 (Question 1)
Transactional letters 2

SB pages 106–107

1 When writing their answers to the transactional letter, students often have little awareness of the register they are writing in. It is important to keep it consistent all the way through the letter – either formal or informal. Another point that students should bear in mind is the reason for writing. In the letter to Pete it shows how to begin a letter with a reason. Students often miss this out and instead go into great detail about how their family is and what they got for their birthdays. This is irrelevant and they will get lower marks because of it.

Ask students which register the letter to Pete is in (informal). Then they should decide their answers to the gaps.

Answers

1 b 2 b 3 a 4 a 5 b 6 b 7 a 8 a 9 a 10 b

---

2 This is a sample exam question. Ask students to read through all the information. Check they understand what would be required of them.

3 Students read through the answering letter to find the main problems. The letter includes:
 – register errors
 – grammar errors
 – repetition
 – limited structure and vocabulary
 – no ending

These are all errors that FCE candidates commonly make when doing the transactional letter. All the points are included, but just doing that doesn't merit a pass mark.

Students reread the letter and rewrite it.

Sample answer

Dear Anna,

Thank you very much for inviting me to your party. I'd love to come. The restaurant sounds lovely. You may not know that I've recently become a vegetarian. Do you know if the restaurant does vegetarian food?

Thank you for the map. I shall take the train but I don't know whether to walk or take a taxi from the station. You said it was only five minutes away from the restaurant – is that on foot or by taxi? Could you also let me know the name of the road the restaurant is in as it wasn't on the map?

I will have a friend staying with me at the time you will be having the party. Would it be all right if she came too? She's called Elisabeth and she's a student from France. She is taking a course at my university and I feel it would be rude for me to disappear for a weekend while she is here. She's also 21 and very nice.

Hope to hear from you soon. What would you like for a birthday present?

Best wishes,

---

4 Students read through the information and using a highlighter pen underline all the points they think are necessary to mention in their answers. They should make sure they cover these points in some way:
- weather
- instructors
- accommodation
- price
- food

The main point of this example letter is to get students to write a persuasive letter. They should be enthusiastic about the trip. Tell them that they need to use a wide range of vocabulary and structure. They should try not to repeat themselves.

This exercise could be set for homework.

Sample answer

Dear Liz,

I'm writing to tell you about a trip to the Lake District I'm organising for a weekend in the spring. Sue and Alice are also going to come along – you remember them from my party, don't you? We thought it'd be really great if you could come too, as we all get on so well together.

The weekend is at a special activity centre where fully qualified instructors teach you how to climb or go sailing and swimming. I'm sure it'll be too cold to go swimming in the lake but there is an indoor heated swimming pool in the nearby town. It'll be just the thing for us to get some exercise after a long winter of studying.

We will be staying in heated wood cabins and we would have to do all our own cooking. There's a town nearby so we could get food there or go to a restaurant if we feel lazy! The cost is £150 between the four of us, which I think is very reasonable. Do say you'll come!

Love

UNIT 17 Collectors and creators

Unit topic	Hobbies
17.1	
Exam skills	Speaking Paper 5 Part 2
	Listening Paper 4 Part 1
Vocabulary	Phrases and phrasal verbs with *look*
17.2	
Grammar focus	Relative clauses
	Use of English Paper 3 Part 4
Pronunciation	Contrastive stress
Workbook contents	
1, 2, 3, 4	Reading and vocabulary
5	Use of English – Part 2

17.1 SB pages 108–109

Lesson plan

Speaking	30–40'
Listening	20–25'
Vocabulary	15–15'

SV Omit 5.
LV See notes below for 5.

1   In this unit, the long turn (Paper 5 Part 2) is practised in full. Refer students to the Exam spot and, if necessary, to the information about the Speaking test on page 7.

Explain that it is better for a candidate to keep talking for the full minute, rather than 'drying up'.

Ask students to read their instructions and allow them a minute or so to think about the notes for Student A, which are there to help them on the first long turn.

Start them talking and keep an eye on the time yourself. Stop the A students after one minute. Then ask Student B to make a brief comment as instructed.

Have a brief class discussion before starting the next long turn with the second pair of photos. Check that the Student As did compare and contrast the two photos. Elicit the type of comments made by the Student Bs. Refer them to the useful language for giving opinions in Unit 6 if necessary (page 39).

2   The pictures show a model-maker and a collector (Hub Cap Annie). As students do the task, walk round and listen to some of the pairs. Do not interrupt or correct them, but make a mental note of any feedback you can give later.

After the minute is up, Student A should make a brief comment as indicated. Then elicit the ideas that came up in the pairs, listing the main ones on the board. Show students that there is in fact a lot that can be said about a pair of photos.

3   Set a time limit of three minutes for the team activity. Check which team has the longer list and write some of the hobbies on the board under the two headings: *Collectors* and *Creators*. Then ask students to decide on the four most interesting from these lists. Elicit opinions from the class afterwards.

4   Explain that students are now going to do a complete set of listening short extracts, the eight multiple choice questions in Paper 4 Part 1. Refer them back to Exam folder 6 (pages 74–75) if necessary before they start. Then play the tape straight through. Each question is recorded and each extract is repeated.

Go through the answers and deal with any problems, quoting from the tapescript or replaying the extracts concerned. The photograph on page 109 shows slot-car racing (question 4).

Answers
1 B   2 C   3 B   4 C   5 A   6 C   7 C   8 A

Tapescript

1   You hear a man giving a talk about his hobby. Where does he find his best fossils?
A   at shops
B   on beaches
C   up cliffs

I've been collecting fossils for about fifteen years. Lyme Regis on the Dorset coast is a good spot and you see a lot of professionals there with all the equipment, chipping away half way up some rock or other. I don't know, though. I mean I've got a special hammer, but my finest pieces have been just picked up by the shore, usually after a storm. 1987 was the year I found the most – the year the hurricane struck Britain. If you're not feeling at all adventurous, you can buy some excellent fossils in the shops in Lyme Regis. I was very tempted to get a magnificent dinosaur's tooth once.

2 You overhear this conversation in a café. What sort of postcards is the woman keen to collect?
A ones that are in good condition
B ones from the 1930s
C ones with a printed message

Man: Here are those cards I bought for you in Oxford, to add to your collection. I hope you don't think they're too tatty – they must be at least fifty years old …

Woman: Thanks. The condition they're in doesn't bother me. And actually, looking at the stamps, they're older than you say, which is brilliant because I haven't got many from the 1930s.

Man: Oh, so you're looking for cards from a certain period?

Woman: Well, I collect all sorts, but I'm on the lookout for older ones that have text on the picture. Like this one, which says: 'Thinking of you in St Ives' …

3 You hear a woman talking on the radio. Why were the wooden objects she describes unusual?
A They were painted with beautiful designs.
B They were made from different types of wood.
C They were carved from a single piece.

I knew someone once who had an absolute passion for making things out of wood. He spent hours and hours on his hobby – whatever the object was, he always took great pride in doing it well and making it unique, by choosing a special wood. He never chose the same kind twice. He would make all sorts of things – a new handle for a fork, with a pattern cut into it; enough models to fill several glass cases … He even made an electric guitar, which he painted designs on – something he didn't normally do. One piece I remember well is a polar bear. The way it was carved really captured the look of the animal, walking heavily through the snow.

4 You hear this radio interview. Who suggested the boy took up slot-car racing?
A his father
B his friend
C his cousin

Int: Jamie Eagle, who is the outright winner of today's slot-car racing, is with me now. Congratulations, Jamie, and this is now your tenth win! So where did it all begin? I know your father was also racing here today. Did he know what he was doing when he persuaded you to take up such a time-consuming hobby?

Jamie: Er, actually, it was me who persuaded him – he's only been racing this year. He's pretty hopeless at it, too! No, it was my cousin who's to blame. He used to take me along when he went to race meetings – I was five at the time – and I thought it was just brilliant!

Int: And if your father's racing his own car, who do you have as back-up today?

Jamie: I've introduced my friend Ian to slot-car racing – at the moment he's free to help me, though next year he hopes to have a car of his own.

5 You hear part of a radio programme. Which kind of beads does the girl have most of?
A glass
B wooden
C plastic

Int: This is Radio QB, the phone lines are open and we want to hear about *your* hobbies. And here's Eleanor, from London. What are you into, Eleanor?

Eleanor: Beads. I've got several hundred, in all shapes and sizes – glass, metal, plastic ones … They're from all over the world, too: I've got a handful of beautiful wooden ones, from India, and some very unusual African ones carved out of bone. A few of them I've made up into earrings and necklaces, but what I really like doing is collecting! Especially coloured glass ones, which I've got loads of.

Int: And you say you've got several hundred – how long has it taken you to get so many?

Eleanor: Not that long, really… I had lots of plastic ones when I was a kid, but I gave those away so they don't count! I suppose I got serious about beads three years ago. Since then, my family have given me tins of beads as presents, and I spend most of my pocket money on them too.

6 You overhear a man talking on the phone. Who is he talking to?
A an assistant at a shop selling kits
B a journalist working for a magazine
C a member of staff at a factory

Now look here, you're not going to pass me on to anyone else … I have … I have been back there twice but they said I must take the matter up with you. It's clearly your responsibility – the model kit was sealed, so it can't have been the shop's fault, can it? … No, I'm quite sure. This is crazy, I mean I buy a lot of your kits, you know. Do you want me to contact Model-Makers magazine and describe the story so far? … No, I didn't think you would. Listen, you have all my details, so please get on and sort it out!

7 You hear part of a radio interview. Which opinion does the interviewer express about Jenny's pictures?
A They are well-researched.
B They are carefully chosen.
C They are extremely detailed.

Int: Jenny Braintree, whose bedroom I'm sitting in right now, has a rather unusual hobby. Jenny, you took up this hobby four years ago and …

Jenny: Er … it was four months ago, in fact. I was on a beach holiday with my parents, and there were all these nice, smooth pebbles. I brought loads home and started to paint them. I've done 89 so far.

Int: In only four months! My, you have been busy. You take a lot of care to select the flattest pebbles, for obvious reasons. And then what do you paint on these stones?

Jenny: I … I'm trying to paint a scene from every country in the world, most of which I haven't been to. So I've done this pebble, which has the Eiffel Tower in France on it … and this one of a Swiss mountain … and I'm working on a picture of the Brazilian rain forest at the moment.

Int: Which is just exquisite. Jenny, who has a library book open in front of her now, sometimes uses references for the things that are in her pictures. Incredibly, no picture is more than five centimetres across, but they contain so much in miniature. Well done, Jenny, I'm tremendously impressed by your enthusiasm and hard work …

8 You will hear a man talking on the radio. How does he spend his weekends?

A pretending to be a soldier
B studying a history course
C producing different plays

People think it's a bit odd that I spend my weekends dressed up in anything from metal armour to old uniforms, out in the open air. But it's good fun! The group that puts on these events was only formed about four months ago. I joined in April and we've already performed five battles! You learn a great deal about history, because everything is researched properly – from the costumes to the actual battle tactics. My girlfriend's not too pleased with me at the moment. I'm going to have to miss her birthday 'cos we're doing the Battle of Naseby. That's not the reason she's mad at me though. She wanted to come too but I wouldn't let her!

5 Encourage students to give reasons for their choice of hobbies that would interest them least.

Extension activity

Include some vocabulary work on negative adjectives before this discussion. Put these adjectives up on the board and ask students to organise them in four meaning groups.

tedious time-consuming dull expensive silly boring fiddly overpriced tricky costly trivial unimportant

> **Answers**
> expensive, overpriced, costly
> tedious, dull, boring
> silly, trivial, unimportant
> time-consuming, tricky, fiddly

---

6 Check students understand the phrases and phrasal verbs in a–i before they go through questions 1–9. Encourage students to use their imagination to the full. Elicit at least one answer from everyone in the class (there are 27 in all!).

> **Suggested answers**
> 1 A dentist B immigration/customs officer C plumber
> 2 A sewing B cooking C translating
> 3 A coastguard B detective/police C accountant
> 4 A shiny and expensive B dark brown C dull and grey
> 5 A a doctor B a gardener C an MP/ the city council
> 6 A My account is not in the red!
>   B You can't stay up to watch that programme on TV.
>   C My private life is my own concern.
> 7 A dishes, tins of food B that your friend was lying to you
>   C distant galaxies; new stars
> 8 A someone was crossing the road
>   B a big wave was about to hit you
>   C a pot of paint was in danger of toppling over
> 9 A his older brother or sister B a professor
>   C the head chef

17.2 SB pages 110–111

> **Lesson plan**
>
> | | |
> |---|---|
> | Grammar | 30–40' |
> | Use of English | 5–20' |
> | Pronunciation | 30–30' |
>
> **SV** Set 5 for homework.
> **LV** See notes below for 4.

1 Students discuss examples *a* and *b* in pairs. Check understanding before referring them to the Grammar folder, page 204. Then elicit the difference in meaning between *c* and *d*.

> **Answers**
> a Only some of the children were tired, so not all of them went to bed. (Defining clause)
> b All the children were tired and all went to bed. (Non-defining)
> c They decided to stay at the first hotel which had a pool, so they probably passed several which didn't have pools.
> d They stayed at the very first hotel they came to and fortunately, it had a pool.

2

> **Answers**
> a is a non-defining clause b is a defining clause
> c N which d D who e D who f N whose
> g N (most of) which h D that

3 Elicit the missing pronoun and refer students to the Grammar folder, page 204 if necessary. Students can work through a–e in pairs.

Answers

Here are those cards which / that I bought for you in Oxford.

a that/which I wanted …
b who/that I really …
c that/which I can't stand …
d who/that you met …
e that/which we stayed …

4 Ask students to read the explanation and then work through the examples a–e.

Answers
a where b when c who d which/that e where

(E)xtension activity

Ask students to write five sentences containing *where, when* and *why* on a piece of paper, one under the other. These should be a mixture of defining or non-defining clauses. They should fold the paper over so that only the bottom sentence is visible. Then ask them to get into groups of four or five and pass their sheet to the person on their right. Each person should tick the sentence if they think the pronoun can be omitted. If they are right, they stay in the game. If not, they sit back and advise the others. The winner is the person who continues to give the right answer for the most turns.

5 If done in class, ask students to skim the text for its general meaning. Elicit opinions on the hobby described.

Answers
1 than 2 ✓ 3 it 4 ✓ 5 with 6 ✓ 7 and
8 so 9 the 10 that 11 since 12 away 13 being
14 ✓ 15 as

6 Explain the importance of stress patterns in English. Contrastive stress allows the speaker to reinforce the correction of a factual error, or underline a different opinion.

Play the tape and ask students to follow the examples, where the stressed words are underlined.

Tapescript

Int: Did he know what he was doing when he persuaded you to take up such a time-consuming hobby?
Jamie: Er, actually, it was <u>me</u> who persuaded <u>him</u> – he's only been racing this year.

Int: Jenny, you took up this hobby four years ago and …
Jamie: Er … it was four <u>months</u> ago, in fact.

Play the tape again, but this time ask students to listen with their eyes shut, so that they can concentrate on listening out for the stressed words.

7 Play the tape and ask students to underline the stressed words as they listen. They should do this on their own and then compare answers by reading aloud. The stressed words are underlined below.

Tapescript

a Would you like a coffee?
   No thanks – it stops me sleeping. I wouldn't mind a <u>cold</u> drink though.
b I'm going to wear my red dress to the interview.
   Oh no, <u>red</u>'s much too bright. I'd wear your <u>blue</u> one – with the grey jacket.
c Hello, Jan? Listen, I've been waiting outside the cinema but no one's turned up.
   The others said they'd meet you <u>inside</u>, didn't they?
d Why is it always <u>my</u> turn to empty the dishwasher?
   It <u>isn't</u>. I did it <u>yesterday</u> – and I cleaned the <u>cooker</u>, too.

8 Ask students to work through the exchanges in pairs, taking it in turns to respond.

Suggested answers
a Let's go and play tennis – it's not too cold, is it?
   It's **freezing!** I think we should go and see a **movie** instead.
b Why not stay in and do your homework this evening?
   Not **again!** I'd much rather go out **clubbing**.
c Paint your room yellow – it would look really good.
   Ugh! Yellow's too **loud**. I think **pale blue** would be much better.
d You know, you could have that magazine sent to you every month.
   But it's so **expensive**. I think I'll just buy it **occasionally**.
e Brian's the one who's interested in model cars.
   No he isn't, that's **Jerry**. **Brian's** keen on **power-kiting**.
f Here's the CD I bought in town. It was only £12.99.
   £12.99? I've seen it for only **£8.50**.

Exam folder 9

Paper 4 Part 4 Choosing from two or three answers

SB pages 112–113

There are seven questions in this part of the Listening paper. There may be a choice of two answers or of three:

    True/False
    Yes/No
    Three-option multiple choice
    Who said what?
    Which person/car/holiday, etc. is good at/famous for, etc.

This part lasts about three minutes and there may be one or more speakers. The questions follow the order of the conversation.

Ask students to read the information in the Advice section.

For practice purposes three different exam types have been included in one listening. In the exam you would only be given one type of question i.e. seven True/False or seven multiple choice questions, etc.

The interview is about the problems of living on a small island. There are three people speaking – the interviewer, Rebecca Laing and Philip Lawson.

Ask students to read through the questions carefully, taking note of the different question types and thinking about possible answers. Play the tape twice.

The parts giving the answers are underlined in the tapescript.

> **Answers**
> 1 F 2 T 3 B 4 C 5 A 6 N 7 P

Tapescript

Interviewer: Welcome to *Around Britain*. On the programme today we are going to be looking at not only the pressures and problems, but also the positive aspects of life on a small island. Now, Rebecca, you were born on the island and lived there until you moved to the mainland last year. Can you tell the listeners a little bit about life there?

Rebecca: In many ways, it sounds idyllic – there's no crime, no roads, no unemployment. Most people live in houses grouped around the harbour and you can walk around the whole island in twenty minutes. Unlike what has happened on other islands, many of the houses were bought as holiday homes, but the families liked it so much they decided to stay, as a result the permanent community is thriving.

Interviewer: Philip Lawson you moved here from London. Why was that?

Philip: Well, because of computer technology I realised I didn't have to stay in London to do my job – I could go anywhere. All I seemed to do in London was work – here the social life is brilliant because you go and see each other more, especially in summer. It's a different story in winter though.

Interviewer: What kind of people do you think are attracted to life on the island Rebecca?

Rebecca: They need to be a bit eccentric and perhaps more determined and organised than normal. The school also only educates the children until they are nine. After that they spend the week at a school on the mainland and only come home at weekends. It teaches them independence, but not everyone would like that.

Interviewer: How do you see the future of the island, Philip?

Philip: Things are okay for this generation. However, the challenge is to provide employment for our children and their children or else they'll leave. We also need to keep development in tune with island life – we can't allow just any business to set up here.

Rebecca: Yes, one reason everyone likes it here is because of the wonderful bird and animal life. Any development needs to take that into consideration – we get a lot of tourists in summer (they come to see us as much as the birds) and they would disappear if any dramatic changes were made, although I believe that the islanders worry too much about that.

Interviewer: Do differences of opinion get out of hand when you're living in such a small community?

Philip: Well, of course, they can do so easily. You just have to go for a walk and not let things get on top of you. It's important not to bottle things up.

Rebecca: That's true. But I've found life easier on the mainland – you're not living in each other's pockets all the time – everyone knowing what you're up to every minute of the day … .

Philip: Personally I don't think that's right. I …

Interviewer: Well, I guess everyone is different. My thanks to Rebecca and Philip. Now onto another problem affecting …

UNIT 18 What's in a book?

Unit topic	Books
18.1	
Exam skills	Reading Paper 1 Part 2
Vocabulary	Phrasal verbs with *come* and *go*
18.2	
Listening	Matching books to speakers
Exam skills	Use of English Parts 2 and 3
Grammar focus	*enough, too, very, so, such*
Workbook contents	
1, 2	Reading – Part 3 gapped sentences
3	Vocabulary – word formation
4	Phrasal verbs
5, 6	Grammar – *enough, too, very, so, such*

18.1 SB pages 114–115

Lesson plan

Speaking	10–10'
Reading	35–45'
Phrasal verbs	15–15'
Writing	5–20'

SV Set 6 for homework.
LV See notes below for 4 for extra vocabulary work.

1   The illustration supports the reading text, which is an extract from *The Old Man and the Sea* by Ernest Hemingway. Elicit answers from students.

Answers
Marlin, open sea, cloudless sky, sun (therefore tropical?)

Background note

Ernest Hemingway (1899–1961) received the Nobel prize for literature in 1954. Born in Chicago, USA, he spent some time in Europe as a journalist in the 1920s. He also lived in Spain for a while, and was passionate about bull-fighting. His other great love was deep-sea fishing, which is the subject of *The Old Man and the Sea*. In later life, he lived mostly in Cuba, and this is where the story is set.

2   Ask students what they know about Ernest Hemingway or tell them a little about his life. Then ask students to read the three reviews and summarise what they learn from them.

Answers
It is a short story; it is economically written; it is about an old man fishing with a line.

3   Refer students to the Exam spot and stress that they do not need to understand every word in a difficult text. Then ask them to skim the extract.

4   Ask students to read the questions and reread the text. Suggest they then work through the questions in pairs, taking their time and examining all the options. Allow them at least ten minutes for this. Check answers when they are ready.

Answers
1 B   2 C   3 B   4 D   5 A   6 D

Extension activity

In this extract, Hemingway describes something in the natural world by comparing it with an everyday thing, as in these two examples:
... the white cumulus clouds built like friendly piles of ice cream ...
His sword was as long as a baseball bat.

Ask students to match these everyday objects and things in nature, explaining why they are similar in appearance.
1 a pane of glass   a mud
2 soap bubbles   b trees
3 broccoli   c ice on a lake
4 chocolate sauce   d surf from breaking waves

Answers
1 c   2 d   3 b   4 a

Then write up the adjectives below on the board and ask students, in groups, to make as many statements as they can using the structure *as ... as*. They should use their imagination to the full.

cold   warm   wide   narrow   thin   tiny

For example:
as cold as ice / snow / a mountain lake / a packet of frozen peas / a polar bear's nose

5

Answers
a come in for b going without c go through
d went after e came up against; go through
f come out g go in for h gone through i went out
j coming through

6 Students get into groups of three or four. Ask them to share their ideas and prepare one description per group. They should continue from the sentence given and write about 20 words. Ask one person in each group to read out their description for the class. All the descriptions can be put on the wall at the end of the lesson.

Sample description
I imagine the hand looks like a bird's claw, or the end of a twisted wooden branch. It is rough and scarred, and hangs uselessly from his arm.

18.2 SB 116–117

Lesson plan

Listening   15–20'
Grammar   55–70'

SV Set 5 or 6 for homework.
LV See notes below for 2.

1 Ask students to identify the books. Remind them to look at the covers and think about the titles.

Answers
a historical novel b thriller c play d non-fiction
e science fiction f short stories

2 Play the tape straight through and ask students to decide on their answers. Check answers, playing the tape again if necessary.

Answers
1 a 2 d 3 b 4 f 5 e

Tapescript

1 All of her books are really well-researched and they're full of amazing details about what life used to be like there. I never realised they lived in apartment buildings, for example! The storyline is very inventive too; you're kept guessing right up until the last few pages. This is the fifth one I've read and I can't wait to get my hands on another!

2 I found the book really interesting, because we've got two now. It explains their behaviour and the relationships they have with their owners. You can find out all sorts of things, like why they purr and how they use their whiskers … and whether they can see colour. Honestly, I've learnt such a lot, just from one paperback!

3 Once I started it, I just couldn't put it down. The plot is quite complicated and it moves along at a really fast pace. What I like best is the dialogue; it's so realistic somehow. Many people say there's no better writer on crime at the moment and I certainly think so. There's lots of other titles I haven't read yet – some of them have been made into films, too.

4 I don't have enough time to read much at the moment, and as I prefer to finish something at one sitting, this book was perfect for me. There are some real classics, too. I must admit that sometimes I felt a little uneasy turning the pages late at night on my own, though. The worst occasion was when I'd almost got to the end, and my cat suddenly jumped up at me out of nowhere, which scared the life out of me!

5 This is an excellent read! I like the way the characters are so well-developed. It's one of three, and I've got them all now. They're so imaginative, and at the same time, they seem strangely accurate. They really make you think about our imminent future, which is not necessarily that wonderful. One of the best people writing at present, I'd say.

Extension activity

Include an optional class discussion about everybody's favourite type of book, referring to the categories listed in 1 and using some of the expressions from the extracts.

3

Answers
Yes, the writer does believe the book has a future. Reasons (in second paragraph): people have more leisure time to read in; the book has a strong tradition; it's very practical.
1 were/posed 2 which/that 3 as 4 would
5 besides 6 like 7 why 8 or 9 less 10 single
11 used 12 well 13 on 14 much 15 be

4 Ask students to find the examples and then match them to a–k. They can do this on their own or in pairs.

Answers
a enough reasons b small enough
c (extra – common expression of this type are: *funnily enough, strangely enough*, etc. For example, *Funnily enough, my friend had bought the same book for me*.)
d too dismissive; too much e and the video game, too
f very badly injured; very strong pull g so effective
h (last hundred years or so) i If so,
j such alternatives to books as k such a practical tool

Refer students to the Grammar folder, page 205.

5

Answers
a enough time **b** large enough **c** enough books
d had had enough of **e** not enough people
f got enough to **g** quite enough **h** Funnily enough

6

Answers
1 such cold weather (that) we **2** too little time to give
3 so well you should/ought to/could **4** is very good at
getting **5** takes such a lot of **6** (this is) so, a refund

Writing folder 9

SB pages 118–119

Refer students to the Exam spot and explain that, as with
any other Paper 2 question, it is important that a relevant
answer to the task is written.

1 Ask students to correct the composition, reminding
   them that there are twenty errors altogether.

Answers
stories; containing; character; unnamed; set in; different;
advertising; environment; completely; its; mixture; bizarre;
surprise; particular; campaigns; Marcovaldo's; friends;
neighbourhood; river; memorable

2

Answer
Yes, it is a reasonable attempt at the task set, although it
gives too much plot description in the second paragraph.
There is no conclusion, which would help to link the
answer back to the question that has been asked.

3 Ask students to reread the extract on page 114 and then
   look at the notes. Ask them to suggest other ideas from
   the extract to add to the notes.

Suggested answers
Realistic scene – fishing on the ocean.
Description of the fish supports this realism.

4 Students can do this in pairs, sharing a dictionary.

Answers
Characters: personality, qualities, defects, reputation,
temper, attitude, sympathy, humiliation, determination
Events: atmosphere, incident, adventure, episode, climate,
impact, surroundings
Both categories: mood – you can talk about someone's
mood or the mood of an event; risk – you can say a person
takes risks or refer to an event being a risk

5 If time is short, students can think about this on their
   own, using a dictionary if necessary. Make sure they
   have an example, as below.

Answers
personality – serious, great, shallow, interesting, strong,
weak, difficult, dangerous

6 Explain that the book title should be written at the top
   of the question paper and the opening paragraph
   should make early reference to the book, so that the
   examiner is clear which book has been chosen.

7 Ask students to write about 30 words for their opening
   paragraph. They can compare ideas when they have
   finished.

Sample opening paragraph
For me, the most memorable episode in 'The Old Man and
the Sea' is when the fish first appears. The description of
this great purple fish emerging from the sea has an
enormous impact.

8 Remind them that their final answer should not contain
   too many plot details.

ⓣeaching extra

Working with a set text can be time-consuming, but it
needn't take up too much class time. In a non-intensive class,
where you will be spending six to nine months preparing for
FCE, give students the option of reading the book on their
own. Check regularly to see how much of the book they have
read, and ask for extra written assignments on the text if
appropriate. Use Question 5s from recent UCLES past papers
for this.

UNITS 13–18 Revision

SB pages 120–121

Lesson plan

Topic review	10–15'
Vocabulary	15–25'
Grammar	15–20'
Phrasal verbs	20–30'

SV Omit the topic review and set the phrasal verb crossword for homework, with an English-English dictionary.

LV Ask students to write a short composition, 100 words, on one of the subjects in the Topic review.

The aim of this unit is to go over some of the main points covered in Units 13–18. With the exception of the Topic review, this unit can be done as a test or for homework.

Topic review

1   In pairs, students look at questions a–j and talk about whether the statements are true for them or not. Encourage them to go into detail, not just say 'yes' or 'no', and to recycle structure and vocabulary they have covered in the preceding units.

ⒺExtension activity

Make a twelve by twelve square crossword grid and ask each student to make a crossword using five down and five across clues. The words asked for should all be in Units 13–18. They should then give their crossword to another student to do for homework.

Vocabulary

2   This is exam practice for Paper 3 Part 1.

Answers
1 B   2 A   3 D   4 A   5 C   6 B   7 A   8 C   9 A   10 C
11 C   12 A   13 B   14 C   15 D

Grammar

3   Students need to read through the sentences and correct them. The mistakes include grammatical errors, punctuation and vocabulary.

Answers
a   There is too much traffic in our town.
b   I have such a lot of/so much work to do, I don't know where to start.
c   The United States and Switzerland have high levels of productivity.
d   Her house, whose roof is thatched, is twelfth century. Her house, the roof of which is thatched, is twelfth century.
e   John plays the piano and football, whereas his brother prefers playing chess.
f   Let me give you some/a piece of advice – don't go on a journey/trip without checking whether you need a visa or not.
g   That shop has stood on that corner for ten years.
h   There's a man over there who has been standing watching us for about half an hour.
i   I have lived in Las Vegas for ten years and I still find it exciting.
j   By this time next year I will have taught for twenty years.
k   He asked me where the police station was.
l   I saw a flash of lightning when I was out in the garden.
m   Have you got enough information to object to the factory noise?
n   He's the one to whom I gave the book. He's the one who I gave the book to.
o   My eldest son, who lives in Paris, is a physicist.

4   Students need to match the first part of the sentences in A with the second part in B.

Answers
1 e   2 c   3 g   4 d   5 a   6 b   7 f

Phrasal verbs

5   This exercise is in the form of a crossword. Explain how to do a crossword for students not familiar with them. The first clue across is done for them. Students need to find an ordinary verb which means the same as the phrasal verb in bold. This exercise can be set for homework.

Answers
Across
1 searching   2 sank   3 count   4 save   5 prepare
6 kept   7 raised   8 control

Down
9 organise   10 examine   11 respect   12 cut   13 start
14 accept   15 chased   16 vomit   17 propose

Paper 1 Part 3

You are going to read a newspaper article about the hobby of collecting things – big and small. Seven paragraphs have been removed from the article. Choose the most suitable paragraph from the list **A–H** for each part (**1–6**) of the article. There is one extra paragraph which you do not need to use. There is an example at the beginning (**0**).

The Collectors

One in three adults indulge in collecting. Amanda Roy writes about the things she collects and the reasons why so many people enjoy the same hobby.

Since the beginning of time, people have had the urge to collect. When primitive man collected pebbles, he hung them around his neck. Attracted by their shapes and colour, these pebbles represented man's first attempts to gather objects for intellectual and spiritual reasons.

0	H

I have been collecting all my life. Everything from flowers such as tulips, to pottery and paintings. My first collection was of stones picked up in my parents' garden. Aged six I had the good fortune, although it did not seem so at the time, to be sent to a school in a remote part of England, a cold and windy place surrounded by hills.

1	

Surprisingly I am not alone in being interested in collecting objects. One in three adults indulges the same passion. The reasons why people collect has became a subject of great interest.

2	

One famous collector was the Duc de Berry in France. He owned a 'room of wonders'. This was a collection of natural and artificial curiosities.

3	

However, you do not have to be rich and powerful to start a collection. I have collected items as different as tulip bulbs and china cups, searching out examples of each type with incredible determination.

4	

One collection that I made was of American rag dolls – 350 of them. I looked all over America for these dolls, searching out each variation in design with delight. This collection was destroyed when my house caught fire.

5	

It is, I suppose the way that collections change hands that has always interested me. A silver spoon that once belonged to a king, a poet: it is this that gives value to the goods that are traded in the markets of the world. As small objects become a popular collector's item, so they begin to rise in price.

6	

I have always loved collecting and collectors. It is a world of passion, envy and enthusiasm and delight. However, if you enter this world, remember one thing: in the end, if you do not fall in love with an object, do not collect it.

A There were cups made from coconut shells, carved ivory beads and pieces of Oriental china. Another aristocrat, Catherine the Great of Russia, collected more than 4,000 paintings.

B I once owned a copy; there are, I believe, only three in existence. It reveals why some objects are more sought after than others.

C When my parents came to visit me they used to take me to the local museum, which was full of objects collected by people in the past. I was fascinated by these objects.

D The toys of the 1950s are now positively an investment, provided of course, that you did not throw away the original boxes. (Not only did I throw away the boxes, but I also threw away the contents.)

E I remember the day that I persuaded a fellow collector of tulips to part with one which I wanted to add to my collection. I planted it and watered it until one year it vanished – stolen by another collector.

F The current thinking is that, for some individuals, it is the only aspect of their lives where they have complete control. For me, it's just something I enjoy doing.

G Next morning, I stood inside the front hall and saw the remains of furniture and collection. I am not certain which saddened me more!

H Over the intervening centuries, nothing much has changed. Small boys and girls still collect stones and seashells just for the beauty of their forms and colours.

Paper 2 Part 1

Next month, you and two English friends are meeting for a day's walk in a beautiful part of your country. Below is part of your friends' letter, together with some notes which you have made.
Read all the information carefully and then reply to your friends, answering all their questions.

We're really looking forward to the walk on the 12th! Unfortunately, Bill has hurt his knee, so has difficulty walking up steep hills. Can you choose a suitable route for us all?

We'll bring a picnic lunch – could you suggest a quiet place to stop, away from the crowds? Also, we're not sure what the weather is like in that part of the country – can you tell us and also advise us what clothes to wear?

Finally, where are we meeting and at what time?

See you!

Elaine and Bill

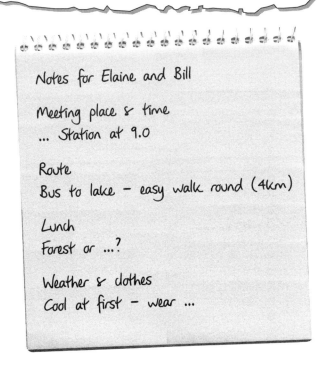

Notes for Elaine and Bill

Meeting place & time
... Station at 9.0

Route
Bus to lake – easy walk round (4km)

Lunch
Forest or ...?

Weather & clothes
Cool at first – wear ...

Write a **letter** of between **120** and **180** words in an appropriate style.
Do not include any postal addresses.

Paper 3 Part 1

For Questions **1–15**, read the text below and decide which answer **A**, **B**, **C** or **D** best fits each space. There is an example at the beginning (**0**).

Example:

0 A ran **B** held **C** kept **D** possessed

THE DRIVING INSTRUCTOR

I'm a driving test examiner. I (**0**) ..... my own driving school for twelve years before applying to become an examiner in 1996. Since then I've (**1**) ..... to examine lorry and bus drivers and instruct trainee examiners. I (**2**) ..... that I've assessed 16,000 people and passed around half of them. The first lorry driver I passed (**3**) ..... tears. However, the most (**4**) ..... reasons for failing are not being ready and being too (**5**) ..... . Inwardly I'm telling the candidates not to do something stupid like (**6**) ..... out into moving traffic, but I am not (**7**) ..... to tell them how to drive.

When I (**8**) ..... my own test I was extremely nervous and had to (**9**) ..... with a very strict and unfriendly examiner. We're taught nowadays to put people at their (**10**) ..... . We pass everyone who's up to (**11**) ..... , but people often present themselves too soon. I've never been offered money to pass anyone, (**12**) ..... one man asked me if he could make me change my (**13**) ..... . I then (**14**) ..... him to the police. My ambition is to be a supervising examiner in (**15**) ..... of test centres in a large area.

1	**A** resulted	**B** succeeded	**C** qualified	**D** mastered
2	**A** count	**B** number	**C** judge	**D** estimate
3	**A** burst into	**B** turned back	**C** carried on	**D** set off
4	**A** simple	**B** regular	**C** average	**D** common
5	**A** tense	**B** tight	**C** stretched	**D** stiff
6	**A** make	**B** pull	**C** pick	**D** stand
7	**A** admitted	**B** let	**C** allowed	**D** enabled
8	**A** took	**B** performed	**C** achieved	**D** effected
9	**A** suffer	**B** meet	**C** experience	**D** deal
10	**A** rest	**B** ease	**C** peace	**D** leisure
11	**A** limit	**B** test	**C** measure	**D** standard
12	**A** while	**B** even	**C** although	**D** despite
13	**A** mind	**B** thoughts	**C** attitude	**D** view
14	**A** reported	**B** declared	**C** announced	**D** notified
15	**A** responsibility	**B** care	**C** duty	**D** charge

Paper 3 Part 3

For Questions **1–10**, complete the second sentence so that it has a similar meaning to the first sentence, using the word given. **Do not change the word given**. You must use between two and five words, including the word given.
Here is an example (**0**).

Example:

0   I have never been to Paris before.

      time

      This .... have been to Paris.

      The gap can be filled by the words 'is the first time I' so you write:

0	is the first time I

---

1   'Mary didn't throw the rubbish out of the window!' the boy said.
    who
    'It .... the rubbish out of the window,' the
    boy said.

2   The curry was too spicy for us to eat.
    such
    It .... that we couldn't eat it.

3   Mark's company has proved successful, thanks to his hard work.
    made
    As a result of his hard work, Mark ....
    his company.

4   'Why don't we go to that Russian restaurant this evening?' said Elaine.
    suggested
    Elaine .... to that Russian restaurant this
    evening.

5   'Have you seen my library books anywhere?' Hilary asked her mother.
    if
    Hilary asked her mother .... library books
    anywhere.

6   My job is so badly paid that I can't afford music lessons.
    enough
    I .... to afford music lessons.

7   Mr Jones started teaching when he was twenty-six.
    been
    Mr Jones .... was twenty-six.

8   In Key West we visited Hemingway's house.
    lived
    We visited the house .... when we were
    in Key West.

9   'I saw you hit that new boy in the playground!' the teacher told him.
    accused
    The teacher .... new boy in the playground.

10   The first time I used e-mail was last week.
    had
    I .... last week.

Paper 4 Part 4

You will hear an interview with a writer called Anson Drew. For Questions 1–7, decide which of the choices **A**, **B** or **C** is the best answer.

---

1 Anson says his success has meant he has
    A made new friends.
    B little time to write.
    C had to install an extra phone.
                                          `1`

2 What does Anson say about the press?
    A They broke into his neighbour's flat.
    B They wrote some lies about him.
    C They failed to get any negative information. `2`

3 What's Anson's attitude to publicity?
    A He's interested in what people say about him.
    B He dislikes gossip columns in newspapers.
    C He is unwilling to publicise his books. `3`

4 While he was at university Anson
    A felt he didn't fit in.
    B made a few friends.
    C began to write novels. `4`

5 What does Anson say about his writing?
    A He's getting worse at it.
    B He's finding it harder to do.
    C He's going to give it up. `5`

6 What does Anson say about his radio play?
    A It was very popular.
    B It's going to be rewritten for TV.
    C It was enjoyable to write. `6`

7 What are Anson's plans for the future?
    A To move closer to his family.
    B To buy a bigger flat.
    C To spend more time on his hobby. `7`

© Cambridge University Press, 2000

Paper 1 Part 3

1 C 2 F 3 A 4 E 5 G 6 D

Paper 2 Part 1

> **Sample answer**
>
> Dear Bill and Elaine
>
> It was great to hear from you so quickly. I'm sorry to hear you've hurt your knee, Bill. Never mind – I'll make sure the walk is fine for us all.
>
> Let's meet at Frampton Station at 9.0. There's a bus leaving from there just after nine, which will take us all the way to Lake Morrell. If we catch that, you won't have any hills to climb, Bill – I promise!
>
> It's about four kilometres to walk the whole way round the lake and there's a good footpath, so it'll be no problem. For our picnic, we could either wander into the forest (which would involve a short, gentle climb) or sit by the lakeside. At this time of year, it rarely gets crowded, and I know a beautiful spot near the sailing club.
>
> Although it should be sunny, it could be quite chilly first thing in the morning, so I'd bring warm sweaters. Make sure you've got comfortable boots, too (that's especially important for you, Bill!)
>
> Looking forward to seeing you.
>
> Love

Paper 3 Part 1

1 C 2 D 3 A 4 D 5 A 6 B 7 C 8 A 9 D 10 B
11 D 12 C 13 A 14 A 15 D

Paper 3 Part 3

1 wasn't/was not Mary who threw
2 was such (a) spicy curry
3 has made a success of / has made a go of
4 suggested going/that we go/that we should go
5 if she had seen her
6 don't/do not earn enough / 'm/am not paid enough
7 has been teaching since he

8 –/which/that Hemingway had lived in / where Hemingway had lived / in which Hemingway had lived / where Hemingway used to live / where Hemingway (once) lived
9 accused him of hitting that
10 had never used e-mail until/before

Paper 4 Part 4

1 B 2 C 3 A 4 A 5 B 6 C 7 A

Tapescript

Int: For a man who has dreamed since the age of twelve of being a writer, Anson Drew is not as happy as he should be. He has sold more than a million copies of his novel *The Dreamer's Story*, and a film of the book is being made. Anson, you couldn't be doing much better, but is the price of success too high?

Anson: People just won't leave me alone. They're on the phone all day. Publicity people wanting you to do this or that, readers wanting bits of information, wanting money and every time the phone goes I scream because I'm trying to concentrate on my new novel.

Int: Has fame affected your relationships with friends, at all?

Anson: Well, I've seen a few recently I never thought I'd see again. You don't know whether they want to know you because they like you, or want to tell everyone they're your best friend.

Int: What about the press, have they been a problem?

Anson: Two weeks ago a Sunday newspaper sent a team of journalists to track me down after I'd refused to give them an interview. They found out my address and questioned the people who live underneath my flat. They asked about me in the local baker's, even in the local bookshop. They found my ex-girlfriend, my parents and also my old English teacher. It felt as if I'd been burgled.

Int: Did they find out anything you'd rather they hadn't?

Anson: Funnily enough, no.

Int: I've heard it said that you hate all publicity. Is that right?

Anson: I'm ashamed to say I have nine boxes of newspaper clippings. But one thing I can't bear are those book launches and literary gatherings you get invited to. They're just gossip machines, all gossiping about each other. You can't leave the room in case someone starts talking about you.

© Cambridge University Press, 2000

Int: When did you decide to become a writer?

Anson: When I was 20 I returned from teaching abroad and decided to go to university to study Philosophy. However, I seemed like a foreigner in my own country. My old friends and I had drifted apart and I became something of a loner. I didn't know what was fashionable or what music to listen to. Anyway, I finished my degree and then decided to write and I haven't stopped since. Sometimes I write all day and all night for a week. Other times I can't write a thing. The problem now is feeling I have to write something as good or better than my last book. It's making me more of a perfectionist, which is not a good thing. My writing does make me quite miserable – I sometimes think of abandoning it entirely.

Int: You've written a radio play recently, haven't you?

Anson: Yes, it was about a mouse called Pietro and I was quite pleased with it. Unfortunately, despite getting okay reviews, very few people got to hear it as they broadcast it on the same night as a popular TV series reached its climax. It was good to do something different like that – made me feel quite cheerful.

Int: Well, one good thing, you must have made a lot of money from your writing?

Anson: Most of it's in the bank. I might buy a house one day – somewhere near my parents. At the moment I still like the flat I've lived in for the past ten years, although it could do with being a bit bigger. I love the workshop I have downstairs, where I can make and restore musical instruments – I guess it's what some people would call a hobby, although I suppose writing is a hobby too! The money's helped me buy better tools, but that's about it.

© Cambridge University Press, 2000

UNIT 19　An apple a day ...

Unit topic	Health

19.1
Grammar focus　　Advice and suggestion
　　　　　　　　　It's time
Vocabulary　　　　Parts of the body
　　　　　　　　　Health
　　　　　　　　　Phrases with *on*

19.2
Speaking　　　　　Medicine
Exam skills　　　　Listening　　Paper 4 Part 4
Grammar extra　　*To have/get something done*
Pronunciation　　　Silent letters
Exam skills　　　　Use of English　　Paper 3 Part 1
Vocabulary　　　　Word formation

Workbook contents

1　　Reading – Part 3 gapped paragraphs
2　　Vocabulary – health
3　　Use of English – Part 3
4　　Writing – informal transactional letter

19.1 SB pages 122–123

Lesson plan
Grammar　　　　50'–60'
Vocabulary　　　20'–30'

SV Omit 4 and 5.
LV See notes below for 2.

1　The aim of this questionnaire is to elicit phrases associated with advice and suggestion. Ask students to read through and choose an answer. Where there is no exact answer for them, ask them to choose the nearest right answer. They should add up their score at the end and compare results with another student. The results are not meant to be taken seriously!

2　Ask students to underline the verbs and phrases in the 'How did you score?' section which are used to express advice and suggestion. They should pay particular attention to the structure which follows. For example:
You should + infinitive without *to*
If I were you + *would do*
You ought + infinitive + *to*
etc.
Refer students to the Grammar folder, page 205.

Answers
Mostly As
You are fairly healthy and have a good attitude to life. You should try to watch what you eat a little more and if I were you I'd try to do a little more exercise. Too much work and not enough play isn't good for you! I think it's about time you thought about your diet.

Mostly Bs
You are obviously in the peak of condition! I recommend you relax as you ought to get some rest even if you don't need much sleep. Overdoing things can lead to illness! Why don't you try doing more reading or have you ever thought of playing a musical instrument?

Mostly Cs
Oh dear! It's time you took a good look at your lifestyle. Missing meals and not getting enough sleep and exercise are very bad for you. My advice to you is to start right away – you'd better book a place in the gym. I also suggest cutting down on coffee and drinking more water and fruit juice. Too much caffeine will keep you awake!

Students should now work with a partner and take it in turns to give advice and make suggestions in response to the problems a–j. Anything appropriate will do here.

Suggested answers
a　I suggest holding your breath.
b　You ought to see if you're allergic to anything.
c　You should stop worrying.
d　Why don't you take a relaxation class?
e　If I were you, I would see a doctor.
f　You'd better have an injection.
g　What about putting your head between your knees?
h　I recommend buying some spray from the chemists'.
i　You should go on a diet.
j　My advice to you is to run it under the cold tap.

Extension activity

This exercise could be extended. Students could write a paragraph giving advice and making suggestions for people in these situations:
1 Coming to your country for the first time.
2 Studying for the FCE examination.
3 Winning the lottery.
4 Learning your language.

3 The expressions, *It's time, It's about time* and *It's high time* are often tested at FCE level. They express strong advice or opinion. The past tense used after these phrases is, in fact, the subjunctive. It is not referring to the past, but to the present.

Teaching extra

The subjunctive is not as important in modern English as it is in some languages. The present subjunctive has the same form as an infinitive, and the past subjunctive looks like a simple past tense (except for the verb *to be*, when *were* is used for all persons). The past perfect subjunctive is identical to the past perfect indicative in form. Modal auxiliaries are often used instead of the present subjunctive.
Examples:
I suggest you should get a job.
If I were you I would work harder.
I wish I were on holiday.
I'd rather he went home.
I wish I had never come here.

Suggested answers
(Students might use *he* or *she* in their answer, which is fine.)
a It's time you gave up smoking.
b It's time you walked a bit more.
c It's time you read a book occasionally.
d It's time you applied for another one.
e It's time you ate something healthier.
f It's time you bought your own house.
g It's time you had it mended.
h It's time you paid for something.
i It's time you bought your own.
j It's time you got up earlier.
k It's time you bought a new one.

4 Ask students to look at the drawing and name as many parts of the body as they can.

Answers

1	forehead	8	stomach
2	cheek	9	wrist
3	chin	10	waist
4	neck	11	hips
5	throat	12	thigh
6	shoulder	13	knee
7	elbow	14	ankle

5 This is a matching exercise. It also recycles the second conditional. There may be some debate about what is the right thing to do in each case.

Suggested answers
If I broke my leg, I'd have it put in plaster.
If I had a headache, I'd take an aspirin.
If I cut my knee badly, I'd have stitches.
If I grazed my elbow, I'd get an elastoplast/a plaster/a Band-Aid.
If I sprained my ankle, I'd put a bandage on it.
If I had flu, I'd go to bed.
If I had a cough, I'd take some cough syrup/mixture.

6 Draw students' attention to the phrase *on holiday* in the questionnaire. Explain that the following phrases are frequently tested and should be learnt.

Answers
a on foot   b on fire   c on purpose   d on duty
e on time   f on the whole   g on sale

19.2 SB pages 124–125

Lesson plan

Speaking	5–10'
Listening	15–20'
Grammar	5–10'
Pronunciation	15–20'
Use of English	10–15'
Word formation	10–15'

SV Set 6 and 7 for homework.
LV See notes below for Grammar extra.

1 Ask students to look at the photos and talk about what is happening in them. If they are not familiar with acupuncture, explain that it is used frequently in China. It involves putting needles into certain parts of the body, which correspond to pressure points.

2 Ask students if they have any personal knowledge of acupuncture.

3 Try to find out how open the class is to alternative medicine. Have they tried herbal medicine for example?

4 Students are going to hear part of an interview with a doctor. The doctor is being interviewed about acupuncture. Students should look carefully at the questions before they listen to the tape. Remind students that some of the answers may be true, but are not answering the question.

Tapescript

Interviewer: Good morning. On the programme this morning we have Dr Sylvia Carpenter, who is a family doctor. Dr Carpenter, you're a great believer in Chinese medicine, aren't you?

Doctor: Yes, I am. When I was a medical student I spent a wonderful month at a hospital in Hong Kong, where they use acupuncture as well as western medicine, which is of course, what I was studying. I saw how effective acupuncture could be, especially for people with digestive disorders, asthma, back pain or stress.

Interviewer: Now, you're not qualified to practise acupuncture yourself, are you?

Doctor: Oh, I'm just an ordinary GP or General Practitioner. I work in a small community, with about 3,000 people on my list. In the past we only referred patients to specialists at the local hospital for treatment – you know, to have their chests X-rayed or have a blood test done. Now I often suggest they see an acupuncturist as well, if I feel it would be of benefit. I can't actually recommend one specifically, but I keep a list of qualified ones.

Interviewer: So, say I go to see an acupuncturist about my backache. What would happen to me?

Doctor: Well, first of all the acupuncturist will ask you for very detailed information, not just about your medical history, but about your lifestyle, what you eat, what sort of exercise you do, how much sleep you get. The treatment you need is then decided and he or she will insert needles in various parts of your body. If you have a back pain, you won't necessarily have a needle in your back, though. It might be in one of your limbs – maybe in a knee or a wrist.

Interviewer: How often would I have to go?

Doctor: It depends on your problems. For some conditions one or two treatments a week for several months may be recommended. For less acute problems, usually fewer visits are required. There aren't usually any side effects. You might feel worse for a couple of days, but that just means the treatment is working. It's quite common to feel exhausted after the first treatment, and this can be overcome with a bit of extra rest.

Interviewer: Now, the big question. Does it hurt?

Doctor: Well, it'd be wrong to say 'No'. It depends where the needles are inserted. Some areas are more sensitive than others. Once the needles are in place there's no pain at all.

Interviewer: Are any positive benefits all in the mind, do you think?

Doctor: No, not at all. Acupuncture has been successfully used on cats and dogs. These animals don't understand or believe in the process that helps them to get better. A positive attitude towards the treatment may reinforce its effects, just as a negative attitude may hinder the effects.

Interviewer: It's a relatively new type of treatment, isn't it?

Doctor: Only in the West. It was first discovered in China in 2696 BC! In 1671 a French Jesuit priest wrote about his experiences in China and was the first westerner to see acupuncture in use. In 1820 acupuncture was actually being used in a Paris hospital! Acupuncture received a lot of publicity in the West when James Reston, a reporter for the New York Times, was covering the visit of President Nixon to China in 1971. Reston developed appendicitis and his appendix was removed using acupuncture as the anaesthetic. He felt no pain during or after the operation because of acupuncture. But, in some ways, your question was right. Acupuncture is still a fairly new subject in the West, but growing all the time.

Interviewer: Thank you, Dr Carpenter. Now we're …

Grammar extra

This part of the unit deals with causative *have*. Point out that *to get something done* is more informal than *to have something done*.

❼xtension activity

Ask students to imagine they are millionaires with lots of servants. They should think of what they would have done for them. For example:
I would have my breakfast brought to me in bed.
I would have my bath filled with champagne every day.

5 Silent letters can prove a problem to students. Even though they don't need to read aloud in the examination, it is important that they know which types of word have silent letters. Refer students' to the Vocabulary spot.

Play the tape. Students listen to the words from the interview.

Tapescript

limb
though
knee
wrist

Put students in groups and ask them to think of other words with a similar pronunciation.

Suggested answers
a knuckle, knot, knife, knight   b comb, lamb, thumb
c wreck, wrap, wriggle   d fasten, castle, listen
e reign, neighbour, resign   f dough, thought, thorough
g chalk, folk, yolk   h rough, tough

6 Ask students to look at the illustration of someone doing yoga. Ask them to tell you what they know about yoga. Do any of them do it themselves? If they are not sure what it is about, some background information can be found in the text itself.

Make sure that students read through the text a couple of times before they try to answer the questions.

Answers
1 A   2 B   3 B   4 D   5 A   6 B   7 B   8 C   9 D   10 C
11 A   12 B   13 C   14 A   15 B

7 This exercise can be set for homework if time is short. The sentences are all taken from the interview. Students need to change the form of the word in capitals so that the sentence makes sense.

Answers
a believer   b specialists, treatment   c medical
d effective   e various   f sensitive   g successfully
h operation

Exam folder 10

Paper 1 Part 1 Multiple matching

SB pages 126–127

In this part of the examination students are asked to read a text which is divided into paragraphs. They might be asked to do one of two tasks **either:**
match a heading to a paragraph **or**
match a summary sentence to a paragraph.

The paragraphs may have more than one idea in them. The students' task is to identify the most suitable heading or summary sentence for each paragraph.

Ask students to read through the Advice section and check their understanding.

Background information

The magazine article they are going to read is about the publishers of the *Lonely Planet* Guidebooks. The *Lonely Planet* series are travel guidebooks, carefully researched, but sometimes controversial in what they say about various places in the world.

Refer students to the example paragraph and heading. The words which give the answer have been underlined in the example paragraph. Ask students to underline those parts of the remaining text which they think includes the main point or points.

Answers
1 C   2 F   3 A   4 G   5 H   6 E   7 D

UNIT 20 No place to hide

Unit topic	Crime
20.1 Exam skills	Speaking Paper 5 Parts 3 and 4
	Reading Paper 1 Part 1
20.2 Grammar focus	Gerunds and infinitives 2
Workbook contents	
1, 2, 3	Vocabulary – crime, word formation, idioms
4, 5	Grammar – Paper 3 Part 4, gerunds and infinitives
6	Writing – error correction

20.1 SB pages 128–129

Lesson plan

Speaking   30–40'
Reading   40–50'

SV Set 5 for homework.
LV See notes below for 2 and 5

1   The introduction to this unit gives practice in Paper 5, Parts 3 and 4. Refer students to the Exam spot. Students are given some information and they have to talk together to come to some conclusion. They needn't agree with each other, but they must be polite, not keep interrupting and show they have the ability to hold a discussion. Students need to have completed the task in the time allowed, so they mustn't spend too much time on one point.

Ask students to look back at Unit 9 to remind themselves of some useful language.

The five photographs show clues in a police case and are (left to right): a fingerprint, hair and a bloodstain, a footprint, teethmarks in cheese, a DNA analysis.

Put students in pairs and ask them to decide which two clues are the most reliable, giving reasons for their choice. If they are not sure what DNA is, they just need to say so. It is included here so that students have a chance to see something they are not familiar with and

realise they can say they don't know. They will be familiar with the other clues so they can talk about them.

The discussion should take about three minutes and the interviewer is not involved in this part of the test.

2   In Part 4 of the exam students are encouraged to broaden their discussion and the interviewer will join in and ask questions.

Here students have four questions which they should discuss in groups of three. Help them with vocabulary or other relevant questions. The conversation can go on to talk about capital punishment or the death penalty.

B ackground information

In the UK the death penalty used to be carried out by hanging. This was abolished in 1965, although this decision is frequently reviewed by parliament.

E xtension activity

Put these categories on the board:
Car   People   Property   Money

Ask students to say which of the following crimes go in which categories. (There is more than one answer, depending on your point of view.)

kidnapping	hijacking	shoplifting
joyriding	burglary	speeding
con tricks	bank robbery	manslaughter
drug pushing	pickpocketing	vandalism
blackmail	arson	mugging
rape	fraud	

Suggested answers
Car
joyriding – stealing a car and driving it as fast as possible for fun
speeding – going too fast

People
kidnapping – usually for money or political reasons
rape – sex without consent of the other person
manslaughter – murder by accident
con tricks – confidence tricks – someone tells you a story to trick you out of money or goods
mugging – stealing and assaulting someone in the street
drug pushing – selling of illegal drugs

Property

shoplifting – stealing from shops
burglary – breaking into a building to steal
pickpocketing – carefully removing money from someone's pocket
arson – burning a building
vandalism – destruction of property
joyriding
hijacking – usually a plane or a ship for political reasons

Money

fraud – cheating a company or people of money – non-violent
bank robbery – stealing from a bank – usually violently
mugging
pickpocketing
blackmail – using information to obtain money from someone
con tricks

To round up this exercise students, in groups of three or four, should decide which five crimes they think are the worst and put them in order (1 = the worst).

3 Some of the more difficult vocabulary from the article is studied here so that students can understand its meaning before doing the reading task.

Students can use an English-English dictionary to decide which word or phrase fits in the gaps in the sentences a–h. They may have to change the form of the verb.

Answers
a a forensic scientist   b to prove   c caught red-handed
d guilty   e genetic code   f evidence, the suspect
g to cover your tracks   h taken to court

4 The article is about detecting crime. It is practice for Paper 1 Part 1 – summary sentences.

Answers
1 C   2 G   3 A   4 F   5 D   6 E

5 This exercise practises back reference. This is tested in Paper 1 Part 2.

Answers
a the traces of evidence   b the old techniques   c an item
d the dusting of surfaces

Extension activity

Students need quite a lot of practice in linking pronouns with what they are referring to, both forward and back references. It is a good idea to spend some time looking at pronouns in newspaper and magazine articles for extra practice.

20.2 SB pages 130–131

Lesson plan

Listening	30–40'
Grammar	60–70'

SV Set 4 for homework.
LV See notes below for 3.

1 In Unit 7, students looked at verbs which were followed by an infinitive or gerund. The aim of this unit is to introduce verbs which take a gerund or an infinitive with a resulting change of meaning. Many of the verbs are heard in the listening exercise.

Before students listen to the tape they should read through the questions a–j very carefully.

Background information

The students are going to hear a true story about three men who tried to escape from Alcatraz, a prison on an island in San Francisco Bay in the USA. The island was a prison from 1934–1963 and few people managed to escape from it.

Answers
a Everyone had to stop talking.
b 10 years.
c Some preferred to paint, others to try to learn to play a musical instrument.
d He began to plot.
e To cover the hole in the wall.
f To turn into a drill.
g By swimming.
h They remembered to keep absolutely quiet.
I He stopped to listen.
j They probably escaped.

Tapescript

The long corridors of cell block B were buzzing. Behind cell doors, convicts were calling to each other, or getting undressed and ready for bed. Everyone had to stop talking at half past nine, when the lights were switched off. Frank Morris, bank robber and burglar, stared at the ceiling, alone in his cell. His world measured three paces by five. Day one of his ten-year sentence on Alcatraz Top Security Island Penitentiary was over. All around him were men regarded as the most hardened desperate criminals in the entire USA.

After lights out, the stillness was broken only by the distant boom of a foghorn and the footsteps of a patrolling guard. Morris noted the time it took the guard to walk the length of the corridor before he turned around. Already he was planning his escape.

Morris's pleasant face and friendly manner hid a ruthless determination and a brilliant brain. As the days went by he became accustomed to the routine of Alcatraz. After the evening meal the men were locked in their cells. They had four hours to themselves before the lights went out. Some liked to paint, others to try to learn to play a musical instrument.

In conversation with another prisoner, Morris learned that three years before, a large fan motor had been removed from a rooftop ventilator shaft above his cell block. It had never been replaced. He immediately saw a way of escape. Morris began to plot. It seemed impossible to reach the shaft from his locked cell but one day he saw a way.

He tried picking at the concrete around a small air vent in his cell. It was slow work and he had to hide the hole he was making with a large accordion, a musical instrument that he had bought with money he'd made in the prison workshop.

The more he plotted, the more he realised that the plan would work better if he had others to escape with. He recruited three other inmates. One of them worked as a cleaner and Morris got him to steal a vacuum cleaner, which Morris turned into a drill. This made digging much faster, but they could only use it during the music practice hour.

They knew that if they managed to get down to the shore, it would mean swimming across the Bay. So one of the four managed to steal plastic raincoats to make into water wings.

Seven days before they were all due to escape, one of the four decided he could wait no longer. He forced the others to climb through the holes they had made in their cells and climb up to the roof. They remembered to keep absolutely quiet but as they were crossing the roof a slate was dislodged and fell to the ground. Below, one of the guards heard it and stopped to listen. However, he heard nothing more and continued walking.

The route from rooftop to shore passed by brightly floodlit areas, overlooked by gun towers. Carefully, they moved forward. Crouching in the damp sand, the escapees inflated their raincoat water wings, then waded through a sharp wind into the dark, freezing waters of San Francisco Bay.

Nothing was ever heard of them again. Whether they are still alive or were swept far out to sea, no one ever found out.

Photocopiable tapescript activity (**P ···⫶ page 188)**

Ask students to underline all the vocabulary connected with crime and punishment.

> **Answers**
> cell block, cell doors, convicts, bank robber, burglar, cell, sentence, criminals, patrolling guard, locked, prisoner, escape, plot, plotted, inmates, steal, floodlit areas, gun towers

2   Either individually or in pairs ask students to talk about the difference in meaning between *stop* and *try* with a gerund and *stop* and *try* with an infinitive.

> **Answers**
> *stop* + gerund means to *cease* – They ceased talking.
> *stop* + infinitive means *in order to* – He stopped in order to listen.
> *try* + gerund – it was an experiment to see if it worked.
> *try* + infinitive – it was difficult to learn to play so it was an attempt.

3   Students should read the information in the box and then look in the Grammar folder, page 206 to check on the difference in meaning.

Extension activity

Students usually need quite a bit of practice in the use of these verbs. When students have looked through the Grammar folder, give each of them one of the verbs which change meaning. Tell them to write down two sentences which exemplify the rules. They then have to read their sentences out loud and explain the difference in meaning. This can be done in teams, as a class or in pairs.

Students could also try to retell the escape story from memory, taking it in turns to tell the story or listen for mistakes.

When you are happy that students are clear about the use of these verbs they can do the written exercise.

> **Answers**
> **a** fitting   **b** reading   **c** to inform   **d** walking   **e** to hurt
> **f** to pay   **g** telling   **h** drinking and driving / to drink and (to) drive   **i** to keep   **j** to talk   **k** to do up
> **l** to run/running – possibly either here.

4   This exercise revises this work done in Unit 7 and this unit. If time is short, it could be set for homework.

> **Answers**
> **1** to make off   **2** to be   **3** to fasten   **4** checking   **5** to see
> **6** to avoid   **7** carrying   **8** to take   **9** reporting   **10** lead
> **11** know   **12** to sign   **13** to turn   **14** taking

Writing folder 10

Paper 2 Part 2

SB pages 132–133

1 In this exercise there is a sample question with a sentence which students must use to begin the story. It is important that students realise that they will lose marks if they forget to include the given sentence, or include it in the wrong part of the story ('begin' means first sentence; 'end' means final sentence).

Ask students to read through the first part of the story and ask them to decide which of the endings A, B or C would be the best.

> **Suggested answers**
> Both A and C end quite well. B is rather boring. Remember you are writing a story and the reader has to be involved in what is happening. You get more marks if your story is interesting and ends well.

2 Students often lose track of which tense they are writing in, when writing a story. This exercise is to make them more aware of tense changes.

> **Answers**
> 1 is happening   2 had arrived   3 found   4 am I going
> 5 thought   6 had been looking   7 had come   8 had told
> 9 was   10 has   11 need   12 had said   13 wanted
> 14 did I decide   15 knew   16 had   17 had been kidnapped
> 18 heard   19 was   20 was wearing   21 have decided
> 22 said   23 continued   24 are   25 hope   26 enjoy
> 27 untied   28 didn't have

3 The text in 2 has different colours. The first is a phrase describing the place, the second describes the person and what they are wearing, and the third describes what happened in the end.

In pairs, students should discuss how to change the three parts to make the composition more interesting. They should keep the other parts of the composition and still end with the sentence:

For Joe, life at the office would never seem stressful again!

When they have finished students could read out what they have written to the rest of the class.

4 This exercise could be set for homework if time is short. Students are given another story ending and need to think of how they would plan out their story. It is important in the examination that they don't just start writing a draft composition in pencil, and then redo it in pen when they think it's perfect. They will probably not finish in time and also it won't be properly planned.

For this exercise students need to think about:
a the people
b the place
c the action

Refer students to the Advice section. Impress upon them the need to keep within reasonable word limits – twenty/thirty words over is acceptable, but under is not. Try to get them to judge how much of their handwriting makes up 120–180 words.

It is probably not a good idea for students to use direct speech in a story, unless they are very good at punctuation. One or two sentences properly punctuated is acceptable and might add to the interest, but a whole page of badly punctuated conversation is not.

> **Sample answer**
> When Pat got up that morning he was looking forward to seeing Jack's face when he saw the huge present he had bought for him. However, before he saw Jack, Pat had to go to the bank.
>
> He caught the bus into the centre of town and got off in the High Street. He went into the bank and joined the shortest queue. As he was waiting, he noticed that the man in front of him was doing a lot of talking to the cashier.
>
> Suddenly the man in front turned round and nervously pointed a gun at Pat. 'Don't move or I'll shoot,' he said. Pat was so surprised he dropped the heavy parcel. It fell on the man's foot and he dropped the gun with a yelp of pain. Pat picked up the gun and took to his heels.
>
> He ran out of the bank and into the street. He could hear the bank robber behind him and he began to panic. Pat threw the gun away and ran down a sidestreet and climbed over a wall into the park. Pat could hear no one following him, and realised that he was safe at last.

UNIT 21 To have and have not

<table>
<tr><td colspan="2">Unit topic   Shopping</td></tr>
<tr><td colspan="2">21.1</td></tr>
<tr><td>Exam skills</td><td>Listening   Paper 4 Part 3</td></tr>
<tr><td>Vocabulary</td><td>Collocation</td></tr>
<tr><td colspan="2">21.2</td></tr>
<tr><td>Grammar focus</td><td>Clauses: concessive clauses; purpose, reason and result clauses</td></tr>
<tr><td>Exam skills</td><td>Reading   Paper 1 Part 1</td></tr>
<tr><td colspan="2">Workbook contents</td></tr>
<tr><td>1, 2, 3</td><td>Reading – Part 2 multiple choice</td></tr>
<tr><td>4</td><td>Grammar – conjunctions</td></tr>
<tr><td>5</td><td>Vocabulary – money and banking</td></tr>
</table>

21.1 SB pages 134–135

Lesson plan

Speaking	10–15'
Listening	30–40'
Vocabulary	25–35'

SV Set sentences in 5 and text in 8 for homework.
LV See notes below for 2, 6 and 7.

1 Ask students to discuss in pairs. Elicit more differences between necessities and luxuries.

2 Ask for suggestions of other weekly luxuries and put them on the board. Check understanding of the phrase *on impulse* (without thinking or planning in advance). Elicit examples of impulse buys students have made and find out whether they have been pleased with their purchases.

Ⓔxtension activity

Impulse buys are often regretted by the purchaser later. Why? Write these examples of impulse buys on the board and elicit reasons why they might not be satisfactory.
   sale-price shoes
   a cheap computer
   10 kilos of fresh spinach
   a year's supply of coffee
   an out-of-date guidebook

3 Ask students to read through A–F. Then play the tape. Check whether students got all five answers at the first listening.

Answers
1 B 2 F 3 E 4 A 5 C

Tapescript

1 Some people only buy flowers very occasionally, on impulse, but to me, a house looks bare without flowers. They brighten up your living space and they've always been important in my life. When I was small, my father travelled a lot in his job. Whenever he came home, he was always carrying an armful of flowers for my mother, even though sometimes he'd only been away for a couple of days. So I grew up with fresh flowers. After I left home, I was a penniless student. Despite being hard-up, I would still try to buy flowers, though my limit was usually a pound bunch of daffodils. Now, with a steady income, I spend at least £20 a week and I wouldn't dream of cutting back on this – I've been doing it for so long that the outlay has become part of my life, like the phone bill or food shopping.

2 For two years now, I've been going to a private gym. I used to be really unfit – I er … liked my food rather, and I smoked quite heavily, too. My doctor told me I had to get myself in better shape and suggested dieting. Well, even though I cut down on what I ate – and cut out the cigarettes entirely – I still didn't feel particularly healthy, so I enrolled at this gym. The joining fee was quite steep, and I pay a monthly membership. While not exactly loaded, I can afford it – and I can't imagine life without my twice-weekly visit! If I do a full work-out, I use the pool afterwards. It's nice to be able to socialise a bit. When I walk out of the place I feel great, you know, totally relaxed. It's a small price to pay for feeling good about yourself.

3 There is nothing more wonderful after a difficult day than sinking into a well-made bed with freshly laundered sheets. Utter bliss! It's an indulgence I picked up when I was young. Every year we would travel to Europe as a family and always stayed in delightful hotels, with excellent bedding. After buying my own place, I was broke. My grandmother gave me all her handmade cotton sheets and pillow-cases, dating from around 1910. In spite of being given all this, I didn't use any of it for ages, because I was frightened that it might get damaged in the

wash. Finally, I decided it was crazy to have it all sitting there in the cupboard, while I was in an old sleeping bag! Having it laundered gives me confidence it's in safe hands. They collect every Friday morning, and I get it back the following Friday, beautifully packed in a box. Well worth the expense, definitely.

4 My girlfriend and I work really long days, plus it takes us over two hours to get home some evenings, as the traffic's so bad. So, the last thing either of us wants to do is rush out again and do the weekly shopping. We used to, of course. It was terrible – more often than not we'd have some silly row about what to buy. We were just too tired and it got to us, whereas now it's much more civilised. Armed with a glass of wine, we sit in front of the computer in the flat, and dial up the Tesco Internet site. We can usually decide on our order quite quickly, even if we still argue over some things! It's all delivered to the door for a weekly charge of £5. I consider it's money very well spent. Anyway, with our joint spending power, money isn't exactly tight.

5 I can't remember the last time I went on public transport. I can't stand it – it's so crowded and dirty. I do own a car, although I much prefer taking a taxi. To begin with, I only used to get one after being out late with friends, because I wanted to be safe. But as my spare cash grew, so did my taxi habit. Now I have an account with Dial-a-Cab, who are very reliable. Much as I appreciate the convenience of taxis, it's the luxurious side that really appeals to me – the exclusiveness, if you like. I jump in and shut the door – and I'm in my own little stress-free world. And if I'm taking my son out for the day somewhere and can't easily park, I just add the cost of the fare to the day out without a second thought, even if it's a lot.

4 Play the tape a second time for students to check their answers. Then ask students to say what the five luxuries were (flowers, membership of a private gym, sheets cleaned at a laundry, shopping on the Internet, using taxis). Elicit views on whether they are all luxuries.

5 Ask students to suggest differences in meaning (*cut back* and *cut down* both mean reduce; *cut out* means stop completely). Ask if students know the other phrasal verbs given. If not, they can make a guess at their meaning, looking at each particle.

Ask students to complete the sentences.

Answers
a cut ... out   **b** cut across   **c** cut down   **d** cut in
e cut off   **f** cut out   **g** cut off   **h** cut back

---

6 Explain that students will hear the listening extracts again and should note down the phrases they hear.

Photocopiable tapescript activity (⋯⟶ page 189)

Alternatively, hand out copies of the tapescript and ask students to underline the phrases.

Answers
Good value: well worth the expense; money very well spent
Having money: loaded, spending power, spare cash
Cost: outlay, fee, expense, charge, fare
Badly-off: broke, penniless, hard-up, (money) tight

Extension activity

If you have photocopied the tapescript, divide students into five groups and ask each group to think about one speaker. The group should build up a 'profile' of that person, listing facts from the extract and suggesting what he or she might be like. Each group should then report their views to the class.

7 Elicit examples of collocations from students. Then ask them to read the explanation and work through sets a–h in pairs. Check answers at the end.

Answers
a account   **b** road   **c** thought   **d** break   **e** belt
f wasp   **g** mood   **h** belief

Extension activity

Either in class, or for homework, ask students to suggest adjectives that do collocate with the other words in sets a–h.

8 Students use the phrases to complete the story.

Answers
1 tight schedule   **2** spare time   **3** fresh air   **4** safe side
5 steep path   **6** delightful square   **7** full swing
8 utter horror   **9** tight fit   **10** safe place

21.2 SB pages 136–137

Lesson plan

Grammar 1	15–25'
Reading	20–30'
Grammar 2	15–15'
Use of English	15–15'

SV Omit 5.
LV See notes below for 1.

Refer students to the introductory paragraph on page 136. Encourage students to use longer and more complex sentences in their own writing. Units 21 and 22 are designed to show them the variety that is possible.

1 Ask students to discuss the differences in pairs.

Answers
a and *b* are examples of 'finite' clauses, where each contains a subject and verb; *c* and *d* are 'non-finite', that is, they do not include a subject and verb. Also, *c* and *d* start with the concessives.

Explain that *although* is used a lot in English. It can be used in all four sentences. In *c*, the sentence would have to be amended slightly: *Although hard-up,…*
Elicit other conjunctions like these (many came up in the listening in 21.1). Then refer students to the Grammar folder, page 206 to look at the full list and read the section.

ⓔxtension activity

Use the tapescript to illustrate the other conjunctions. The following occur:

Speaker 1
… though my limit was usually a pound bunch of daffodils.
Speaker 2
… even though I cut down on what I ate
Speaker 3
In spite of being given all this …
… while I was in an old sleeping bag.
Speaker 4
… whereas now it's much more civilised.
Speaker 5
… although I much prefer taking a taxi.
Much as I appreciate the convenience of taxis…
… even if it's a lot.

2 Explain that common errors with these conjunctions are often tested in Paper 3 Part 4. Ask students to correct the sentences.

Answers
a despite making … b Even though department stores …
c whereas Iceland … d In spite of wanting …
e even if they … f they usually pick up …

3 Ask students to read the questions in A–I. Remind them that I is the example heading in the exam and may help them predict what happened to Faye.

Answer
A lot of money ended up in Faye's account and the bank took a long time to sort the matter out.

4 Allow students a maximum of ten minutes to match the headings correctly.

Answers
1 F 2 D 3 H 4 A 5 B 6 E 7 G

5 Ask students to take it in turns to reread a paragraph, summarise what happened to Faye, and say whether they would have done the same as her or not. This gives students plenty of opportunities to practise the second conditional!

6 Ask students to look through the examples and then find other examples of these clauses in the article.

Answers
I knew it wasn't mine <u>so</u> I went into the bank … (Purpose)
Two weeks later I again checked my balance <u>so as to</u> be sure … (Purpose)
<u>Since</u> my boyfriend John works for another bank …
(Reason)
… that's the interest, <u>so</u> I wouldn't have been touching the capital. (Result)
I … contacted head office, <u>in order to</u> sort it out … (Purpose)

7 Students should write the new sentences on their own and then compare with a partner.

Answers
a Supermarkets give their customers loyalty cards so as to get more information about what they/people buy.
b There weren't many stalls at the market yesterday because it was a public holiday.
c Some daily newspapers cut their prices in order to get a bigger circulation.
d Since I like filling the house with flowers, I buy a lot of them.
e Harrods is seen as a very exclusive shop so it can charge a lot.
f I went to London to buy a special present for Ellen.
g It's always worth trying clothes on before you buy them in case they're too tight.
h Some supermarkets create the smell of freshly-baked bread so that they (can) make a good impression on their customers.

8

Answers
1 despite it being (so) cold OR despite the coldness (of) OR despite the cold weather
2 in case it doesn't
3 even if they charge
4 since it is commonly/often
5 whereas British people do OR whereas in Britain they do

Exam folder 11

Paper 1 Part 2 Multiple choice
SB pages 138–139

Ask students to read through the Advice section.

There are various types of item which are tested in this part of the Reading paper.
a detailed understanding
b global understanding
c backwards and forwards reference
d vocabulary

The questions are all in the order in which you read the text, with the global question, if there is one, at the end.

This article is about a woman who goes on a painting holiday to Africa. Ask students to read through the article to get a general feeling of what it is about. They should underline the words or sentences that they think contain the answer and when they have finished discuss their answers with a partner.

UNIT 22 | A little night music

Unit topic	Music
22.1	
Exam skills	Speaking Paper 5 Part 2
	Reading Paper 1 Part 3
Vocabulary	Music and concerts
22.2	
Grammar focus	Complex sentences
Exam skills	Use of English Paper 3 Part 4
Workbook contents	
1	Use of English – Part 1
2	Vocabulary – music
3	Writing

22.1 SB pages 140–141

Lesson plan

Speaking	30–40'
Reading	35–50'

SV Limit discussion in 4.
LV See notes below for 8.

Ask how many in the class enjoy listening to music or playing it. Find out whether there are any pianists in the class. If there are, you can ask them for expert explanations to some of the words and phrases in 8 later.

1   Ask students to look at the two pictures. They show a Heavy Soul concert and a special event where 2,740 young musicians played in the Birmingham Symphony Hall.

Allow students three minutes to compare and contrast the pictures.

2   Remind students of the format of the Speaking test and of Paper 5 Part 2, referring them to the explanation on page 7 if necessary. Explain that on the tape they will hear two FCE-level students, Carmen and Jurgen, together with an Interlocutor (the examiner who asks the questions). Carmen will be doing the long turn and Jurgen will comment briefly at the end. Ask students to listen out for the views of both students. Either play the tape straight through or pause after the long turn to summarise Carmen's views.

Answers
Jurgen prefers taking part whereas Carmen dislikes playing in large orchestras and enjoys listening to music at festivals.

Tapescript

Examiner: Carmen, here are your two photographs. They show a lot of people in one place. Please let Jurgen have a look at them.
Carmen, I'd like you to compare and contrast these photographs, and say how you would feel in each situation. Remember, you have only about a minute for this so don't worry if I interrupt you. All right?

Carmen: Yes, fine. Well, the pictures have two things in common. The first, which you mentioned, is the huge number of people. The other is that they both show music taking place. This one is at a major rock festival – it's outdoors, of course. The other one is indoors and it looks like an enormous orchestra. There must be hundreds of performers there, I mean er ... there are over a hundred cellists taking part! I don't know where it is but all the musicians are quite young, so maybe it's a concert organised by several schools?
The main difference between the two scenes is that in the first one, there is an audience – people are watching a band on stage – while in this one, everyone is a performer. I really like being part of a large audience, sitting back and relaxing to the music.

Examiner: Thank you Carmen. Now, Jurgen, which situation would you prefer to be in?

Jurgen: Oh, the orchestra, definitely. I'd rather participate than watch music. I actually belong to a large choir and we sing as a group of about a hundred and twenty. It's really good fun and because there are so many of us, it doesn't matter if you make a mistake sometimes.

Examiner: Thank you.

Elicit comments on the recording: is this long turn more difficult or easier than they expected? Reassure them if necessary!

3   Play the tape again for the vocabulary check. Many of these words will come up in the gapped text which follows.

Answers
Perform: take part, participate
Performers: musician, band, orchestra, choir
Performance: concert, festival

4   Allow students to discuss in pairs or groups.

5   Ask students to skim the skeleton text with the example paragraph in place, to find the answer. This should take them no more than three minutes.

> **Answer**
> He chopped at the piano with the axe.

6   Suggest that students time themselves and allow them up to six minutes to underline key words. Elicit some of these. Then refer them to the Exam spot and explain that this task is like fitting a jigsaw together.

7   Ask students to comment on paragraph A and suggest where it fits, giving reasons for their answer.

> **Answer**
> Gap 6 (late part of the narrative: *he had no intention of going on with the concert*; link between *axe* in previous paragraph and *chop* in A.)

Students now scan the remaining paragraphs on their own, referring back to the sections they have underlined in the main text. Allow them up to six minutes to note down their answers, which they can then compare in groups.

> **Answers**
> 1 G   2 C   3 B   4 D   5 F

If there are differences of opinion, elicit possible ways of checking answers.

> **Suggested answers**
> Discussing the links before and after a paragraph.
> Reading through the whole text with the answers in place, to check that everything makes sense.
> Checking that the extra paragraph does not fit anywhere.
> Mention that Exam folder 12 (pages 150–151) deals with Paper 1 Part 3 and suggest they run through the Advice section at home.

8   Work through a–j with the class, giving them the extra information below.

> **Answers**
> a those parts in the piece that particularly show the pianist's feelings about what he is playing – *expressive* is an adjective; the verb is *express*; the noun is *expression*
> b needs looking after the whole time – *constant* commonly collocates with *attention*, and also with *pressure* and *demands*
> c he didn't have much patience left – he had started to become *impatient*
> d to take the axe away from him – noun: *disarmament*

e a piano key which was sticking particularly badly
f should be strongly told off
g calmed down; stopped laughing – adjective: became *composed*
h an idiom: meaning to reach the end of something difficult unharmed
i having sat down on the stool as comfortably as possible
j appearing weak and unhealthy. Explain that *-looking* can be added to a number of adjectives in English in this way, for example: *tired-looking*, *sad-looking*

Elicit reactions to the story. How would it have felt to be a member of that audience? Do students feel sorry for the performer?

ⓔxtension activity

Ask students to complete this informal spoken narrative about the concert, which revises the specific vocabulary and informal expressions. Read it out, stopping at each gap to elicit possible answers. This could be done as a competitive task, dividing the class into two teams and alternating which team answers first. When you come to number 12, ask teams to give as many possible answers as they can in turn (one point per answer). All other answers score one point each.

When Myron Kropp first came on (1) ....., he looked really (2) ....., although he proved how strong he actually was later! Things got off to a bad (3) ....., as he couldn't find a proper (4) ..... to sit on. The (5) ..... he used made him turn sideways at times – it was hilarious, you could hear him (6) ..... under his breath, not just because of this, either. You see, some of the piano (7) ..... were sticking, mainly (8) ..... to the humidity. There was an awful moment when he ended up face to (9) ..... with the audience. Someone started giggling and the whole audience (10) ..... in, which left him quite shaken. When the laughter finally (11) ...... down, he went on to the next piece, but guess what happened next! The third octave G started sticking, too. Well, this drove him completely (12) ..... and he started to (13) ..... the piano really hard. He then went off and came back with – wait for it – an (14) ....., which he proceeded to use to (15) ..... the legs off!

> **Answers**
> 1 stage   2 frail/ weak   3 start   4 bench   5 stool
> 6 swearing   7 keys   8 due   9 face   10 joined
> 11 died   12 mad/nuts/bonkers/insane/spare/berserk/ bananas/up the wall   13 kick   14 axe   15 chop

22.2 SB pages 142–143

This lesson focuses on ways students can produce more complex sentences, particularly in their writing. All of the material could be done at home and reviewed at a later class. If so, check answers or hand out copies of a key.

1 Ask students to do the matching task in pairs.

Answers
1 a 3 b 8 c 2 d 6 e 4 f 1 g 5 h 7

2 Refer students to the example and then ask them to rewrite the sentences, using the information in brackets.

Answers
a As it was late, we decided not to stay for the final band.
b Beautifully hand-made, with a reddish-brown colour, the cello has an excellent sound.
c Having learnt the recorder for three years, Ellen went on to the flute.
d Despite being technically brilliant, his playing has no feeling.
e Due to the conductor's mistake, the soloist had to miss out a whole verse.
f This is especially noticeable in recordings of live concerts.
g Although a low-priced guitar, the Squier sounds very similar to a proper Stratocaster.
h It is appropriate to add that he lived to the age of 86.

3

Suggested answers
a Due to the delay in the band's arrival, we insisted on a refund for the tickets.
b Since the last train left at eleven thirty, we sadly had to miss some of the performance.
c Despite feeling unwell, the singer decided not to cancel the recital, although it was shortened.
d Instead of playing what was printed in the programme, the pianist improvised quite brilliantly for over 40 minutes.
e An oboe has a very suitable tone, even if it is underused as a jazz instrument.
f As the violinist suffers from stage fright, he rarely gives performances to large audiences.

4 This is another example of an unusual concert. Ask students to skim the paragraph and elicit which is the opening sentence. Then ask students to decide in pairs where the sentences should go.

Answers
b is the opening sentence.

Complete paragraph:
(b) Although for the wrong reason, the Chicago Symphony Orchestra's Centennial concert in 1991 was a memorable event. Three of its most famous music directors participated: Solti, Barenboim and Kubelik. Immediately before the concert, a celebration dinner was held for special donors. *(d) There were some 400 of these, each paying at least $500 for the privilege of attending.* At an event like this, it is customary to give diners a small gift, so each person was presented with an attractive alarm clock, gift-wrapped. Why some of the clocks were put in their boxes with the alarm switched on is a mystery, but this was the case. It is appropriate to remind the reader that the dinner guests went straight on to the concert, armed with these ticking timebombs! *(a) During the first half there were few problems, with only an occasional beep being heard.* However, after the interval more and more alarms were going off, so the concert had to be temporarily stopped and an announcement made. As the clocks were inside boxes and gift-wrapped, nobody in the audience had realised what the problem was. *(c) Once the laughter had died down, they were instructed to take their gifts outside to the lobby.* The rest of the evening then proceeded without incident.

Extension activity

This paragraph contains some of the clauses in Unit 21, as well as some types of complex sentences given at the beginning of this lesson. Students could identify these in pairs, underlining the relevant parts of the paragraph.

Answers
Concessive clause:
(b) Although for the wrong reason, the Chicago Symphony Orchestra's Centennial concert in 1991 was a memorable event.

Rhetorical question:
Why some of the clocks were put in their boxes with the alarm switches on is a mystery, but this was the case.

Emphasising new information:
It is appropriate to remind the reader that the dinner guests went straight on to the concert, armed with these ticking timebombs!

Reason clause:
As the clocks were inside boxes and gift-wrapped, nobody in the audience had realised what the problem was.

Refer students to the Grammar folder, page 206 for
further examples.

5   Suggest students do the error correction task
    individually and then compare answers.

Answers
1 with   2 such   3 ✓   4 the   5 off   6 ✓   7 too
8 has   9 all   10 they   11 ✓   12 that   13 ✓   14 most
15 to

Writing folder 11

SB pages 144–145

1   If possible, ask students to reread WF 6 (SB pages
    80–81) at home before working through WF 11.
    Alternatively, ask them to spend a couple of minutes
    in class, skimming its content and reading the
    Advice section.

    Then ask students to read the exam task and the
    report. They should discuss improvements in pairs,
    working through a–c. Remind them to use complex
    sentences in b.

Answers
a   Add something to make it clear what the report is
    about, for example, *on last year's festival.*
    Add a concluding sentence, for example, *I hope you will
    find this information helpful.*

b   Even though there was some car parking, many people
    had to park ...
    Although there was some choice of catering at the site,
    very little vegetarian food was offered.
    People seemed to enjoy the performances, so perhaps
    each band ...
    Since several members ... thought the tickets were
    unusually cheap, the price could be raised next year.

c   To the festival organisers
    The site
    Catering facilities
    people were forced to go from one end of the site to
    the other when buying food and drink, which they
    were not pleased about.
    This would give the festival useful additional funds.
    It is clear that ... is needed, as well as some changes ...

2   In pairs or small groups, students decide on suitable
    types of shopping for each of the target groups.

Suggested answers
1 f, h, i   2 a, d, j   3 c, e, j   4 b, d, g

3   If time allows, ask students to make a paragraph plan
    in class.

Sample answer

This report covers the main shopping facilities in
Newtown.

Food
There are three supermarkets: Sainsbury's is in the centre
of town near the market, and also sells videos; Waitrose is
only five minutes from the college and has a large car
park; Tesco's on the edge of town is the biggest of the
three, but is difficult to get to. It is best to buy fresh fruit
and vegetables in the market, which is held every day
apart from Sunday.

Study materials
In Bridge Street, there are four bookshops. There is also a
massive stationery shop called Staples in the main square,
where you can buy everything from files and pens to CD-
roms. There is a small bookshop on the college campus,
which also sells basic stationery items like paper.

Souvenirs
Newtown doesn't have as many souvenir shops as
London, but the castle has its own shop, and so does the
museum. Additionally, the market stalls often have cheap
souvenirs.

UNIT 23 Unexpected events

Unit topic	Disasters
23.1	
Speaking	
Exam skills	Listening Paper 4 Part 2
Pronunciation	Intensifying
Grammar extra	Intensifiers
Vocabulary	Phrasal verbs with off
Exam skills	Use of English Paper 3 Part 2
23.2	
Grammar focus	Wish/if only
	Hope
	As if/as though
	Would rather
Exam skills	Paper 3 Part 3
Vocabulary	Collocations with un
	Weather vocabulary
Workbook contents	
1	Vocabulary – weather
2, 3, 4, 5	Reading – Part 4 matching
6	Grammar – *wish/I'd rather/hope/ if only*

23.1   SB pages 146–147

Lesson plan

Speaking	5–10'
Listening	15–20'
Pronunciation	15–20'
Grammar extra	15–20'
Vocabulary	10–20'

SV Set 4 and 5 for homework.
LV See notes below for 4.

1   Ask students to discuss the photos in pairs. They shouldn't describe them, but talk about which event worries them most. They then have to decide which set of vocabulary items goes with which photo. Check they understand the vocabulary.

Answers
1 volcano – c   2 lightning – a   3 floods – b
4 earthquake – d

2   Two people are interviewed about an experience they had when camping some years ago. This is practice for Part 2 of Paper 4. Students need to complete the sentences with a word or short phrase.

ⓑackground information

The conversation is based on a true story of what happened when Mount St Helens in Washington State in the USA erupted in 1980.

Answers
1 forest fire   2 smoke cloud   3 silent   4 handle
5 the tent   6 (falling) trees   7 shirts   8 ash
9 rotten/bad eggs   10 radio

Tapescript

Int: On the morning of May 18th, 1980, Liz Nielson was camping with a friend about 18 kilometres from Mount St Helens in Washington State in the United States. She was making coffee and her friend Dave was fishing. So, Liz, when did you realise that something was wrong?

Liz: Well, Dave lost the fish and came up to replace his line. He looked up and saw a small black cloud on the horizon and said there must be a forest fire. Within 30 seconds it was absolutely enormous and then it just kept getting bigger and bigger, and coming at us faster and faster, and it was very dark and black. The cloud of ash was the first sign we had that anything was happening.

Int: What were your thoughts at that moment?

Liz: I'm not sure I had any – apart from maybe wishing I were somewhere else! It wasn't like a smoke cloud, it was as if it were alive and it was massive and dense, and very black. It was the strangest thing. It was totally silent until it got down into the canyon where we were and then there was a huge roaring. I remember looking at the fire and the wind just blew the flames out low along the ground, and watching the handle of my coffee pot just kind of melt in the flames, and then this awful cold – it just surrounded us.

Int: I expect you were very frightened by then, weren't you?

Liz: Frightened! I was absolutely petrified, and so was Dave. Well, we started to run back towards the tent. Stupidly I thought that if only we could get in the tent we'd be safe! Then the cloud hit us. It was like an explosion of sound and I fell over backwards and was covered with dirt. I remember wishing it would stop and almost immediately it did, and then Dave reached over to me and asked me if

I was OK. We got up and realised that there were trees all around us. In fact, we'd fallen down into a hole left by the roots of a tree and then other falling trees had covered us. Dave tried to climb out of the hole but it was too hot. Then, when we did get out we were met with such a scene of total devastation. Everything had happened so fast. When we set off it was difficult to breathe so we took our shirts off and wrapped them around our heads. There were flashes of lightning across the sky.

Int: Was it difficult getting out of the valley?

Liz: The ash was nearly a metre deep and it was so hot underneath you could only stay in it for a short period of time. Then we had to get up on a tree stump and take our shoes off and unroll our trousers, but within a few minutes they would be filled up again. It gave off a terrible smell – like rotten eggs. Anyway, we were really lucky. A falling tree could easily have crushed us. I wish now that we'd taken a radio with us, then maybe we would have had some warning. Even a couple of hours warning would have helped. We went back a few days later and found the site where our tent had been. Thank goodness we fell in that hole instead of reaching the tent!

Int: A lucky escape indeed. Now in the studio we also have …

3   Play the extract from the listening. Students should listen to the intonation pattern used when an adjective is intensified in this way.

Tapescript

Int: I expect you were very frightened by then, weren't you?

Liz: Frightened! I was absolutely petrified, and so was Dave.

In pairs students take turns to role play each of a–j.

T eaching extra

Explain that students do not have to shout or use a funny voice to stress a word. They should lengthen the word slightly. The stress on *absolutely* is on the first syllable for emphasis.

Grammar extra

This exercise practises the grammar of intensifying. Some adjectives are 'gradable', that is they can be made weaker or stronger. Others are 'absolute', that is they can't be qualified. You use *very* with gradable adjectives, and *absolutely* with ungradable adjectives.

Refer students to the Grammar folder, page 207.

Answers
a very **b** very **c** absolutely **d** absolutely **e** very
f absolutely **g** absolutely **h** very **i** absolutely
j very **k** very **l** absolutely

4   Draw students' attention to the Vocabulary spot. It is important for students to realise that phrasal verbs are really individual vocabulary items and that they can't be used indiscriminately to replace a verb.

Answers
1 produced **2** removed **3** began the journey

a broke off **b** called off **c** write off **d** wore off
e pay off **f** put off **g** run off **h** dropping off
i come off

E xtension activity

Students should write out sentences of their own which show they know how to use these phrasal verbs correctly.

5   Ask students to read through this article about volcanoes carefully before they start to complete the gaps. This exercise can be set for homework.

Answers
1 as **2** after **3** in **4** without **5** over **6** less **7** and
8 called/named **9** the **10** down **11** which/that
12 set **13** anything/everything **14** was **15** this

23.2 SB pages 148–149

Lesson plan

Grammar	50–60'
Vocabulary	25–30'

SV Set 7 and 8 for homework.
LV See notes below for 5.

1   Unit 19 looked at expressions with *time* with a verb in the past tense. This unit deals with *wish, if only, would rather* and *as if/as though*.

Refer students to the Grammar folder, page 207 for more details. Students usually readily understand the use of *wish* + past perfect for past regrets. They have problems with *wish* + past simple and *wish* + would.

2   Students need to think of five other things Liz would have wished for after the eruption.

Suggested answers
I wish we had realised the mountain might erupt.
I wish there had been a cave nearby.
I wish we had left the area before the eruption.
I wish we had never decided to go camping.
I wish it hadn't happened to us.

They then need to move on to talk about themselves and the things they regret doing or not doing.

3 Students have to talk about what they wish for at this very moment, using *wish* + past simple or *could*.

T eaching extra

After *I wish*, the form of the verb *be* is *were*. Nowadays you will hear and see *was*, but for examination purposes use *were*. Take care that students don't use *I wish I would*, which is a very common mistake. It is possible to say *I wish he would*, or *I wish they would*, but the object must be different from the subject.

4 *Would* after *wish* or *if only* is usually used for complaints or criticism. Ask students to write down some examples of things they are annoyed about at the moment. For example:

I wish the teacher would stop giving us so much homework.
I wish my parents would send me more money.

5 *Wish* is often confused with *hope*. *Hope* is usually a wish for the future and takes a present tense with future meaning.

Answers
a I hope the rain stops soon.
b I hope you can come to my party.
c I wish I could speak Arabic.
d I wish Peter would finish writing his book.
e I wish I had remembered to bring the sleeping bags.

E xtension activity

If it is possible, tape the news in English from the BBC World Service and get students to take notes. They should then form pairs and talk about what they wish and hope for their country or the world as a result of what they have just heard.

6 a The use of the past tense after *as if/as though* is for hypothetical situations – they express unreality.

Answer
In the first example you aren't an expert, and in the second you are.

b There is often some confusion of *would rather* with *had better*, usually because they are often seen in contracted forms as *I'd rather, You'd better*.

Answers
a I wish I had/could have more money.
b correct
c If only he would stop smoking – I can hardly breathe.
d correct
e I would rather you went now.
f Liz wishes she could go home now.
g I wish I had learned the violin when I was at school.

7 This exercise is exam practice for Paper 3 Part 3. If time is short, this exercise can be set for homework.

Answers
1 wish I had taken
2 would/'d rather the children stayed
3 only we had seen some
4 wish I lived/could live
5 wish you wouldn't walk
6 would/'d rather you didn't

8 Students need to familiarise themselves with these collocations. The negative prefix *un-* is commonly used in these phrases. This exercise could be set for homework with a dictionary.

Suggested answers
a a knot b a cardigan c a knot d a parcel
e a secret/a clue f a Roman coin, treasure
g a seat belt h some wool/your hair i a window

9 Students will probably need help with this exercise. If they are finding it difficult, you could fill in some of the spaces to help them. It could be set for homework.

Answers
a tornadoes b snowdrifts c gale warning
d forecast e overcast f shower g hurricanes
h drought i damp, humid

Exam folder 12

Paper 1 Part 3 Gapped text

SB pages 150–151

If discussing the task in class, stress to students that this part of the Reading paper is double-weighted. Explain too that if they fill one gap wrongly, this may affect several answers. It is essential to spend adequate time on this part in the exam. Refer students to the Advice section, which includes recommended times for each stage.

Answers
1 D 2 G 3 H 4 C 5 F 6 B 7 E

UNIT 24 Priceless or worthless?

Unit topic	Art
24.1	
Exam skills	Reading Paper 1 Part 2
Vocabulary	Collocations
Exam skills	Listening Paper 4 Part 1
24.2	
Grammar focus	Adverbs and word order
Vocabulary	Words often confused
Exam skills	Use of English Paper 3 Part 5

Workbook contents

1	Use of English – Part 2,
2	Grammar – word order
3, 4, 5, 6	Vocabulary – collocations, definitions

24.1 SB pages 152–153

Lesson plan

Speaking	5–10'
Reading	20–30'
Vocabulary	20–30'
Listening	15–20'

SV   Omit 4 and 7; set 5 for homework.
LV   See notes below for 4.

1 Ask students to think about which famous paintings or artist they like best. You could take in some pictures of famous paintings in different styles so that they could talk about them.

The two photos have two very different types of painting. Ask students to work in pairs and discuss the questions in this exercise.

2 Ask students to read the title and opening paragraph and to decide what the article is going to be about. The article is a true story about a boy who has made a lot of money from his paintings.

3 Students should now read through the article and answer the multiple choice questions.

Answers
1 D   2 A   3 C   4 B   5 C   6 B   7 A   8 C

4 Ask students what they think about what they have read.

Extension activity

Put these sentences on the board and ask students to complete them, using vocabulary from the article. Remind them to read the opening paragraph, too.

a I couldn't see the spelling mistake until the teacher .... it ....

b Doctors can .... up to £100,000 a year if they treat patients privately.

c Houses where I live are .... to £250,000 at the moment.

d I sold my car for a three .... sum.

e In parts of Africa rain has been .... and the crops have failed.

f Can you lend me some money? I'm a bit .... at the moment.

g The Mona Lisa is supposed to be ....

Answers
a pointed out   b make   c fetching up   d figure
e scarce   f short   g priceless

5

Answers
to break a promise
to sit still
to get a holiday / better
to spend a fortune / a week / a holiday
to taste funny
to keep a promise / still / awake / a secret
to have a conversation / an expression / a look / a fortune / a secret / a holiday
to do 20 kilometres to the litre / better
to wear a look / an expression

6 These are three short listening extracts to give practice for Paper 4 Part 1. Play the tape twice.

Answers
1 A   2 B   3 C

Tapescript

Speaker 1: I went to see the Mona Lisa when I was in Paris. Well, it's so famous, I felt I couldn't not go, though it's better to go earlier in the day when there's more natural light. You just have to follow the crowds really – I don't think most tourists look at anything else, which is a shame as there are probably much better pictures on display there. Anyway, I went along too, though it was a bit pointless really – the picture is so small, I could hardly make it out.

Speaker 2: They've decided to brighten up our offices at work by letting us choose a painting to hang up. Sounds like a good idea you might think, but you'd be amazed at some of the things people have chosen. I've got something fairly neutral, because of the nature of the job I do. Had I not been so high profile, I would have felt able to choose more freely, like some of my colleagues have.

Speaker 3: Well, it was a great exhibition from my point of view – lots of interesting paintings, which seemed to be going down well with the public, and I saw some friends I hadn't seen for ages. The artist looked a bit down at one stage and later I found out that someone had bought a portrait which had sentimental value – it'd been put at an astronomical price in the hope of dissuading anyone, but anyway, that's life isn't it?

24.2 SB pages 154–155

Lesson plan	
Grammar	40–50'
Vocabulary	30–40'

SV Set 4 and 5 for homework.
LV See notes below for 2.

1 Although some adverbs have already been covered in Units 1, 2 and 6 of this book, this unit extends that coverage to include inversion and gives students more practice in word order.

ⓣ eaching extra

Be careful when teaching inversion. It is important for students to understand how it is formed, but it is usually only used in formal writing and speaking. The one form of inversion that students should use in their writing is the *Not only … but also* construction.

Check that students understand the word order after a negative adverb.

2 The sentences a–p include examples of common word order mistakes. There is one correct sentence. Ask students to work individually or in pairs to correct the sentences. They can refer to the Grammar folder, page 207 if they are having problems. The position of adverbs in English is very variable and the rules can get quite complicated. Below are the answers with a summary of the rules.

Answers
a I like Van Gogh very much. (*very much* always goes after the object)
b Yesterday I visited a gallery in London. OR I visited a gallery in London yesterday. (Time at the beginning or end)
c She would never have suggested buying it. (adverb between two auxiliaries)
d He is still hoping to have an exhibition. (adverb between auxiliary and verb)
e I asked him not to stand in front of the painting. (negative before infinitive)
f There is always a queue for the Summer Exhibition. (adverb after verb *to be*)
g I often go to Los Angeles. (adverb between subject and ordinary verb)
h The price is high enough, so don't bid any more. (enough after adjective)
i Correct (inversion after negative adverb)
j Can you tell me what the price is, please? (question form in first part of sentence)
k I don't know what it is called. (not a question)
l It was such a heavy frame that no one could carry it. (*such* before article)
m The artist gave the small portrait to my father. (order of objects – something to somebody)
n How magnificent it is! (an exclamation)
o He described the photo to me. (describe something to somebody)
p She drew the sketch quickly. (adverb of manner after object)

ⓔ xtension activity

Students have to describe what the following people do using as many adverbs of time, manner and place that they can. Ask students to form teams and get them to think of ten animals/people/jobs, etc. They then ask the other team to define the word in one sentence. For example:

A politician – A person who often goes to parliament to earn a lot of money for hardly doing any work.

A bee – An insect which frequently flies out of its hive looking very hard for some nectar to sip.

3 Most of this exercise will be familiar to students, especially the part on irregular adverbs. Students are often confused by *hard/hardly* and don't know how to use *friendly* as an adverb. In the exercise a–l they need to use the word in capitals to form a word or phrase that makes sense grammatically. Some words do not need changing.

Answers
a silly b well c in a friendly way d better e fast
f better, well g more carefully h more interestingly
i lonely j worse k hardly l straight

4　Refer students to the Vocabulary spot. In the article was the word *priceless* which is one of the words in English that students often confuse. This exercise looks at other common examples. Below is an explanation of the differences:

> at the end – of the story/film/book
> in the end – finally
> priceless – so valuable it has no price
> invaluable – usually about something abstract like help; means very useful
> valuable – worth a lot of money
> nowadays – is happening currently
> actually – in fact
> to raise – transitive – takes an object
> to rise – intransitive – no object
> to lie – takes no object
> to lay – takes an object – to lay eggs, to lay the table
> to tell – someone something
> to say – something to someone
> a cook is a person
> a cooker is a machine
> to steal something from someone
> to rob somewhere or someone of something
> to damage something
> to injure someone
> sympathetic – kind if you have a problem
> friendly – pleasant and sociable
> sensible – full of common sense
> sensitive – feels very deeply

Teaching extra

Students often confuse phrases such as:
except for/apart from
by car/on foot
on my own/by myself
by hand/on hand/in hand

It's a good idea for students to keep a list of the mistakes that they regularly make in their vocabulary books.

5　This is exam practice for Paper 3 Part 5. The subject is Pablo Picasso. Before students start reading ask them to tell you everything they know about Picasso.

Background information

Pablo Picasso 1881–1973
Born in Malaga, Spain.
Blue period 1902–1904
Pink period 1904–1906

1906–7 cubism – helped develop this style with the painter Braque. Picasso's major work is *Guernica* 1937, a cubist painting expressing the horror of war.

Answers
1 different　2 cheerful　3 successful　4 inspiration
5 African　6 expressive　7 angular　8 beginning
9 unrealistic　10 symbolising

Writing folder 12

Paper 2 Part 2

SB pages 156–157

1　Ask students to look carefully at the painting by Vermeer of *The Cook*. Then, in pairs, students should describe what is in the picture and comment on how they feel about it.

Tell them to read through the answer to the question and to choose a title from A, B or C.

2　This exercise type used to appear on Paper 3 before FCE was revised. It is useful for making students aware of certain words needed in a sentence, such as prepositions and articles.

Suggested answer

The walls are fairly bare and they have been painted white. There is a window high up on one wall with a basket hanging next to it. Under the window there is a table with a basket of bread, a bowl of milk and cakes set out on it. Both the jar of milk and the bowl are made of brown pottery. There are some blue and white tiles along the edge of the wall where it joins the floor. On the floor is a box containing a pot with a handle.

3　Students can try this exam question in class or for homework. It is always a good idea to discuss the question in class first and to plan out what they should write. The sample answer is based on a rather boring type of severe weather condition, so that students shouldn't feel that if they haven't been in a hurricane or earthquake recently they can't answer the question!

Sample plan and answer
Introduction – Yes, thick fog
Where – coming home from a party
What I did – got out of the car and walked slowly in front

Sample answer

Walking through a cloud

I remember very well the night I went to a party in town but had to spend six hours getting the five kilometres back home. It was my friend's birthday party and she had hired a disco. The weather was fine when we left for the party and it only took us twenty minutes to get to the disco by car. I was driving there and my brother was going to drive back.

We had a great time at the party – good music, lots of friends and a brilliant birthday cake. Every now and then someone would arrive and tell us the weather was getting worse. We just kept on partying – we weren't interested in what was happening outside. Then, around two-thirty in the morning, it was time to go home. We

couldn't believe it when we got outside. Where was the car? Luckily we had parked near to the disco, so we followed the walls round to the back and went from car to car, looking for ours.

We got in and my brother drove. I had to walk in front of the car, all the way home, following the side of the road. It was a good thing that I knew the way very well.

---

4   The aim of this exercise is to get students to widen their vocabulary so that they don't keep repeating the same words. This exercise can be used for dictionary work.

Suggested answers
a large, enormous, huge, gigantic, vast, immense
b tiny, minute, little
c wealthy, well-to-do, affluent, well-off, prosperous
d badly-off, impoverished, penniless
e sweltering, boiling, burning
f chilly, icy, cool, freezing
g heavy, plump, stout, tubby
h bony, skinny, slim, slender
i attractive, charming, good-looking, lovely
j awful, terrible, unacceptable, rotten

Units 19–24 Revision

SB pages 158–159

Lesson plan

Topic review	15-35'
Vocabulary	25-25'
Grammar	30-30'

LV   Extend Topic review (see 1).

Topic review

1   Follow the standard procedure, using the Extension activity on page 73 for the longer version.

Vocabulary

2   Suggest that students work through 2 and 3 in three teams of up to five students (have more teams if your class is larger than 15). The winning team must not only finish first but have the most correct answers.

Answers
1 C   2 A   3 C   4 B   5 C   6 B   7 A   8 B

3

Answers
● **illness or injury**
1 sprain   2 cough
● **volcanoes**
3 erupt   4 ash   5 lava
● **musical instruments**
6 oboe   7 piano   8 guitar   9 flute
● **serious crimes**
10 rape   11 fraud   12 mugging   13 arson
14 hijacking
● **adjectives to describe works of art**
15 worthless   16 expressive   17 priceless
18 valuable   19 garish   20 symbolic

a flute   b lava   c garish   d sprain   e arson

Grammar

4   Ask students to work through the task in pairs. If there is any time at the end, have a class discussion on everyday things that might become valuable.

Answers
1 not   2 of   3 who   4 although   5 might/could/may/should   6 few   7 enough   8 so   9 up   10 a
11 than   12 it   13 at   14 being   15 if

Paper 1 Part 4

You are going to read a magazine article about four women's lifestyles. For Questions
1–15, choose from the women (**A–E**). There is an example at the beginning (**0**).

Which woman

is a saleswoman?	**0**	C
is concerned that her children should look good?	**1**	
depends on someone to make the right choices for her?	**2**	
finds that her regular treat allows her to relax?	**3**	
feels she has to do well because of the money she has spent?	**4**	
gets pleasure from making food?	**5**	
sometimes feels uneasy about what she is spending?	**6**	
orders goods to be driven to her home?	**7**	
has to make an appointment by phone?	**8**	
believes that employing someone to keep her house spotless is essential?	**9**	
initially planned to pay for only a few sessions?	**10**	
feels better about herself now?	**11**	
is in charge of a business?	**12**	
recently noticed something different about herself?	**13**	
has a young child?	**14**	
says she dislikes spending more than she has to?	**15**	

Not so much a luxury, more a way of life

A — Lenor

A year after having my baby, I still needed to lose weight, but I felt awkward about going to a gym. I thought that if I booked two or three appointments with a personal trainer, I'd learn what to do and then I could continue on my own. However, I became addicted. I found that it was so much better having someone to encourage me. I've been seeing my trainer twice a week for three years now. We tend to work out at the gym because it has childcare, but sometimes we go for a run in the park. Even though I do worry about the cost from time to time, she's worth every penny. I'm more focused and I work out more effectively. I also feel motivated to work harder because of the expense!

B — Sheila

When I was younger I felt I ought to do all the cleaning, shopping and ironing myself, but now I don't. I have a pressured but well-paid job, so I can pay someone else to do these chores so that I am free to do the things I enjoy, like cooking. I have a cleaner who comes three mornings a week and she also does the ironing. Coming home to an immaculate kitchen is wonderful, better than any facial or massage treatment, and well worth the money. Recently, I decided to cut out my weekly supermarket visit too, and now have organic food delivered instead. I use local shops for other groceries, so I never have to go to the supermarket at all now. Although I like shopping for clothes, having my house cleaned is more important to me. If I had to cut back, cleaning would be the last thing to go.

C — Jane

Having a personal shopper takes the hard work out of clothes shopping. I need lots of smart outfits for work as I'm involved in selling, but I don't have the time to wander round the shops looking for them, so I go to a personal shopper at a big London department store. She knows my tastes exactly. All I have to do is ring her to tell her what I want, then arrange a convenient time to go along to the store, to try on the clothes she has selected for me. If I'm really busy, she'll even send me things to try on at the office! I rely on her totally. She keeps a record of what I buy each time so I don't end up with things that don't match. It's a free service, and I actually spend less on clothes than I used to, because she steers me in the right direction and stops me becoming a fashion victim.

D — Sarah

A while ago, I started having facials because I was getting more wrinkles, and my face was very dry. At first, I treated myself to a six-week course, but now I go once a week after a session at the gym. The whole process lasts about an hour and really helps me to unwind. I regard it as a worthwhile investment. I didn't look after my skin when I was younger, but now I have to do things properly. I've picked up some good habits and tips from the beauty consultant, but I could never do the facials myself. I'd far rather spend money on a facial than having a cleaning lady. As well as improving my appearance, facials have given me greater self-esteem.

E — Frances

While the children were small, there was just about enough time to keep on top of all the washing and ironing. Now, with three teenagers and a company to run, I've come to realise that it's impossible to do everything. I also feel that I deserve better than piles of dirty washing after my working day. It's a wonderfully efficient service; they pick up two mornings a week before I leave for work, and deliver everything back, laundered and ironed to perfection, within 24 hours. Of course, it's quite an outlay each week, but I have no problem with that at all. Keeping the family presentable is more important!

Paper 2 Part 2

Write an answer to one of the Questions **1–3** in this part. Write your answer in **120–180** words in an appropriate style.

1 You have been asked to write a story for a student magazine ending with these words:

   I was really thankful to see the police car arrive.

   Write your **story**.

2 Your college principal has asked you to write a report for new students coming to the college. He would like you to write your report on what students should do to keep fit and healthy while they study.

   Write your **report**.

3 You have just seen the following advertisement in an English newspaper.

Do you speak English?

Are you interested in art?

Would you like a holiday job where you could meet people from all over the world?

We are looking for someone to work in the City Art Gallery shop during the holidays. No experience is necessary but you must be friendly and helpful and have some interest in art.

Contact Mrs Donovan at the City Art Gallery.

Write your **letter**. You do not need to include postal addresses.

Paper 3 Part 3

For Questions **1–10**, complete the second sentence so that it has a similar meaning to the first sentence, using the word given. **Do not change the word given**. You must use between two and five words, including the word given.
Here is an example (**0**).

Example:

0   I have never been to Paris before.
    time
    This .... have been to Paris.

    The gap can be filled by the words 'is the first time I' so you write:

0	is the first time I

---

1   I strongly advise you to see a dentist if you have toothache.
    better
    You .... a dentist if you have toothache.

2   It's a pity I didn't buy that dress I saw yesterday.
    wish
    I .... that dress I saw yesterday.

3   It's best to ask an expert to value that painting if you are really thinking of buying it.
    have
    You ought .... by an expert if you are really thinking of buying it.

4   I usually find it very difficult to lose weight.
    difficulty
    I usually .... weight.

5   I still play in a rock band from time to time, even though I have a full-time job nowadays.
    spite
    I still play in a rock band from time to time
    .... full-time nowadays.

6   You really should get your hair cut.
    about
    It's .... your hair cut.

7   The pianist decided to appear less in public as he grew older.
    appearances
    The pianist decided to .... as he grew older.

8   It's a shame she can't decrease the number of cigarettes she smokes.
    cut
    If only .... the number of cigarettes she smokes.

9   The concert was cancelled due to the small number of ticket sales.
    called
    They .... of the small number of ticket sales.

10   I'd prefer to go to Venice with a friend, than to Florida with my aunt.
    rather
    I .... to Venice with a friend, than to Florida with my aunt.

Paper 3 Part 4

For Questions **1–15**, read the text below and look carefully at each line. Some of the lines are correct, and some have a word which should not be there.
If a line is correct, put a tick (✓) **at the end of the line**. If a line has a word which should not be there, write the word **at the end of the line**. There are two examples at the beginning (**0** and **00**).

Examples:

0	the
00	✓

THE FESTIVAL

0	I've always enjoyed listening to the music. It helps me calm down after	_the_
00	a busy day, and I'm also one of those people who can listen and study	✓
1	at the same time. I'm not keen on jazz, but apart from that, I like many	....
2	different types – depending on how that I feel. Last year I went to a	....
3	pop festival. It lasted since three days so we decided to camp on the	....
4	field provided by the concert organisers. The weather it was awful and	....
5	it rained all weekend. We were being soaking wet and I began to wish	....
6	that I would had stayed at home or booked into a hotel! The organisers	....
7	were making up a fortune selling umbrellas and plastic raincoats. Anyway,	....
8	the concert continued despite of the weather. They advised us to keep to	....
9	the special walk-ways that they built above the mud and gave to us plastic	....
10	sheets to put over our tents. In spite of all that, the music was very brilliant.	....
11	I particularly enjoyed some of the supporting bands – I always find they	....
12	perform better than the main star. It's probably because most of the	....
13	supporting bands are not well known and as this is their great opportunity	....
14	to get their music heard. I'd really advise anyone who to go to one of these	....
15	pop festivals, if only I wish I had booked into a hotel rather than sleeping	....
	in a tent!	

Paper 4 Part 1

You will hear people talking in eight different situations. For Questions 1–8, choose the best answer, **A**, **B** or **C**.

---

1 You overhear a woman talking on a mobile phone.
What is her job?

   A a journalist
   B a firefighter
   C a photographer

   [ ] 1

2 You hear a man talking to his doctor.
What is wrong with him?

   A He has a sprain.
   B He has a broken bone.
   C He has a bad cut.

   [ ] 2

3 You hear a radio report about a music festival.
Which event does the man have a ticket for?

   A a solo piano recital
   B jazz improvisation
   C a classical concert

   [ ] 3

4 You overhear a conversation in an art gallery.
What does the woman think of the painting?

   A It's too bright.
   B It's very powerful.
   C It's quite disappointing.

   [ ] 4

5 You hear part of a news report on the radio.
What has happened?

   A a flood
   B a tornado
   C an earthquake

   [ ] 5

6 You hear a woman talking on the phone.
Why is she calling?

   A to arrange a delivery date
   B to report a delay
   C to place another order

   [ ] 6

7 You hear this radio report about a crime.
Why will the suspect escape conviction?

   A There is insufficient evidence.
   B The suspect is too young.
   C A witness cannot be found.

   [ ] 7

8 You overhear this conversation about a party.
What do the couple agree about?

   A how quickly the time passed
   B what the catering was like
   C who was interesting to talk to

   [ ] 8

Paper 1 Part 4

1 E **2** C **3** D **4** A **5** B **6** A **7** B **8** C **9** B **10** A
11 D **12** E **13** D **14** A **15** A

Paper 2 Part 2

Sample answers

1

I had decided to stay in my flat for the weekend, rather than go to a music festival with my flatmates. I had spent Saturday cleaning the flat and doing some reading for a lecture I had to go to on the Monday morning. I went to bed about midnight after watching a movie on the TV.

At three o'clock in the morning I heard a noise. It sounded like a dustbin lid falling on the ground. I didn't think much of it at first – maybe it's a cat, I thought. Then there was the sound of footsteps, although very quiet ones. I was immediately wide awake and reached for the phone by my bed. Quickly I dialled 999 for the police. I told them where I was and that I thought I had a burglar. Then I got out of bed and locked my bedroom door. A few minutes later came the sound of breaking glass. Nervously I looked out of the window, but I was in luck. There was a flashing blue light coming up the road. I was really thankful to see the police car arrive.

2

How to keep yourself fit and healthy

Getting enough exercise
The aim of this report is to give advice to students at the college. It's very easy to get out of condition while you're studying. There never seems enough time to do any exercise – you always seem to have to be at a lecture or in the library. However, we're very lucky as we have excellent sports facilities. The gym is open from 7.00 in the morning until 10.00 at night, so I would recommend that you try to fit in some exercise twice a week.

Eating to stay healthy
Most people say that the stress of exams and having to write essays can make you want to eat food which is bad for you, like chocolate and cream cakes. They make you feel better and after working hard you often feel the need for a reward. Try to resist the temptation! Instead keep lots of fruit in your room and have a banana when you feel hungry. The college canteen has a wide variety of healthy food to choose from, so don't buy an expensive take-away if you're short of time and money, eat in the canteen.

3

Dear Mrs Donovan,

I'm writing to apply for the holiday job which you advertised recently in the newspaper. I am a twenty-year-old student and I speak English quite well. At present I am in my third year studying Mathematics at Redstone College and I am very keen to have a holiday job this summer. I am extremely good at adding up so I think I would be an asset to your shop.

My term finishes on 3rd July and I am free until 18th September. Last year I worked in a restaurant serving tourists from all over the world and I enjoyed it very much. I would like to have the opportunity to meet people and practise my English again.

I enjoy going to art galleries and am particularly keen on paintings by the Impressionists. Last year I went to the Monet exhibition which was held in London. I have often been in your art gallery and am familiar with the paintings you have. I do hope you will be interested in my application.

I look forward to hearing from you in the near future.

Yours sincerely,

Paper 3 Part 3

1 had/'d better see **2** wish I had bought **3** to have that painting valued **4** have (great) difficulty (in) losing **5** in spite of working **6** about time you got/had **7** make fewer (public) appearances / make fewer appearances in public **8** she could cut down on **9** called off the concert because **10** would/'d rather go

Paper 3 Part 4

1 ✓ **2** that **3** since **4** it **5** being **6** would **7** up
8 of **9** to **10** very **11** ✓ **12** ✓ **13** as **14** who **15** if

Paper 4 Part 1

1 A **2** C **3** B **4** B **5** C **6** B **7** B **8** B

Tapescript

1 You overhear a woman talking on a mobile phone. What is her job?
  A a journalist
  B a firefighter
  C a photographer

Woman: We're still at the scene … I've tried to get a closer look, but I can't get near the building because of the smoke. John's taken a lot of pictures, so hold some space on page five, could you? Amazingly, there seem to be no serious casualties. It's just about under control now, so I'm going to hang around for a bit, and hopefully speak to the chief fire officer.

2   You hear a man talking to his doctor. What is wrong with him?

   A He has a sprain.
   B He has a broken bone.
   C He has a bad cut.

   Dr: You're in the wars, Graeme. It seems only yesterday you were in with that nasty ankle injury. What's happened this time?

   G: Another bad tackle. Our coach checked me over when I came off the field and he's sure there's nothing broken. Will I need stitches?

   Dr: I'm afraid so. At least you won't be out of action for six weeks, like with the sprain.

   G: Mmm, I'll have to rest the leg for a while though, won't I?

3   You hear a radio report about a music festival. Which event does the man have a ticket for?

   A a solo piano recital
   B jazz improvisation
   C a classical concert

   Male: This year's concerts are more popular than ever and several are already sold out, including Sunday afternoon's piano music and tomorrow's jazz at St John's Church. I played safe and bought my ticket for this one well in advance. Surman will be playing on his own, and a wonderfully inventive evening seems in store. Finally, there are a few tickets left for tonight's performance by the Bournemouth Symphony Orchestra, which is taking place in the main concert hall.

4   You overhear a conversation in an art gallery. What does the woman think of the painting?

   A It's too bright.
   B It's very powerful.
   C It's quite disappointing.

   Brian: So what about this one, Paula? Looks like an enormous orange bobbing about in a turquoise pool to me! Talk about garish use of colours … ugh …

   Paula: Oh come on Brian, that's unfair. I agree the colours are quite loud, but they're actually rather effective … they strengthen the image, make it more symbolic. I'm sorry you're disappointed … I thought you'd like his work.

5   You hear part of a news report on the radio. What has happened?

   A a flood
   B a tornado
   C an earthquake

Woman: … This happened at 5.23 a.m. and there have since been two smaller tremors, within twenty minutes of each other. The centre is quite close to a populated area and several people have already been moved to temporary accommodation in windproof tents. Cracks have appeared on the major north-south highway and there is also growing concern that the river, swollen by the spring thaw, may burst its banks. More on this story after the break.

6   You hear a woman talking on the phone. Why is she calling?

   A to arrange a delivery date
   B to report a delay
   C to place another order

   Woman: Well, it was supposed to come by 10.30. I remember specifically asking for Thursday morning, as I work from 2 o'clock. So what are you going to do about it? It's all very well promising a door-to-door service, but you never deliver when you say you're going to. I waited all day for the last order, and I'm not prepared to do that again. … You will? Okay, I'll give it another half an hour, but I have to say that my patience is wearing a little thin.

7   You hear this radio report about a crime. Why will the suspect escape conviction?

   A There is insufficient evidence.
   B The suspect is too young.
   C A witness cannot be found.

   Male: Last week's arson attack on a local supermarket by a nine-year-old boy has led to the store being closed for good. Even though the boy was caught red-handed by the manager, he's unlikely to be taken to court because of his age. However, evidence from the in-store video camera suggests that the lad was aided by an older teenager, and police are confident of making an early arrest.

8   You overhear this conversation about a party. What do the couple agree about?

   A how quickly the time passed
   B what the catering was like
   C who was interesting to talk to

   Woman: Well, that was a boring party, even though the food was very tasty. I kept looking at my watch all night – I couldn't believe how slowly the time was going.

   Man: Oh I wouldn't say that … and we were there almost five hours, you know. You were just unlucky in who you got to speak to, whereas I met some rather interesting people …

   Woman: If you mean that self-centred man who called himself a poet, I couldn't disagree with you more! He went on and on about his latest book, I thought he was trying to sell me a copy at one point. I crept off back to the kitchen in the end.

   Man: … to have some more of those deliciously mouth-watering fishy things, no doubt!

   Woman: Mmm.

UNIT 25 | Urban decay, suburban hell

Unit topic	City life
25.1	
Exam skills	Listening Paper 4 Part 4
	(Who says what?)
	Speaking Paper 5 Part 4
Vocabulary	Words with *up*
25.2	
Grammar focus	Mixed conditionals
Exam skills	Use of English Paper 3 Part 1
Vocabulary	Prefix *re-*

Workbook contents

1, 2, 3	Reading – Part 3 gapped sentences, vocabulary
4	Grammar – mixed conditionals
5	Use of English – Part 5

25.1 SB pages 160–161

Lesson plan	
Listening	30–40'
Vocabulary	15–20'
Speaking	20–30'

1   The pictures show a suburb in Melbourne, Australia and a street in Greenwich Village, New York.

Allow students to complete one long turn (and brief comment from the other candidate), but tell them when one minute has passed.

2   Play the first part and elicit the two answers, as well as a prediction about how the discussion might continue.

Answers
- The expert is an architect – the profession is architecture.
- Gareth believes that architects are out of touch and irresponsible, referring to modern buildings as 'eyesores'.
- Gareth may go on to exemplify this criticism.

Tapescript

Part 1

Presenter: Good evening. Well, with me for the next thirty minutes on *Do they really know best?* are Jennifer Ralston and Gareth Webster. Jennifer is a fully-qualified architect with the London-based firm Kinnaird and Partners, a company which has been responsible for some of the most innovative buildings of the last ten years. Facing her – and ready to do battle with the profession he describes as out-of-touch and irresponsible – is Gareth, an undergraduate at the University of London, who is surrounded by, in his own words, those eyesores that pass for modern buildings. Gareth, state your case.

3   Ask students to read questions 1–7 and then play the tape.

Answers
1 J   2 J   3 G   4 B   5 G   6 J   7 G

Tapescript

Part 2

Gareth: Right, well it's as you've said really. I walk past these awful 60s concrete blocks every day and I just can't believe the mistakes that have been made … people have been uprooted and forced to live in high-rise buildings against their will. Architects and planners have never talked to the public, er, they feel they have the right to decide what's best for us.

Presenter: Is that how you operate, Jennifer?

Jennifer: Not at all, and in my view, lack of consultation over new buildings is not an issue with the public. Gareth, you're describing a time when many people wanted to be rehoused, because their living conditions were so bad. Uh, this was a policy upheld by government, rather than decided by architects.

Gareth: But the fact is that people still have to live in high-rise accommodation. I grew up in the suburbs where everyone had a garden, it was a pleasant environment. How can you expect people to enjoy life on the twenty-third floor with a bleak view and a lift that's out of order? If we were meant to live up in the sky, we would have been born with wings!

Jennifer: Well, joking apart, I was in a tower block in a run-down part of Bristol for six years of my childhood, so I do know what it's like. That's largely what drove me to become an architect, actually. Yes, some 60s architecture is poor, but the point is, if it hadn't happened, we would be making similar mistakes today, whereas …

Gareth: They *are* being made!

Presenter: Gareth, let Jennifer finish!

Jennifer: … whereas, as it is, we have been able to learn from the recent past. Look, we do have a serious problem: our cities are getting bigger, we call it urban sprawl, with suburbs that go on for ever. Okay, everyone has a garden, but at a huge cost to the tax-paying public, in terms of basic services and upkeep.

Gareth: You mean drainage, road-maintenance, that sort of thing? I hadn't thought of that … And I suppose city expansion isn't very good news for the countryside either, it's sort of … disappearing?

Jennifer: Absolutely. And at the same time, there's sometimes appalling decay in the middle of our cities as a direct result of the move outwards. Shops have closed because of out-of-town shopping facilities, and people often have little left to support them locally.

Presenter: Gareth, do you fancy living right in the city centre?

Gareth: Hmm. I must confess I would really like to move further in one day, there's so much going on, you know, entertainment, concerts and stuff, but any housing in central London that's nice to live in is so upmarket that it's completely unaffordable for someone like me.

Jennifer: That depends, Gareth, on whether you would be prepared to live up in the sky. What I believe in – and what many architects are trying to work towards – is the regeneration of our cities' core, and this can only happen if we build vertically – there's no space to do anything else! It's a really exciting development that could give city centres the uplift they so badly need. Gareth, imagine if your building was a multi-use one, where you could just go downstairs to see your live music, or pick up some shopping late at night … this is the housing of the future, where everything is on the doorstep. No-one will need to own a car.

Gareth: Yes, but again is that what people want? I mean having a car is every person's dream, isn't it? I know traffic's a problem, but you can't change how people are, how they want to live.

Jennifer: Well, it may surprise you that in a recent TV phone-in, 67% of callers thought that the car should be banned altogether from central London – one example of public consultation, incidentally. I think people are ready for this, Gareth, they understand that traffic congestion is killing us. Living in the city has to become a healthier and more acceptable option.

Gareth: Oh, I don't know, you do sound as though you know what you're talking about.

Presenter: Gareth, Jennifer, good to see you getting on so well now! I'm going to have to stop you briefly, while we take a few calls on this topic from listeners, but …

4 Play Part 2 of the tape again so that students can check their answers. Pause after each question has been covered (see underlined parts of the tapescript). Elicit key phrases that supply each answer.

Photocopiable tapescript activity (P ⋯⋗ page 190)

Alternatively, give out copies of the tapescript and ask students to underline the key phrases. They can also refer to the tapescript for 5 below.

5 Students listen again to Part 2 for the words with *up*.

> **Answers**
> **a** 3 **b** 5 **c** 1 **d** 2 **e** 4

6 Ask students to discuss the statements in small groups.

7 Refer students to the Exam spot and in particular to the information about turn-taking. Then ask students to decide on the purpose of each turn-taking move in pairs.

> **Answers**
> i: b, c, g
> ii: a, d, f
> iii: e, h

Ask students to decide which are offensive.

> **Answers**
> **d** is too direct for a discussion and might give offence.
> **g** is a rather abrupt question.

Elicit other examples of the three categories i–iii.

> **Suggested answers**
> Other non-verbal strategies for directing a conversation include:
> nodding or shaking one's head; making eye contact; raising a hand; leaning forward.

8 Students now discuss the questions as described, using some of these techniques. Remind them to change roles after every question.

25.2 SB pages 162–163

Lesson plan

Grammar	40–50'
Use of English	25–35'

SV Keep 4 brief and set 6 for homework.
LV See notes below for 4.

1 Ask students what the term 'mixed conditional' might mean. Then ask them to identify the tenses used.

2 Allow students three to four minutes to write out the full sentences. Then ask for examples. Write up some on the board, correcting them if necessary. Be sure to explain why you are making any corrections.

Possible answers
a would look much worse.
b wouldn't be starving now.
c would be less well-informed.
d wouldn't behave so appallingly.
e would still be living at home.

3 Ask students to look at the example. They can finish these sentences in pairs and then report to the class.

Possible answers
a would have chosen to live in them.
b would have tidied up your bedroom by now.
c wouldn't have been so high for the last 20 years.
d would have gone out at 3 am this morning to buy you some paracetamol.

Refer students to the Grammar folder, page 207.

4 Remind students to use turn-taking skills in their discussion.

5

Answers
1 C 2 A 3 C 4 B 5 D 6 A 7 C 8 B 9 D
10 B 11 C 12 A 13 D 14 D 15 A

6

Answers
reconsider/reconsideration; reconstruct/reconstruction; regenerate/regeneration; reopen/reopening; repossess/repossession; rewrite/rewritten

a regenerated	c reopening
b reconstructed	d reconsider

Exam folder 13

Paper 1 Part 4 Multiple matching

SB pages 164–165

1 This type of multiple matching differs from the multiple matching in Part 1 of the paper. There are usually 13–15 questions and students need to scan the text to find the answers. Often there are two multiple choice questions which test global meaning. These come at the end.

Ask students to read through the Advice section. It is useful for students to have a highlighter pen so that they can highlight the part of the text with the answer in.

This text is about four people who have jobs that other people might envy.

To introduce the topic it might be a good idea to ask students what they see as a dream job. The ideas don't have to be serious, e.g. working in a chocolate factory.

Tell students to read the questions and then scan the texts for the answers. There are clues to help students if they get stuck on a question. When they finish, they should compare answers with another student.

Answers
1 B 2 D 3 C 4 A 5 C 6 A 7 C 8 A 9 D
10 B 11 A 12 D 13 A 14 D 15 A

Unit topic	Transport

26.1
Exam skills	Reading Paper 1 Part 1
Grammar extra	Inversion
Vocabulary	Phrases with *get*

26.2
Grammar focus	Relative pronouns
Vocabulary	Topic words
Exam skills	Use of English Paper 3 Part 4

Workbook contents

1	Use of English – Part 2
2	Use of English – Part 3
3	Vocabulary – topic
4	Writing – proofreading a report

26.1 SB pages 166–167

Lesson plan

Reading	50–60'
Vocabulary	20–20'
Grammar extra	0–10'

SV Set Grammar extra for homework.
LV See notes below for 1 and 4.

1 Ask students to discuss their opinions in small groups. Put some useful vocabulary on the board, reminding students of their discussion in Unit 21 about luxuries and necessities. For example:
car-ownership
essential/ necessity/ luxury
depend on

Extension activity

Ask students to prepare the following task as a long turn. When they are ready, choose two or three to speak to the class, and ask the others to time each long turn. Alternatively, suggest that students record their own long turn at home and then time it.

Compare and contrast the two pictures, explaining which car would suit your lifestyle better, and why.

2 Explain that students are going to hear five unscripted extracts, where people are talking about their own attitudes to car-ownership.

Answers
Speaker 3 has to use the car every day.
Speaker 1 would prefer not to travel by car.
Speaker 4 claims to be a car enthusiast.

Tapescript

Speaker 1: I don't really use my car very much. I use it mostly at weekends when I'm getting out of the city but I don't really like driving very much so I'd much rather take the train if I could.

Speaker 2: I suppose in the week when I'm in the city I could definitely do without the car, in fact I often do and then I use public transport and it's fine. But at the weekends I go to visit my godfather who's … who's not very well and so I have to go every weekend and really he lives in the middle of nowhere so I have to have the car then. I couldn't possibly do the journey without it.

Speaker 3: The car's used all the time now by everybody. My wife and I seem to find that we wouldn't be able to exist if we didn't have the car. We take the children to school in the morning, do the shopping because we're not near any shops any more, pick the children up from school, go to the station to pick up my parents who come down every weekend. It's like a taxi now … it's like one of the family too.

Speaker 4: I love my car. It's a 1976 BMW 1602 in a lemon yellow colour. It's called Moosey and it's really my pride and joy. I … I belong to the BMW members' club and I spend my weekends going to lots of rallies and I'm, you know, I'm a real car lover.

Speaker 5: Well, my car's quite important in my life although I only usually use it at weekends, taking the kids out for day trips, going to the supermarket, visiting the local DIY store. During the week, I tend to use public transport more, I mean I do use the car in the week of course, and use it for work occasionally … but, on the whole it's weekends.

3 Students discuss the headings in pairs.

4 Allow students a time limit of eight minutes to complete the matching task.

Answers
1 E   2 G   3 B   4 A   5 D   6 C   7 H

Ⓔ xtension activity

Ask students to choose a paragraph each and summarise it in one or two sentences, looking for key vocabulary.

5 Students discuss the questions in groups or as a class.

6 Ask students to find the phrases in the article and match them to a–h (the paragraph number is given in brackets).

Answers
a get away from it all (3)   b get at
c (not) get anywhere (2)   d get around (1)
e get going/get moving   f get the message across (2)
g get behind (5)   h get over with

Grammar extra

Remind students that inversion first came up in Unit 24. Refer them to the Grammar folder, page 207 if necessary.

Answers
a Not only has there been a huge increase in the number of private cars on the road – more cars …
b No longer can we depend on the unlimited use of our cars.
c Not only does Brendan ride a bike to work, he also uses it to travel longer distances.
d In no way should the government weaken its transport policy.
e Seldom are members of the public willing to walk to work, especially if it's raining.
f Not only do cars pollute the air but they endanger people's lives too.

26.2 SB pages 168–169

Lesson plan

Grammar	30–30'
Vocabulary	25–25'
Use of English	10–25'

SV Set 7 for homework.

1 Ask students to read the section in the Grammar folder, page 208. Students discuss the examples in pairs.

Answers
a additional; *who* = Richard Simmons
b essential; *who* = visitors
c essential; *for whom* = the people
d additional; *whose* = the countryside
whose does not always refer to people.

2 Ask students to discuss each sentence in pairs and agree the changes which need to be made.

Answers
a Wetherby, with whom I went on several expeditions, was always the perfect gentleman.
b The ranchers for whom cowboys worked expected them to spend at least 12 hours a day on horseback.
c Apollo, in whom the ancient Greeks believed, was supposed to ride a chariot of flame across the sky.
d Teenagers, to whom rollerblading is seen as a quick way of getting around, often take unnecessary risks in traffic.

3 Ask students to read the definitions and identify each one, using the pictures to help them.

Answers
a hydrofoil   b camel   c canoe   d submarine
e helicopter   f tandem   g hovercraft   h llama

4 Explain that it is often better to join two sentences like this, as the ideas are better linked.

Answers
a The Regent's Canal in London, whose towpath is increasingly used by cyclists, runs between Camden and Islington.
b This new jetski, whose size can accommodate four people comfortably, has a top speed of over 100 kph. OR This new jetski, whose seating accommodates four people comfortably, has a top speed of over 100 kph.
c The hot air balloon, whose first flight was made in 1783, was designed by the Montgolfier brothers.
d From 1983 to 1987, the number of cars and trucks in the United States, whose population in that period grew by only 9.2 million, increased by 20.1 million.
e The Brox, a new four-wheel cycle trailer whose seven gears allow it to go up hills and even steps easily, is being trialled by the Royal Mail.
f The American space shuttle, whose heat-proof tiles allow it to re-enter the earth's atmosphere safely, can be used again and again.

5 Ask students to sort the words into columns, giving explanations where necessary.

Answers

Cars and trucks	Boats and ships	Aircraft
bonnet	cabin	cabin
boot	funnel	flap
brake	hull	jet engine
cab	mast	propeller
dashboard	oar	rudder
exhaust	paddle	tyre
gearbox	porthole	undercarriage
indicator	rudder	windscreen
radiator		
steering wheel		
tyre		
windscreen		

---

6 Check understanding of the vocabulary. Students describe each problem in a single sentence, using *whose*.

7 Ask whether students recognise the film or the actor in the photograph.

Background note

Robert Carlyle, whose film appearances include *The Full Monty*, *Trainspotting* and *Carla's Song* , is one of Britain's best-known actors. *Carla's Song*, directed by Ken Loach, is set in Glasgow and Nicaragua. It is both a love story and a political statement.

If any students have seen *Carla's Song*, ask them to tell the class about the character played by Robert Carlyle. Students can do the task for homework or in class.

Answers
1 than   2 of   3 ✓   4 and   5 ✓   6 been
7 to   8 the   9 enough   10 ✓   11 more
12 going   13 ✓   14 across   15 unless

Writing folder 13

SB pages 170–171

1 Ask students to look at the three statements. As they read the composition, they should think about the ideas expressed, and say which statement is being dealt with. Tell students how important it is to clearly address the statement in an exam question. If they don't, they will receive a poor mark, in spite of any good language.

Answer
B – although it is a poor attempt!

2 Remind students that linkers were covered in Compositions 1 (Student's Book page 56).

Answers
There is considerable irrelevance in the first paragraph and the statement is not adequately addressed until the start of the second paragraph.

There should have been an introductory paragraph, and the second paragraph should have been split into two (new idea, cycling as fun).

There is little use of linkers – just 'on the other hand' in paragraph 2.

The writer's view is stated, though unclearly.

There are some inappropriately informal expressions, e.g. 'oh god', 'why not', 'yes, it is'.

3 Ask students to do this in pairs.

Answer
Relevant ideas: all except c, e and i.

4 Remind students about the need to use commas for clarity.

Answers
a Of high priority is the introduction of tighter laws on older vehicles, whose exhaust fumes cause greater pollution.
b In the short-term, it is essential to consult the public, whose concerns have never been fully aired.
c Instant action is needed to reduce the volume of cars in our cities, while in the medium-term, further research should be done on alternative forms of transport.

5 Students can use sentences *b* or *c* above in their answer, editing them slightly if necessary. Ask why sentence *a* is less relevant.

Sample answer
It is obvious that there is too much traffic nowadays. Not only does this affect cities, but the countryside too. The way we depend on our cars is threatening the natural world, because of the high levels of pollution caused. Instant action is needed to reduce the volume of cars, while in the medium-term, further research should be done on alternative forms of transport.

In my view, we desperately need a better public transport system, in order to cut down on the use of private cars. At present, people are not offered a true choice, as travel by bus or train is double the cost of using a car. It is also essential to advertise the services which are available.

Other measures may be needed in the short-term to force people to leave their cars behind, such as higher taxes on road use. Some cities already charge for car entry and I believe this should be done more.

The government should invest heavily in research, so that new forms of transport, which are more environmentally friendly, can be developed. This applies equally to private ownership and public transport.

UNIT 27 Material girl

Unit topic	Madonna
27.1	
Speaking	Discourse markers
Exam skills	Listening Paper 4 Part 4
Pronunciation	List intonation
27.2	
Grammar focus	Revision of tenses
	Time expressions
Vocabulary	Phrasal verbs
Exam skills	Use of English
	Paper 3 Part 5

Workbook contents

1, 2	Reading – Part 1 summary sentences
3	Prepositions
4	Use of English – Part 4

27.1 SB pages 172–173

Lesson plan

Speaking	15–20'
Listening	25–30'
Pronunciation	30–40'

SV Omit 1, 2 and 3.
LV See notes below for 8.

1 Ask students to compare what they know about Madonna. Take in some of her songs and ask them what they think. (It is possible that some might not know who she is or have never heard her songs.)

In this interview a journalist, called Jonas Day is being interviewed about Madonna. Play the tape once and tell the class to make notes.

Answers
Born: 1958
Place: Rochester, Detroit USA
Family: 8 children, mother died when she was young
Education: went to University of Michigan and
             dropped out.

Tapescript

Part 1

Int: In the studio today we have Jonas Day, who's just won an award for student journalism by writing an article about Madonna for his college newspaper. Jonas, welcome. I believe Madonna herself rang to congratulate you?

Jonas: Well, it's true that I had a letter from her PR company, but I haven't spoken to her myself.

Int: So, let's start at the beginning. She was born in Detroit in 1958, is that right?

Jonas: Actually, at a place called Rochester.

Int: What about her family?

Jonas: Well, let's see now, her father was an engineer. I think life was quite a battle for her. You see, she was the eldest of eight children and quite young when her mother died. Anyway, she did ballet, singing and piano lessons and got a scholarship to the University of Michigan.

Int: A scholarship? She must've been quite good.

Jonas: Well, I think, on the whole, she did well. Anyway, it wasn't enough for her and she dropped out after two years and went to New York to find fame and fortune. I guess she didn't want to put the moment of stardom off any longer.

Int: Apparently, I believe the story is that she only had $35 in her pocket when she arrived in New York?

Jonas: I'm afraid I've never got to the bottom of that story.

Int: Oh, right, OK, now tell us how her career took off.

2 Play the tape again and ask students to write down the word or phrase asked for.

Teaching extra

Students should be aware of discourse markers, that is, words which signal to the listener the connection between what the speaker is saying and what they are about to say or have just said. Some words, for example, *apparently* also show the opinion of the speaker. Students are usually familiar with written markers such as *on the one hand, as regards, firstly,* etc. However, they are usually not clear about informal spoken markers.

Answers

taking charge of the conversation	so, right, now
correcting some information	actually
changing subject	anyway
apologising	I'm afraid
partly agreeing	it is true, but
making a generalisation	on the whole
giving some information which may not be reliable	apparently
thinking	let's see now
explaining	you see

3 The aim of this activity is to give practice for Paper 5. Ask students to form pairs and then ask one to choose a famous person. One will interview the famous person, as in the example given in the Student's Book. Possible people to interview:

   President Kennedy
   Lenin
   John Lennon
   Mother Theresa
   Gandhi

4 Students now listen to the rest of the interview with Jonas about Madonna. Ask them to read through the multiple choice questions quickly.

   Play the tape twice and then let students compare their answers.

Answers
1 B   2 C   3 B   4 B   5 A   6 C   7 A

Tapescript

Part 2

Jonas: Well, of course the thing most people don't associate with Madonna is the fact that she's chief executive of a large company called Maverick Entertainment which is a multi-million dollar company and earns her more than her records or her films.

Int: Yes, her image is certainly different, isn't it? She's had a lot of bad publicity about her private life, hasn't she? Especially when she married Sean Penn – the newspapers really put her down.

Jonas: She said at the time that what they said in the newspapers took her by surprise. She'd believed her life to be totally under control. Everything she'd ever done had been carefully planned. You know, in order to get a record contract when she came to New York she went to clubs where she knew record producers went; she even managed to get an appointment with the head of Sire records when he was in hospital! He reckoned she was a very determined lady.

Int: I heard a similar story about how she got her Manager. Apparently she asked herself who managed the biggest act in the world, and of course that was Michael Jackson's manager, and she decided she wanted him to manage her too. She just walked into his office and told him.

Jonas: Well, there you have it – determination, charm, intelligence and above all – talent. Anyway, at the end of the eighties, she decided to move away from just being a pop star back to her first love – acting and dance. Of course, she still needed to make money.

Int: I expect she did – apparently she was spending over a million dollars a month (even her dog had its own psychiatrist).

Jonas: Well that's true enough but her real motivation has been mainly to make a success of her film career. Apart from *Evita*, which won her a few good reviews and a Golden Globe award, she hasn't had much success on this front. She seems to have picked bad projects – things that looked like they were going to be winners and turned out to be no good. Also she put a lot of people's backs up with her desire to shock. Funnily enough it doesn't seem to have done her any real harm – I guess she realises that scandal sells! She constantly bounces back. I think she's very good at putting her ideas across. Like in 1992 after a year of negotiation, she announced a new seven-year deal. Part of this deal was to operate a new multi-media entertainment company called Maverick Entertainment. She was the one who signed up singers like Alanis Morissette and Prodigy. Now the record label is one of the most successful in the business.

Int: Just as well as her own films and records haven't always done too well, have they?

Jonas: Quite. She's diversified at just the right time – she now has a line of clothing and a designer hotel, besides being able to choose which films she might want to do in the future.

Int: Any clues about what she'll do next?

Jonas: Not really. Her new album is really great and it'll probably have sold over 20 million copies by the end of this year. After that, who knows? But that's the thing with Madonna, she's constantly looking for fresh challenges and she's the type who will get on with whatever she puts her mind to.

5 There are various intonation patterns practised in this unit. The aim is to teach very basic awareness of intonation patterns in English. This is not a comprehensive guide to intonation. Impress upon students that the rise and fall is only slight. They needn't be too theatrical about it!

   The first example on the tape practises list intonation. The voice rises with each item in a list and then falls at the end. This can be a whole class activity or could be done in small groups.

   Play the tape with the extract from the interview.

Tapescript

Jonas: Anyway, she did ballet, singing and piano lessons.

6 When we are surprised, our voice rises. Put students in groups of four and ask them to do the example first to practise. They can then make up new conversations.

Tapescript

Int: A scholarship?

7 When a question begins with *Wh* or *How* then the voice tends to fall towards the end of the sentence. If you don't hear clearly what is asked then the intonation pattern changes and the voice rises at the end of the sentence.

Tapescript

Int: What about her family?

Int: Where did you say you live?
   What did you say you do?

8 In English our voices rise and fall to show interest or friendliness. It is easy in English to sound quite unfriendly without meaning to, just because the intonation is too flat. Listen to this man speaking and decide if he's being friendly or not.

> **Answers**
> a unfriendly b friendly c friendly d unfriendly
> e friendly f unfriendly

Tapescript

a It's over there. [flat]
b Make me a cup of coffee. [friendly]
c Thank you. [friendly]
d Hello. [flat]
e Excuse me. [flat]
f See you soon. [friendly]

Ⓔxtension activity

You can easily extend this exercise if you think students need to have more practice at hearing the patterns. Use polite requests to practise with:
   Would you open the window, please?
   Can you help me?
   I wonder if you could help me?
   Would it be possible to tell me how to get to the station?

27.2 SB pages 174–175

> **Lesson plan**
> Grammar   40–50'
> Vocabulary   30–40'
>
> **SV** Set 6 and 7 for homework.
> **LV** See notes below for 1.

1 The aim of this unit is to revise tenses covered in previous units. Students should check in the Grammar folder for Units 2 (present tenses), 5 (past tenses), 10 (future tenses) and 14 (perfect tenses). Students should work in pairs or individually to discuss the differences in the use of tenses in the sentences in this exercise.

> **Answers**
> 1 a Present perfect – she asked you at **sometime** in the recent past.
>   b Past simple – she asked you at **a specific time** in the past which the speaker is referring to.
> 2 a Present simple with verbs of perception, senses, etc.
>   b Present continuous to mean 'meeting' and for arranged future.
> 3 a Past simple – actions happening at the same time.
>   b Past perfect – agreement after he had seen her.
> 4 a Past continuous – at some point when she was making an album she met her producer.
>   b Past simple – She didn't make an album until she met her producer.
> 5 a Past simple – A general statement about the past. Possibly still true.
>   b Past perfect – Before a given moment her life was under control. Now she no longer believes it is.
> 6 a Present perfect – general statement about all her record sales.
>   b Present perfect continuous – her more recent record sales.
> 7 a Future simple – prediction
>   b *Going to* – more probable than future simple here – maybe you have evidence for this statement.

Ⓔxtension activity

Ask every student to prepare a three-minute talk about the career of his or her favourite singer or group. They should pay particular attention to tenses and try not to repeat vocabulary or information. They then give their talks in small groups with the other students listening for errors. They should use notes rather than reading from a prepared composition.

2 This exercise deals with time expressions and when they can be used. Students need to match up the beginning of the sentence with a time expression.

> **Answers**
> 1 j 2 d 3 f 4 b 5 c 6 h 7 i 8 g 9 e 10 a

3 This exercise should pinpoint any problems students are still having with tenses and show you where more work may need to be done. This exercise could be set for homework. Alternative answers are given.

> **Answers**
> a Where were you born?
> b I'm flying to Hong Kong tomorrow./I'm going to fly to Hong Kong tomorrow.

c I was playing football when President Kennedy was shot.
d What are you doing this weekend?/What will you do this weekend?/What are you going to do this weekend?
e I was going to phone you, but I lost your number.
f Shakespeare is/was the greatest English playwright.
g It was the first time I had been to the theatre.
h It is the first time I've heard that record.
i I believe that homework will be abolished by the year 2010./I believe that homework will have been abolished by the year 2010.
j The painter painted the ceiling, while the plumber fixed the pipes./The painter was painting the ceiling, while the plumber was fixing the pipes.
k After the film had finished, everyone clapped.
l I wonder who makes more money – Michael Jackson or Madonna?
m I have been trying to explain how to do it for the past ten minutes.
n This time next week I will be sitting on a ride in Disneyland.
o What time do you think the plane will arrive?/What time do you think the plane is going to arrive?
p He arrived at the party late because he had been working.
q Madonna has produced some great records recently.
r I haven't seen you for ages. What have you been doing?
s This time last week I was in New York.
t Where were you living/did you live/had you lived/had you been living before you moved here?

4 Play the tape of the two interviews once more. Students need to listen for phrasal verbs and complete the sentences a–h. They then need to use the correct form of one of the words or phrases in the box to replace the appropriate phrasal verb.

Answers
a put off – postpone
b got to the bottom – found out the truth
c took off – began
d put down – criticised

e took by surprise – astonished
f put backs up – upset
g putting her ideas across – communicating
h puts her mind to – decides to do

5 Ask students to take turns in asking and answering the questions a–h. They should try to answer using the phrasal verb. The phrasal verbs used here have these meanings:
a postpone b upset c be offended d discourage
e save f stop reading g tolerate h accommodate

6 This is practice for Paper 3 Part 5. The article is about how accent affects the way we sing.

Answers
1 grammatical 2 speech 3 extent 4 singer 5 largely
6 characteristics 7 difference 8 tendency 9 unlike
10 adjustment(s)

7 There are two parts to this word formation exercise. Firstly there is a list of verbs which have to be made into nouns – sometimes there is more than one form. The second list requires students to make adjectives from a list of nouns. The words on both lists were heard in the listening exercises. They could both be set as dictionary work for homework.

Answers
nouns
association belief/believer knowledge
manager/manageress/management decision
actor/actress/action death announcement/announcer
operator/operation choice
adjectives
occasional responsible/irresponsible famous/infamous
determined intelligent/unintelligent talented
successful/unsuccessful harmful/harmless

Exam folder 14

Paper 5 Speaking

SB pages 176-177

Run through the Advice section with students and elicit the format of the test. If necessary, refer students to page 7.

Unless you have plenty of free time and a spare room to use, this complete Speaking test will have to be done as paired

practice in class. Ask students to read the instructions, which would form the basis of what the interlocutor would say. They should swap roles across the two long turns in Part 2.

The Part 2 photographs show the following:
First turn: Leonardo di Caprio out on his own (top) and being mobbed by fans.
Second turn: a remote village in Nepal (left) and the Australian outback.

UNIT 28 Sense and sensitivity

Unit topic	Colour
28.1	
Discussion	Speaking
Exam skills	Reading Paper 1 Part 3
Vocabulary	Phrasal verbs with *out*
Grammar extra	Prepositions after verbs and adjectives
28.2	
Grammar focus	Number and concord
Exam skills	Listening – Paper 4 Part 2
	Use of English – Paper 3 Part 4
Workbook contents	
1	Vocabulary – questionnaire
2	Use of English – Part 2
3, 4	Vocabulary – word formation, definitions
5, 6	Writing – an informal letter

28.1 SB pages 178–179

Lesson plan

Speaking	5–10'
Reading	25–30'
Vocabulary	5–10'
Grammar extra	15–20'
Phrasal verbs	15–20'

SV Set 3 and 4 for homework as a dictionary exercise.
LV See notes below for Grammar extra and 4.

1 This introduction is to focus students' thoughts on the impact colour makes in our lives. The reading deals with an unusual topic, that of synaesthesia, and so it is important to set the scene before they read the article.

Background information

Synaesthesia is a well-documented ability that some people have to hear sounds or see letters in colour.

Ask students to discuss the photos which have different colour schemes. They should then go on to talk about the other ideas raised in a–g. It may be a good idea to take in some examples of the shades of colour that are talked about which aren't immediately obvious. The suffix *-ish* is rather informal and tends to be slightly derogatory.

Examples needed: sky blue, navy blue, deep blue, off white and pea green.

> **Answers**
> f   red   anger
>   blue   depression
>   green   jealousy
>   yellow   cowardice
>
> g The question of which colour represents which feeling or idea can give rise to an interesting discussion in class. In English red can also be used to represent embarrassment and green for sickness. Cowards used to be given a white feather. Red is also used in the expression 'a red-light district', where prostitutes work.

2 The aim of this reading is to practise for Paper 1 Part 3 – the gapped paragraphs. This type of reading is quite hard – usually much harder than the other types of reading. In the examination students only have 1 hour and 15 minutes for 4 different texts and 35 questions. Students should be aiming to spend no more than 15 to 20 minutes on a text at this stage.

> **Answers**
> 1 C   2 E   3 A   4 F   5 B   6 G

3 This exercise can be set for homework as a follow-up to the reading comprehension. It also recycles work done in a previous unit.

> **Answers**
> a a lasting/great impression
> b a plan of what colours you're going to use
> c blind; deaf   d basically
> e a story about something that happened to you
> f someone else writes your biography; you write your own autobiography   g a shade of red
> h sensitive people easily have hurt feelings; sensible people always know the right thing to do – they have a lot of common sense

4 This exercise deals with phrasal verbs with *out*.

Answers
a crossing things out – putting a line through it
b coming out – blooming
c drew out the speech – made the speech longer
d held out – lasted
e make out – distinguish
f missed out on – lost
g worked out – solved
h turn out – produce

Extension activity

Ask students to come up with another example of each of the phrasal verbs above, either in class or for homework.

Grammar extra

Prepositions cause many problems to students of English. This exercise deals with the most common ones. These should be learnt as they are often tested at FCE.

Answers
a from, away b on c to d in e with f for
g on h with i with, for j to k about l to
m from/to

Extension activity

In groups of three or four, students should make up a complete story using as many of the verbs and adjectives as possible. The winning group is the one which has a real story with the largest number of verbs/adjectives and prepositions. They do not have to be in the order given. For practice they should finish this story. For example:
   My mother was very annoyed with me when I came home and told her I was keen on the boy next door. She was worried about my exams and she explained to me that she didn't object to him as a person, she just didn't believe in people of my age having a steady relationship. etc.

28.2 SB pages 180–181

Lesson plan

Grammar	45–55'
Listening	10–15'
Proofreading	15–20'

SV Set 6 for homework.
LV See notes below for 5.

1 The aim of this part of the unit is to make students aware of the need to check their work for agreement of subject and verb.

Teaching extra

The agreement of subject and verb is called 'concord'. Many of the mistakes that students make on the Writing paper and the Use of English paper are the result of not getting this right. It is often neglected as teachers feel that it is something students learn early on in their English studies. Often we teach students to proofread their work for spelling, punctuation, etc. but we often forget to tell them to check for agreement of subject and verb. Many marks can be lost because of this.

Students should refer to the Grammar folder, page 208.

Answers
a has b plays c watches d believe e wants
f are g has h are l are j doesn't seem
k enjoys l was formed m has found/will find/finds
n go o is p likes q is r is

2 This exercise is a word sort so that the rules of which expression takes a singular or plural verb become more manageable. The words with a * can go in both sections. Sometimes their use in one section is for informal use only.

Answers
A

each	*staff	*neither
every	the news	*either
no-one	a series	
one of	everybody	
more than one	*none	

B

all	people	the majority of
both	*staff	*either (informally)
the police	sunglasses	*neither (informally)
a group of	jeans	*none (informally)

3 Students should work through this exercise and then compare notes at the end. Refer students to the Grammar folder, page 208.

Answers
a each b all c Both/Neither d None e either
f Neither g Every h Each i none j Each/every
k each

4 If you think of the family or government as people then you use a plural verb. If they are used as an idea or concept then you use a singular verb. In a, *the family* are people. In b, *the family* is a concept.

> **Answers**
> Other words which follow the same rule are:
> class, bank, England (sports team), firm, orchestra, party, public, school, staff, team, committee

ⓔxtension activity

Ask students to discuss the pair of photographs, comparing and contrasting the families shown.

5 Before listening ask students to say how they feel about hair colour. For example:
> *Do they like their own hair colour?*
> *Would they ever dye their own hair?*
> *Do blondes have more fun? Would Marilyn Monroe or Brigitte Bardot have been famous as brunettes?*

Ask students to read through the sentences 1–6, and then play the tape.

> **Answers**
> **1** eager to please **2** money **3** rebellion
> **4** 30/thirty women **5** carrots **6** discrimination

Tapescript

Presenter: Good morning. And it's now official – blondes really do have more fun. New research has revealed that a woman's hair colour reflects her personality; redheads are wild and fiery, while brunettes have a lot of common sense and are eager to please.

University psychologists believe they have proved that the classic stereotypes attributed to a woman's hair colour have a scientific basis, and that changing the colour of your hair may even help change your personality. According to the research, to be published later this year, dyed blondes – typified most famously by Marilyn Monroe – start having more fun and appear to worry less about money.

Dr Tony Farmer who carried out the study, said it showed for the first time that there are key personality differences between women of different natural hair colour. Whether the differences are genetic or simply a consequence of expectation is less clear. Apparently, people who dye their hair blonde are making a real gesture of rebellion. The researchers interviewed 93 women with natural hair colour, who answered 48 questions to establish their personality traits. They then conducted the same personality analysis on 30 women before and after they changed their hair colour.

Natural redheads were less likely to care about what other people thought of them and had more significant mood swings.

I decided to ask some redheads whether they agreed. First of all, Jenny Alton, the actress. What do you think, Jenny?

Jenny: Well, having red hair has caused me some problems. I remember when I was younger, my classmates would call me 'carrots'. Later on people would shout at me in the street – maybe that's why redheads become so bad-tempered.

Presenter: I wondered if this stereotyping was only aimed at women so I asked the redheaded writer Peter Jameson what he thought.

Peter: Well, I'm fairly famous for being irritable and intolerant, but I do think stereotyping can lead to discrimination. On my first day at school I was surrounded by a group of boys who attacked me so I retaliated. Of course, when a teacher appeared he immediately blamed me.

Presenter: Well, my thanks to both Jenny and Peter. Fortunately, I'm going bald so none of this applies to me. In the studio next week we …

Photocopiable tapescript activity (Ⓟ ⋯⁚ page 191)

Ask students to underline all the character adjectives and write a sentence for each one to explain the meaning.

> **Answers**
> wild, fiery, eager (to please), bad-tempered, irritable, intolerant
> If someone is described as 'wild', they lack control and can behave unpredictably.

ⓔxtension activity

This exercise can be expanded to include word formation. Ask students to complete this chart, referring to the tapescript.

Noun	Verb	Adjective
personality	believe	
		famous
difference	typify	
	change	
	agree	significant
discrimination	appear	
		fortunate
		simple
		clear
	conduct	
	reveal	

6   This exercise gives practice in Paper 3 Part 4 –
    proofreading. It can be done for homework or in class.

Answers
1 an   2 while   3 of   4 to   5 ✓   6 every   7 both
8 ✓   9 still   10 any   11 ✓   12 which   13 up
14 must   15 themselves

Writing folder 14

Paper 2 Part 2

SB pages 182–183

1   Remind students that the letter of application is written to
    an individual or an organisation. The purpose is always
    clear and no irrelevant information should be included.

    Students should read through the advertisement and
    decide what information they need to include in a letter
    of application.

    Things to think about:
       How long the letter should be – 120–180 words
       Should addresses be included? – no!
       Who to write to – Dear Mr O'Hare **NOT** Dear
       Mr/Mister/Mr Dave O'Hare
       Reason for writing – seeing the advertisement
       Paragraphs – three to four maximum
       How to finish – Yours sincerely

2   The example is an answer to the advertisement, but
    there are grammar, punctuation, spelling and
    vocabulary mistakes. This letter revises many of the
    grammar points covered in the previous units.

Answers

Dear Mr O'Hare,

I saw your **advertisement** for a family to spend a month
on a **desert** island and I would like **to** suggest my own
family. **There are six people in my family** – my parents,
myself (I **am** 22 **years old**), my two sisters (12 and 16), and
my brother (8). We **come** from Iceland. My father is **a**
doctor and my mother is **a** sports teacher. **I am doing an
Economics course / I study Economics at** university, and
my brother and sisters are still **studying** at school.

I think we would really enjoy **spending** a month **on** our
own, as we all get on very **well** with each other. We aren't
the kind of **people who watch** TV all day or **need** to be
entertained all **the** time. We are a sociable and **friendly**
family who **are** capable of taking care **of themselves**.

Last **year** we spent in the mountains camping **by**
ourselves, **which** was useful experience for being on a
desert island. As my father is **a** doctor he can look after
any emergencies that **might** happen. My mother is very
interested in sport and we are all very fit and **in good**
condition. I **attended fishing** lessons two years ago and I
have a good knowledge of **which** plants are good **to eat**
and **which are** poisonous.

I **hope** you will consider my **application** and look forward
to **hearing** from you.

Yours **sincerely,**

Magnus Magnusson

3   This is another example of a letter of application
    question. Students should read through the question
    and then look at the planning. This shows how they
    should plan a letter. They need to read through the task
    and answer the questions in the plan. Many of the
    answers to the questions can be found in the last letter.

4   A model answer to the previous task is given here but
    with some of the verbs missing. Students need to read
    through the letter and decide which form of which verb
    to use.

Answers
1 saw   2 have been collecting   3 know   4 enjoy
5 helps   6 write   7 would make   8 try   9 criticise
10 was asked   11 held   12 will consider

5   The final task can be set for homework or done in class.
    Students have two model answers, one for each task and
    they should have a good idea of how to proceed with
    this type of question.

Unit topic	The media
29.1	
Exam skills	Listening Paper 4 Part 3
	Use of English Paper 3 Part 1
Vocabulary	Topic words
29.2	
Vocabulary	Idioms

Workbook contents

1, 2	Reading – Part 2 multiple choice
3, 4	Vocabulary – idioms

29.1 SB pages 184–185

Lesson plan

Listening	40–50'
Use of English	25–40'

SV Keep discussion in 1 brief.
LV See notes below for 5.

1   Ask students to discuss the headlines, which refer to the following stories:
1   Attractive TV star caught stealing underwear from a shop.
2   Paparazzo takes secret photos of footballer beating his wife.
3   Head of company resigns after being charged with bribery.
4   Government minister's son involved in taking illegal drugs.
5   Judge has a hideaway home with another woman.

Ask students to suggest recent examples of invasion of privacy by the press in your own country or elsewhere.

2   Elicit suggestions of what is happening in the photograph, which shows the paparazzi hounding a public figure. Remind students to use some of the vocabulary given (elicit the plural form of *paparazzo* – an Italian word – which is *paparazzi*).

3   Students should read the six statements before you play the tape. Check understanding.

```
Answers
1 C   2 F   3 E   4 A   5 D
```

Tapescript

Speaker 1: The first we knew about it was when the paper phoned us up and asked for an interview. Cathy had said she'd be staying with a friend in London for the weekend. She'd phoned us on her arrival – as we thought – and we were expecting her back on the Sunday evening. To get the call like that out of the blue was terrible. Did we know that our daughter was sailing round the Mediterranean with a bunch of drug-crazed rock musicians? How old was she? Could we let the paper have a school photo to put in Monday's edition? It was a young chap and he went on and on – I mean, he must have known that he was breaking bad news to us, but he just didn't care.

Speaker 2: I was an idiot, but at the time I suppose I was flattered, it went to my head. You know, this famous singer was interested in me, some nobody from the suburbs. I would have phoned my parents again on the Sunday evening and come clean – the yacht had all the technology obviously. I'd just turned 18 the week before anyway, so I <u>was</u> an adult – but where's the story in that? I had to become a silly little thing, a total lie of course, but then that's their trademark, isn't it? We knew something was wrong when this speedboat kept cruising round the yacht on the Saturday afternoon. Nat – the bass player – noticed one guy had a camera with a long lens. It turned out that they'd bribed one of the bodyguards the night before, who got my name and address from my passport and radioed it all through. And the rest is history – a big juicy scandal!

Speaker 3: They run stories on us the whole time – we've got this bad boy image and any dirt they can rake up on us sells newspapers – or so they believe. I feel really bad about Cathy. She's a nice kid and she didn't deserve any of this – nor did her folks. Course the paper deliberately got her age wrong, making it look as though she was this innocent young schoolgirl who was being led astray by the big bad band. You get sick to the back teeth with it, you really do. Nat's got a better attitude, he doesn't let it get to him, but I hate it – I hate <u>them</u>, hounding us the whole time. They never give up, no way. Don't suppose they ever will, while we're flavour of the month.

Speaker 4: Cathy's put a brave face on the whole thing and admits she made a mistake. When she got back last week, I visited her at home – the school's on holiday until Monday next. The family all probably thought I was going to ban her from coming back next term, but I wanted to reassure her really. I mean, the whole thing has been blown rather out of proportion, a three-day wonder. Typical media sensationalism! Cathy's a promising student who should get very good grades in her A-levels. Why let all that go to waste? Everything will have died down soon, and I've every confidence that she'll be able to concentrate on her work again.

Speaker 5: Well, I genuinely believe the public has a right to know these things, I mean it could have been anyone's daughter. It's almost a duty if you like, you know, we don't shy away from the truth, even if it is hard to find. We're ready to show these people up for what they really are. Who knows, if we hadn't got to Cathy when we did, she might not be safely back home now. Perhaps some of the people involved should think about what might have happened, then they might have a change of tune, rather than criticise us as they have done. As for the band, well they're in the public eye, so if they choose to behave as they do, they've got it coming to them. And let's face it, there's no such thing as bad publicity, is there?

4   Explain what idioms are: expressions containing a group of words, where the meaning is not always transparent. Play the tape again and ask students to tick the ones heard. Remind them that some of the verb-based idioms may be in a different tense.

> **Answers**
> Idioms not heard:
> break new ground (comes up in 29.2)
> keep a low profile (comes up in 29.2)
> turn something on its head (in 6 Vocabulary cloze)

Photocopiable tapescript activity (P ⋯⟩ page 192)

Hand out copies of the tapescript so that students can see how the idioms have been used. The tapescript would also be useful for the extension activity in 5 below.

5   Refer students to the headlines and ask them to discuss possible content in small groups.

Extension activity

Students work in small groups. Ask them to put together an article, choosing one of the headlines, or writing a better one! They should first plan the article, listing the information to be included (from the recording or invented). Once they have agreed on content and the ordering of points, the article can be written up for homework. Remind them to bring the articles to the next lesson, where they can be looked at in the same groups.

6   Ask students to skim the article for general meaning. Work through the questions with the class, eliciting the correct answers and reasons why some of the other options are wrong.

> **Answers**
> 1 C   2 D   3 A   4 B   5 B   6 C   7 A   8 D   9 D
> 10 C   11 B   12 A   13 D   14 A   15 C

29.2 SB pages 186–187

Lesson plan
See below.

This lesson concentrates on idioms. It could be given as independent study, out of class time.

1

> **Answers**
> 1 b   2 c   3 d   4 a   5 g   6 h   7 f   8 e   9 l   10 k
> 11 i   12 j   13 o   14 p   15 n   16 m   17 s   18 q
> 19 t   20 r

2

> **Answers**
> break new ground – do something innovative (shows approval)
> make your mark – do something to be noticed
> get to grips with something – become in control of something
> come out of your shell – become less shy
> tighten your belt – economise
> keep a low profile – try not to be noticed
> get your act together – become better organised
> take somewhere by storm – be very successful
> put your oar in – give an opinion (often different to the one being expressed)
> catch someone off guard – surprise someone
> go out of the window – disappear completely (of a plan or idea)
> put something on ice – postpone (a plan or project)

3

Suggested answers
a The paparazzi caught them off guard at their hideaway cottage.
b The government has put many of its proposals for new road development on ice.
c All her promises to her parents about studying hard went out of the window when she met Danny.
d The software breaks new ground with a technique that requires much less memory.
e Some town councils have got to grips with traffic problems.
f Kevin has quickly made his mark in his new job.
g The British film *The Full Monty* took America by storm.
h The argumentative politician had to put his oar in.
i John kept a low profile in the cinema, hoping his teacher wouldn't see him.
j Children are very nervous during the first day at a new school, but they soon come out of their shells.
k Caroline really needs to get her act together and stop letting people down.

4

Answers
a on b in c in d out for e to f at g in
h out on i with j on k at ... with l in m off

5 The four idioms illustrated are:
  1 in full swing (b)
  2 at loggerheads with someone (k)
  3 out for the count (d)
  4 in a tight corner (g)

Answers
a thin on the ground b out on a limb c pie in the sky
d at a loose end e in a nutshell f quick off the mark
g economical with the truth h shocked to the core

Exam folder 15

Paper 2 Writing

SB pages 188–189

Elicit the contents of Paper 2, referring students to page 6 if necessary. Then ask students to get into groups and decide on the important issues regarding this paper. One person in the group should write down a list of the ideas discussed. Students should then look at the Advice section and compare them with their lists.

1 Ask students to read the questions, underlining any key words and phrases.

2 Suggest that students do this activity in pairs, spending about five minutes reading through the answer and the notes, then discussing how the answer could be improved. The final rewriting of the piece could be done for homework, or as a timed task in class.

Sample answer

This composition considers the statement about newspapers today and whether their role has changed. In my opinion, the answer to this depends on which newspapers you read, as some still concentrate on current affairs, while others contain only a minimal amount of news. It is clearly important for any newspaper to report what has happened, but people like to read other things too.

Moreover, it is good to expose scandal occasionally, such as the recent articles on the attempted cover-up by Lord Archer, which has led to him standing down as a candidate for London mayor. Famous people are in the public eye and they must behave appropriately.

At the same time, newspapers should not focus exclusively on the reporting of scandal. Their main role is to inform and this means writing detailed reports on current news and events. I think television can often cover events effectively, with visual images and on-the-spot reports, but with a newspaper, the reader has time to read and reflect on what is printed.

In conclusion, the role of newspapers today is still mainly to inform, but they should shock and entertain us as well.

UNIT 30 Anything for a laugh

Unit topic	Humour
30.1	
Exam skills	Reading Paper 1 Part 4
Grammar extra	Uses of *rather*
30.2	
Grammar focus	Phrasal verbs
Exam skills	Use of English Paper 3 Part 2

Workbook contents

1	Use of English – Part 5
2, 3	Vocabulary
4	Use of English – Part 3

30.1 SB pages 190–191

Lesson plan

See below.

As this last unit is rather different in approach from the others, no formal timings are given. The main aim is for students to have fun!

1   Start by asking students to define the word *funny*. This is a word which is often used wrongly in students' writing. Then suggest each student takes a long turn on the photos, which show stand-up comedian Eddie Izzard (left) and Mr Bean, played by Rowan Atkinson; film stills of *The Nutty Professor*, starring Eddie Murphy (left), and Buster Keaton.

Background information

Eddie Izzard sometimes performs his stand-up comedy in other languages. In France, he recently performed his 'Dress to Kill' act in French. He is currently learning Spanish and German too. See him if you can!

2   Ask whether students know any urban myths. Then give them a minute or so to read through the questions and prepare to scan the texts.

3

Answers

1 B   2 A   3 D   4 C   5 A   6 D   7 C   8 B   9 D
10 B   11 D   12 A   13 D   14 C   15 B

4   Students discuss in pairs.

5   Reassure students that difficult words in the exam texts will not cause them problems, providing they look at surrounding context.

Answers

a loomed   b with gusto   c bewildered   d tossed
e shooed ... away   f all the trimmings   g settled
h fleeing

6   Play the tape and then get students to retell the story in small groups. Ask students what they would do in such a situation. Do they find the story believable?

Tapescript

Cow down below

A salesman was speeding along the motorway one gorgeous summer's day in his new convertible, enjoying the sunshine, the freedom and some good music on the car stereo. Then, out of the blue, a huge black and white Friesian cow landed in the back seat with a thud. He managed to pull over onto the hard shoulder and tried to remove the poor dead beast, but it was unbelievably heavy and was stuck fast. Rather shaken, the man drove off the motorway to the nearest village and found a garage. Once they'd stopped laughing, the garage mechanics managed to lift the cow out with an engine hoist, but the back of his car was covered in unspeakable muck. They offered to clean the car up. So, rather than standing around waiting at the garage, he went off to the local pub for a drink. At the pub, he got talking to the landlord and told him his unfortunate story. As he did so, another customer came over. 'You must have been below me,' he laughed. 'I've just ploughed into a herd of cows with my lorry, on the bridge over the motorway. Sorry, mate!'

Grammar extra

Explain that the recording has several examples of *rather*, a useful word in English. Play the tape again if necessary.

Answers
a 1 than   b 3 would; not   c 2, 4 quite

30.2 SB pages 192–193

1 Tell students that phrasal verbs have different grammatical patterns, which affect word order. Ask them to look at the examples and discuss in pairs. Elicit answers.

Answers
b and **e** are intransitive.
a no change possible (three-part phrasal verb)
c ✓ – He set down the snack ...
d no change possible (pronoun)
f no change possible
g no change possible (three-part phrasal verb)
h no change possible (pronoun)
i ✓ – They offered to clean up the car.
j no change possible

2

Answers
Word order can change in *a* and *d*:
He put up a sign ...
Jenny couldn't keep the payments up ...

3

Suggested answers
a turn off the TV   b get it over with   c made out a car
d has put me off   e picked up Swedish
f look them up   g make for the beach
h got behind the speaker   i worked out the answer
j cut down on cakes

4 Ask students if they know any jokes that they could explain in English. Write up any vocabulary which arises. Then suggest they do the matching task in pairs.

Answers
1 j   2 g   3 o   4 i   5 d   6 m   7 b   8 h   9 k   10 e
11 a   12 l   13 f   14 n   15 c

Ask students which jokes they think are the best, and which are the worst. Take a class vote.

5

Answers
1 bit/little   2 was   3 during/in   4 with   5 at   6 as
7 a/the   8 where   9 up   10 be   11 would/could/might
12 most   13 for   14 since   15 is

Writing folder 15

1 Suggest students decide on the five main points in pairs.

Answers
- information about Larry Hatfield's performance on Friday night
- unfair to call performers second-rate
- Holmes and Watson were improvising
- Ted Grainger's humour was political but not offensive
- not a disaster (give own view)

2 Ask students to read the letter on their own. Then elicit the missing content point. Stress how vital it is for students to include **all** the points in the task.

Answer
No mention of Holmes and Watson's improvisation.

3

Answers
It has far too many idioms in it, most of which are used inaccurately. It is also badly organised.

Suggested answer
I would like to comment on the article about the Festival of Fun, which appeared in yesterday's *Daily News*. I attended this festival and was surprised by the negative tone of the article. Your reporter has been rather economical with the truth, in my opinion.

Sample answer

Dear Editor

I would like to comment on the article about Talentspot, in this morning's edition. I was present at the concert, which I enjoyed.

I think your paper should be more supportive of local music. Many of the bands were performing live for the first time and may have been nervous. As for the poor quality of the microphone used by Jenny Lowe, this is surely the responsibility of the organisers, as your reporter implies in the article. Moreover, it is totally inaccurate to describe Lowe's singing as 'very flat' – she has a perfect voice.

Dingbats played brilliantly, especially when they added the brass section. I don't think your reporter understands the way this band performs: the arguments between the bass player and guitarist Mike Thompson are part of the act!

The criticism of Down and Out is unfair. Your reporter clearly left before their three encores, which brought everyone to their feet clapping and cheering.

Talentspot is a wonderful event, which is very popular with young people. It must continue, as it gives local bands a unique opportunity to show us what they can do.

Yours sincerely

UNITS 25–30 | Revision

> **Lesson plan**
>
> Topic review   15–20'
> Grammar   30–35'
> Vocabulary   30–35'
>
> **SV** Omit the Topic review and set the phrasal verb
> story for homework, with an English-English
> dictionary.
> **LV** Ask students to write a composition of 120–180
> words on one of the review topics.

The aim of this unit is to go over some of the main points
covered in Units 25–30. With the exception of the Topic
review, this unit can be done as a test or for homework.

Topic review

1 Ask students to work in pairs. They need to look at
questions a–h and talk about whether the statements are
true for them or not. Encourage them to go into detail,
not just say 'yes' or 'no'. The point of this exercise is to
get students to use some of the vocabulary and language
they have studied, but in a personalised way. This part
of the revision unit is designed to be integrated with the
other revision exercises if wanted, or to be done
completely separately.

Grammar

2 This exercise gives practice for Paper 3 Part 3. Remind
students they should count the number of words they
put in the space, and that contractions count as two
words. They should also remember not to change the
word given.

> **Answers**
> 1 object to people parking
> 2 is the traffic as bad
> 3 first time I had bought
> 4 apologised for laughing at her
> 5 put up with people
> 6 haven't read either
> 7 all (of) the seats have
> 8 people live in London than
> 9 rather you didn't tell
> 10 bus to town will have

3 The sentences a–m all contain mistakes, with the
exception of one sentence.

> **Answers**
> a Just cross out the word you spell wrongly in your
> composition.
> b That's the man to whom I sold the house.
> c I'd prefer a blue car to a red one.
> d Please turn it off at once – you're making too much
> noise.
> e The police are available twenty-four hours a day.
> f Neither my father nor my mother has/have blond hair.
> Correct
> g It's the first time I have been to the Paris Motor Show.
> h The office block had stood on this street for more than
> a decade when they decided to demolish it.
> i I believe in the trustworthiness of our police force.
> j What time do you think the train will arrive?
> k Seldom do we see new ideas on saving energy.
> l The building whose roof had been blown off by the
> gales is on the next street.
> m If we all shared a car to work, then the motorways
> wouldn't have been necessary.

Vocabulary

4 This exercise tests idioms and expressions.

> **Answers**
> a tune   b end   c keep   d hands   e ice   f feet
> g eyebrows   h eye

Phrasal verb story

5 This article is a true story about a man who was
involved in making the Spielberg film *Saving Private
Ryan*. Students should read through the text and then
decide which form of which phrasal verb should go in
each gap. Students will probably find this quite
challenging and so this task could be given for
homework, to be done with a dictionary.

> **Answers**
> 1 calling up   2 taken on   3 taken aback   4 bring in
> 5 work out   6 ended up   7 put Mr Murgatroyd off
> 8 miss out on

Paper 1 Part 2

You are going to read a newspaper article about the media's treatment of famous people. For Questions **1–7**, choose the correct answer (**A, B, C** or **D**) which you think fits best according to the text.

Week after week, tabloid newspapers carry pictures which intrude into people's privacy and break the newspaper editors' code of practice. Although pop star Liam Gallagher and his wife Patsy Kensit have posed for paparazzi on occasion, such action is not typical.

7 More usually, great damage is done to individuals in the public eye, who see their most private moments captured on the front page. Yet very few call on the services of the Press Complaints Commission, an organisation that was set up to deal with issues of this kind.

Rarely, if ever, are these pictures in the public interest. Did the intimate shots of Gallagher and Patsy Kensit help to detect a crime? In what way did the topless picture of model turned actress Liz Hurley on a hotel balcony protect public health and safety? Hurley has made a fuss about long-lens pictures in the past and since she was in a hotel, a place where, to quote the code of practice, 'there is a reasonable expectation of privacy', she had good cause for complaint, but she didn't take any action.

That the Press Complaints Commission did not launch an investigation itself is a scandal. It should also be looking into the outrageous story published recently about comedian Lenny Henry's love life. Lenny Henry, like Liz Hurley, has held back from making a formal complaint. 25 Shouldn't the PCC take the initiative on this and other shameful attacks?

To begin with, this seems like a great idea. It would surely lead to many decisions against newspapers. These would be reported by their rivals and broadcast on TV and radio. The public would not be sympathetic and editors would have to refuse to publish such material. Even photographers would be affected, no longer finding it financially possible to spend their days hidden behind trees waiting to snap unsuspecting celebrities.

If the PCC decided to take on this role of 'police officer', which it technically could, there would be several problems. How would it decide whether or not to launch an inquiry? Should it approach the victim and encourage him or her to make a complaint? And if the person involved still refused to do anything, should it proceed nevertheless? In addition, celebrities and members of royalty might well expect that any story involving them would be taken up, and then be outraged to find it wasn't. Above all, the role itself is too enormous. How could the PCC realistically monitor the whole of the British press: national, regional and magazines?

Then there is the embarrassment factor to consider. However seriously someone's privacy has been invaded, would they really want the further embarrassment of an investigation? I suspect the majority simply want to put it behind them and get on with their lives. Of course, one or two may have other reasons for keeping quiet. A worse story may exist, that they have managed to keep from the press, and they realise that this may also become public knowledge if they complain. In other words, even the PCC might become the enemy.

Comedian Harry Enfield also suffered at the hands of the press when three years ago, he and his wife were secretly photographed on their honeymoon in the Caribbean. He didn't complain then, nor more recently, when he and his family were again victims of a sneak photographer during a family holiday. His reason for this was fear that the *News of the World* would re-run the pictures with a new story about his 'fury', saying that they thought it was just a bit of fun, and that, being a comedian, they thought he had a sense of humour. This fear is understandable. People believe they will again become targets if they dare to challenge the tabloids. It is hard to see an easy solution to this serious problem.

1   What does the phrase 'in the public eye' in line 7 mean?
    A of great appeal
    B in the news
    C under attack
    D on screen

2   Why would Liz Hurley have had reason to complain recently?
    A The photographer had not used a long lens.
    B Her personal safety had been threatened.
    C The newspaper had criticised her acting.
    D She had been in a fairly private place.

3   What does 'this' refer to in line 25?
    A the story about Lenny Henry
    B the PCC's lack of initiative
    C Lenny Henry's complaint
    D the picture of Liz Hurley

4   If the PCC became more involved, the writer believes that
    A TV and radio would take over the role of newspapers.
    B newspaper editors could no longer behave in the same way.
    C photographers would demand more money for their work.
    D members of the public might stop supporting the press.

5   Why would it be difficult for the PCC to take action?
    A It would never be able to persuade anyone to help.
    B Famous people would regularly object to the PCC.
    C There would be too many cases to investigate.
    D No rules actually exist to allow the PCC to act.

6   According to the writer, most famous people
    A would rather forget about what has taken place.
    B have something further to hide from the press.
    C regard the PCC in a negative way.
    D are used to being embarrassed in public.

7   Harry Enfield chose not to complain because
    A he didn't want to make his wife more upset than she was.
    B he believed the press would link his career with the story.
    C he hadn't really minded the pictures being printed.
    D he was worried that his family might see the pictures.

© Cambridge University Press, 2000

Paper 2 Part 1

1 You recently entered a competition in a magazine for learners of English. Your prize was a visit to a TV studio to see programmes being made. Unfortunately, the visit was not very well organised. Below is the original letter you received about the prize, on which you have made notes.

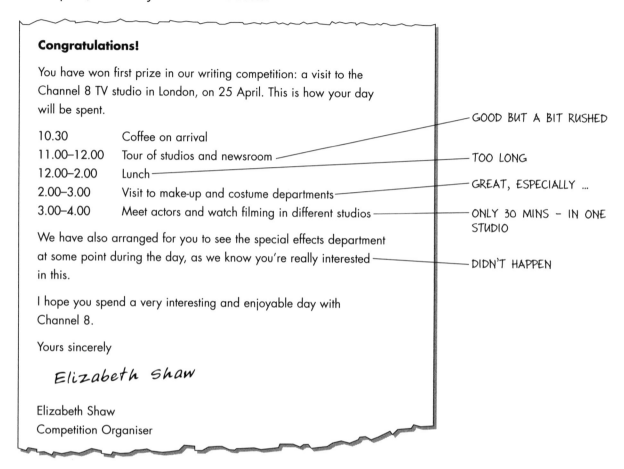

Congratulations!

You have won first prize in our writing competition: a visit to the Channel 8 TV studio in London, on 25 April. This is how your day will be spent.

10.30	Coffee on arrival	
11.00–12.00	Tour of studios and newsroom	GOOD BUT A BIT RUSHED
12.00–2.00	Lunch	TOO LONG
2.00–3.00	Visit to make-up and costume departments	GREAT, ESPECIALLY …
3.00–4.00	Meet actors and watch filming in different studios	ONLY 30 MINS – IN ONE STUDIO

We have also arranged for you to see the special effects department at some point during the day, as we know you're really interested in this. — DIDN'T HAPPEN

I hope you spend a very interesting and enjoyable day with Channel 8.

Yours sincerely

Elizabeth Shaw

Elizabeth Shaw
Competition Organiser

Read the letter and your notes carefully. Then write a letter explaining what happened and making suggestions on how future prizes could be improved.

Write a **letter** of between **120** and **180** words in an appropriate style.
Do not write any postal addresses.

Paper 3 Part 3

For Questions **1–10**, complete the second sentence so that it has a similar meaning to the first sentence, using the word given. Do not change the word given. You must use between two and five words, including the word given. Here is an example (**0**).

Example:

0   I have never been to Paris before.

time

This .... have been to Paris.

The gap can be filled by the words 'is the first time I' so you write:

| 0 | is the first time I |

---

1   As the club manager, you really ought to tell that comedian what you think of his show.
high
As the club manager, it's .... that comedian what you think of his show.

2   I wish I'd complained to the newspaper about the unfairness of their article.
regret
I .... the newspaper about the unfairness of their article.

3   Don't unfasten your seatbelt as we're flying into storms.
keep
It is necessary for you .... as we're flying into storms.

4   There was a fault with the keyboard and the computer wouldn't work.
whose
The computer, ... , wouldn't work.

5   It wasn't attractive for either newspaper to publish the story, so they didn't go ahead with it.
of
The two newspapers both found the story unattractive, so .... with it.

6   John promised he wouldn't tell anyone else about the problem, but he has.
broken
John .... to keep quiet about the problem.

7   Although it was difficult, the family managed to find out the truth about what had happened.
spite
The family managed to find out the truth about what had happened .... difficult.

8   No two people have the same DNA, apart from identical twins.
except
Everyone's DNA is .... identical twins.

9   It was a tight fit, but we parked the car eventually.
deal
There wasn't ...., but we parked the car eventually.

10 I remember finding Benny Hill's jokes very funny when I was a little girl.
used
I remember that when I was a little girl I .... of Benny Hill very funny.

© Cambridge University Press, 2000

Paper 3 Part 5

For Questions **1–10**, read the text below. Use the word given in capitals at the end of each line to form a word that fits in the space in the same line. There is an example at the beginning (**0**).

Example: | **0** | proud |

THE CITY OF CARDIFF

Cardiff, the capital of Wales, is very (**0**) proud of its latest	**PRIDE**
role as the home of the new Welsh Assembly. (**1**) ..... few	**SURPRISE**
tourists visit Cardiff, but it has many (**2**) ..... and it is also	**ATTRACT**
a thriving (**3**) ..... centre. It has an important music industry	**CULTURE**
and offers some of the best facilities for (**4**) ..... anywhere.	**RECORD**
(**5**) ..... Welsh groups like the Manic Street Preachers and	**SUCCEED**
Catatonia still give (**6**) ..... in the city.	**PERFORM**
The city centre may seem an (**7**) ..... place for a castle, but	**LIKE**
there is one, just where (**8**) ..... rush past carrying their	**SHOP**
various bargains. Although (**9**) ..... from 1091, Cardiff Castle	**DATE**
had been in ruins until it was (**10**) ..... around one hundred	**BUILD**
years ago.	

Paper 4 Part 4

You will hear two friends, Alan and Liz, talking about three towns, Bridgeport, Lakeside and Petersfield. For Questions **1–7**, decide which of the following is said about each town. Write **B** for **Bridgeport**, **L** for **Lakeside** or **P** for **Petersfield**.

1   It has the widest range of prices for accommodation.   ☐ 1

2   There's some good scenery on the outskirts.   ☐ 2

3   There's a direct train service to London.   ☐ 3

4   It's closest to where Alan will work.   ☐ 4

5   It's a busy place with lots of traffic.   ☐ 5

6   There are few opportunities for sightseeing.   ☐ 6

7   It has very convenient shopping hours.   ☐ 7

© Cambridge University Press, 2000

Paper 1 Part 2

1 B **2** D **3** A **4** B **5** C **6** A **7** B

Paper 2 Part 1

Sample answer

Dear Ms Shaw,

I was very pleased to win first prize in your competition. I went on the visit to Channel 8, but feel a bit disappointed with what happened.

First of all we had a tour of the studios, which I enjoyed, but I think that in future you should make this tour longer – one hour is not enough. In the afternoon I was taken to see the make-up and costume departments. They were great, especially the make-up artists. They showed me how to use special make-up for victims of accidents and what techniques they use to make people look older. From 3.00–4.00 I was supposed to go to different studios to see programmes being made. However, we only had thirty minutes, and only in one studio. I was very disappointed about this and would recommend that in future you make lunch shorter so that more time is available to see programmes being made.

You said that I would be able to see the special effects department as this is something I am particularly interested in. No one at Channel 8 knew anything about this part of the visit and as a result I didn't get to see it.

I look forward to hearing from you soon.

Yours sincerely,

Paper 3 Part 3

1 high time you told
2 regret not complaining to / regret not having complained to
3 to keep your seatbelt fastened
4 whose keyboard was faulty
5 neither of them went ahead
6 has broken his promise
7 in spite of it being
8 different except for
9 a great deal of room
10 used to find the jokes

Paper 3 Part 5

1 surprisingly **2** attractions **3** cultural **4** recording
5 Successful **6** performances **7** unlikely **8** shoppers
9 dating **10** rebuilt

Paper 4 Part 4

1 B **2** P **3** P **4** L **5** B **6** B **7** L

Tapescript

Alan: Liz, could you spare a few minutes? I've got all this information from the estate agent – I need to talk it through with someone, just to get my head round it. It's … it's really a choice between Bridgeport, Lakeside and Petersfield. They're the main towns in the area I'll be working in.

Liz: Fine. You need to make a decision soon, don't you? After all, you start your new job in a month's time. What sort of place are you looking for?

Alan: Well, somewhere I can afford, for a start. At least the prices should be cheaper than in London!

Liz: That's Petersfield out then – far too exclusive for you! I wouldn't fancy those cheap new flats and houses they're advertising at Lakeside either – not a lot of imagination there! You're left with Bridgeport then, aren't you? It seems to have something for most pockets.

Alan: That's true. But, I think Petersfield has got quite a lot going for it. For one thing, there's all that brilliant countryside surrounding it. The other two can't really compete when it comes to that, can they?

Liz: Hold on, Lakeside will look great when all the building work is done, and I'm sure there must be a park or two in the centre of Bridgeport.

Alan: Ugh! Town parks! Now, what about travel links. There's trains from both Bridgeport and Petersfield stations …

Liz: …Yep, and you can go straight through on the Petersfield train if you're going to London …

Alan: … but no station at Lakeside. That's a bit of a pain, as I'll have to come up to London quite often.

Liz: To see your friends, I hope! As a matter of interest, which place is nearest to your new job?

Alan: Both Petersfield and Lakeside are about the same distance away, although the latter is slightly nearer. Bridgeport is not quite so close.

Liz: Do you have any contacts down there you can ask about the area?

Alan: Well, my brother used to live in Bridgeport, you know – he used to go on about the congestion there all the time. That was after he left college in Petersfield, of course.

Liz: Yes, other people have told me the same thing. I guess it's because it's quite a thriving sort of place – a lot of new businesses have moved there in the last ten years.

Alan: So, what else does all this stuff tell us? What about things to do? I don't want to end up in a place with nothing going on.

Liz: Well, it says here that Lakeside has a new leisure centre – I believe it's got an Olympic size swimming pool and an athletics track, and there's a theatre.

Alan: Sounds good, although that's not really my thing – I enjoy wandering around, looking at places. You'd think Bridgeport would have some decent art galleries and museums, wouldn't you? Bit disappointing really.

Liz: Yes, I was surprised, too. Petersfield may be small but it's got some interesting buildings, I guess it's because of the college being there.

Alan: Umm. OK, so what else should I be thinking about?

Liz: Well, there is shopping. I know it's not something you probably worry about too much, but you'll be working odd hours. Lakeside does seem to have been planned for people like you, while Petersfield isn't quite ready for 24-hour shopping yet.

Alan: Yes, I can't imagine what the citizens of Petersfield would say to that! Come to think of it, Bridgeport doesn't seem to be too great on that front either!

Liz: So, have you come to any conclusion? I know which I'd choose.

Alan: Oh, and where's that?

© Cambridge University Press, 2000

Photocopiable tapescripts

Unit 1, 1.1 Exercise 7 photocopiable tapescript

Speaker 2: I started working this year, so I'm able to get new clothes more regularly than before, when I had to save up for months. I buy a lot, I must confess. My mum thinks I should cut down a bit on what I spend, but my image is really important to me: if someone sees me in something once, I don't like to go out in it again – well, not for a while, in any case. I like to wear bright colours and always dress up when I go clubbing. I buy a big range of styles and I do try to keep up with the latest fashions. Sometimes the things are a bit outrageous!

Speaker 3: Shopping for clothes isn't really my scene, if you know what I mean. I don't really mind what I wear, to tell you the truth. I'm the least fashion-conscious person I know! I suppose if anything I favour the casual look. I've got two pairs of jeans and I wear them mostly, with a T-shirt or something. I have got one favourite top, which a girlfriend gave me. It's red and it's got a sort of abstract design printed in navy blue on the back. She said she gave it to me so I would always stand out in a crowd!

Speaker 4: My clothes have to be comfortable, make me feel relaxed as soon as I slip them on. I often put together outfits from stuff I find in street markets – they're less expensive that way. Second-hand clothes can be real bargains, and usually, they've hardly been worn! I'll change the look of my clothes quite frequently, you know, sew in a new piece of material, swap buttons, dye something a different colour, just for a change. I make a lot of my own jewellery too.

Speaker 5: My friends take far less trouble with clothes than I do – sometimes they wear the tattiest things ever! As my job involves dealing with people, I have to make an effort to look good all the time. I like to present a classy, sophisticated image. I go shopping for clothes about once a month, though if I see something by chance, I'm quite likely to go for it there and then. I think I've got good taste and I very rarely make a mistake when I buy clothes. I did take a jacket back last week, but that was because it was badly tailored.

 © Cambridge University Press, 2000

Unit 3, 3.1 Exercise 5 photocopiable tapescript

Int: Good morning, everyone. Well, in the studio today we have Steve Jackson who's going to tell us about his recent trip to the Antarctic. So, Steve, what was it like? Did you freeze?

Steve: No, I didn't. The temperature was about seven degrees most days and I must say I found it quite comfortable. You should take warm clothes though and you really need a good windproof coat.

Int: Now, tell us a bit about the ship you were on.

Steve: It was called the *Explorer*, and it was built only three years ago. The cabins are very small and at first I did wonder where I was going to put all my stuff. However, whoever designed the ship thought of just about everything a passenger would need and I eventually found plenty of cupboard space under the bed.

Int: What were the other passengers like?

Steve: Oh, the atmosphere on board between the passengers was really great. The crew really tried to get everyone to mix. I was invited to eat with the expedition leader, he was American, on the first night, and then after that I sat at a different table for dinner every night, but you don't have to if you don't feel like it.

Int: Did you get seasick at all?

Steve: Some of the passengers did – the weather can be stormy in the Antarctic. Of course there is a doctor on board and he gave anyone who needed it an injection for seasickness – luckily, I didn't need one and the others got over it pretty quickly once they'd had the injection.

Int: I bet that was a relief! What's your best memory of the trip?

Steve: Well, that's hard to say, but probably it's of the animals we saw – whales, penguins and seals. One day we set off to a place called Cuverville Island, which is famous for its birds. There were ten of us in a tiny rubber boat – that was a bit hair-raising I can tell you! Anyway, once there we had to climb up a steep, icy hill, but the view from the top was terrific.

Int: Did you come across any people apart from your fellow tourists?

Steve: Yes, a few of the scientists at a research station. They gave us coffee and biscuits one morning! There used to be a thriving fishing industry in this area at one time, but all that's left are some deserted buildings.

Int: Did you feel guilty about disturbing such an untouched region?

Steve: Well, yes and no. Cruise ships are not allowed to dump rubbish or to go where they like, and they have to carry scientists to lead the excursions. Only small parties are permitted to land in one area at a time and you've got to keep away from the wildlife. So, all in all I felt that well-run trips, like this one, would do more good than harm. I also felt completely changed by the experience – it was like going to another world.

Int: Well, thank you for telling us about your trip, Steve. Now next …

© Cambridge University Press, 2000

Unit 6, 6.2 Exercise 1 photocopiable tapescript

1

I'd buy a Seychelles blue Bentley convertible. I'd buy a nice, fat house in Holland Park. I'd get a lovely, big house in the countryside. I'd buy a beautiful house in Spain, with swimming pool, palm trees, that sort of thing. I'd get a flat in Manhattan probably. Um … I'd also have a permanent chef … top of the range chef who could cook all different types of food, so I could have whatever food I wanted whenever I wanted it. I'd have my own personal masseur …

2

I don't believe it when people say that if they won the lottery it wouldn't change their lives, because it would certainly change mine. Um, and I think I would just alter my life entirely. I love the sun and I hate English winters so I think I'd buy a yacht. And as I don't know anything about um … sailing, I'd have to buy a crew as well. So, um, I'd … I'd get this luxurious yacht and a very skilled crew – and probably a … a … a skilled cook – who would just take me all around the world going from hot spot to hot spot, so I could have a really great time.

3

Well, I know I'd have a problem with having all that money. I'd … I think it is a problem really, in some ways, because you … you'd have a sort of social responsibility and there are all kinds of people who you need to help, which I would want to do very much. Um, so of course I'd sort out my debts, my family's, but in the end I think what I'd do is buy – depending on how much money I had – buy a huge house, a really massive house somewhere in the country and just surround myself by all the people I want to be with, um and people who perhaps never had a chance to get out into the country at all.

4

Again depending on how many millions I won, um it would change what I would or wouldn't do with it. Frankly, if it was a lot, I mean five million upwards … sort out my own debts, which God knows are bad enough, sort out the family's debts and then invest as much as possible and just try and live off the interest, keep it there, nice little nest egg, growing and growing and growing, developing, flowering bountifully, and holiday, get away, move, anywhere but cold Britain.

Unit 9, 9.2 Exercises 4 and 5 photocopiable tapescript

Part 2

Woman: There's one advert I really like, partly because it's brilliantly put together …

Man: And it's for?

Woman: Bacardi – it's set on a tropical island somewhere in the Caribbean. And there's this radio DJ who's broadcasting in a studio and …

Man: Oh, not Ray on Reef Radio?

Woman: You've seen it too!

Man: Yep. Detest it, actually. All about some friend of Ray's who's leaving for the mainland and how he's going to miss his wonderful life on the island …

Woman: And you see what he's been up to – I adore the way the DJ, Ray, tells the storyline on air and you see flashbacks of the other guy … Like 'I know you're going to miss the way they serve Bacardi around here' – and you see a girl throw a glassful in the friend's face! Such a striking image and totally unexpected.

Man: Mmm, I suppose ads do work well when they contain something out of the ordinary – I guess they stick in your mind that way.

Woman: Right … and of course, the ending itself is unforgettable – quite spectacular, isn't it? Seeing the friend sailing away on the boat, listening to all this on his radio – and then, what does he do …

Man: He dives off the deck and swims back to the island.

Woman: For another night on the town and a glass of …

Man: Yes, yes … You know, I must admit that although I personally loathe the ad, it sells the product pretty well. It's got the right ingredients – you know, exotic location, powerful images …

Woman: So what didn't you like about it?

Man: The characters themselves, I think … especially Ray!

Woman: But come on, the very fact that you remember him now means he made an impact on you … which must mean that the ad has worked.

Man: True enough … And what about you? You said it makes you laugh, is that why you like it so much?

Woman: That … and the way it succeeds in telling a story in such a short time, I think that's quite clever, getting the message across like that. The music's great, too.

Man: But was it truly successful? I mean, did you dig into your pocket and buy a bottle?

Woman: Well, no … I don't drink spirits! I bet plenty of people were persuaded to rush out and buy some, though …

© Cambridge University Press, 2000

Unit 11, 11.1 Exercises 3, 4 and 5 photocopiable tapescript

Presenter: So, Hannah, what was it like growing up in Hollywood as an only child, and having such a famous mother?

Hannah: Well, I guess I was pretty privileged as I had things most other kids only dream about. For instance, when I was 14 I just loved Harrison Ford films, and my mother arranged for me and a few friends to go to the film set to see him working on his latest film, as a treat for my birthday. I don't think I was particularly spoilt though, even though I was an only child, and I didn't get into trouble like some of the kids I knew did.

Presenter: You, yourself, are an actress now. Did she ever try to put you off acting?

Hannah: Not at all. Just the opposite. She felt I should follow my feelings, I guess in the same way she had done when she was younger. My grandparents hadn't wanted her to take up acting you know, especially as she had to move from Europe to Hollywood. I don't think her family took her seriously at first and I think she was quite homesick and felt she could have done with a little more family support.

Presenter: Now, you look very like your mother, don't you?

Hannah: Oh, yes. My mouth, the shape of my face, my jaw line is my mother's. My nose too, but only the tip of it, not the bridge – that is unique, like no one else's in the family. My eyes, my forehead, my colouring, my height are different from my mother's but everyone tells me I look like her. When I say everybody, I mean everybody. People stop me in shops, on the subway, in the street.

Presenter: What does your mother say about this?

Hannah: Well, we both looked in the mirror one day and came to the same conclusion – people exaggerate. Then one day I went into a dress shop. I was alone except for another customer. I thought to myself, 'She looks like my mother.' Then I walked too close to her and crashed into a mirror – the lady was me! I hadn't recognised myself!

Presenter: What qualities do you think your mother possesses?

Hannah: Great physical energy. She used to walk fast, and when she wasn't acting she cleaned and organised the house perfectly. She loved acting more than cleaning; she loved acting most and above all. It took me some time not to feel hurt by this. I wanted to come first. When asked what was the most important thing in her life, she got real embarrassed and nervous, but my mother couldn't lie; she had to say 'acting'; though I know for our sake she wished she could say 'family'. She is terribly practical, and I am too. We consider it one of the greatest qualities in people. We give it the same status as intelligence. Practicality is what made my mother advise me to learn to be an accountant. 'If you know how to do it, you know you'll never be cheated out of any money,' she says. I didn't finish the course as I decided I wanted to act.

Presenter: Did she have any personal experience of being cheated out of money?

Hannah: Well, my mother has always been a very generous person to people she likes. I think another actor who she fell out with started the rumour that she is a bit stingy. She does say that I'm a bit extravagant.

Presenter: Now, you don't sound like your mother, do you?

Hannah: Oh no. She still has a bit of an accent. But her voice is definitely an actress's voice – the clearest speech, the most commanding delivery, and loud. The family used to tell her that she didn't need a phone, she could have just talked to us on the other side of town and we would have heard her. She justifies it with 'I picked it up in the theatre. My voice has to reach all the way to the last row.'

Presenter: Thank you for coming in today to talk to us Hannah and good luck in your new film, which I believe, is released on Tuesday?

Hannah: Yes, that's right. Thank you.

Unit 13, 13.1 Exercise 4 photocopiable tapescript

Int: With me now are Sandra Wilson and Mike Tripp. Mike is owner of a successful new travel company Just Trips and Sandra works for him as Publicity Manager. They were actually in the same class at school, though at that time, they did not get on with each other! They met again by chance last year, when Sandra went for an interview at Just Trips and was surprised to find Mike across the table, asking her the questions. Sandra, when you were at school, did you think Mike would become successful like this?

Sandra: To be honest, no one thought Mike would get anywhere – he was the original under-achiever! That's why we didn't get on. My group of friends were quite hard-working, you know, we did all the homework, made an effort in class, but Mike was the complete opposite. He was bad news, actually.

Int: Is this true Mike?

Mike: I'm afraid so. I wasn't the only one though. It was … uncool for boys to work, a whole group of us were like that. I don't remember being especially horrible to Sandra …

Sandra: Talk about a selective memory!

Int: Why?

Sandra: Well, he would regularly do annoying things like stealing my ruler or hiding my books. You saw it as a big joke, I suppose, Mike?

Mike: Never thought about it. I can see now that I might have been a … a bit of a nuisance.

Sandra: I've forgiven you though!

Int: And you've done very well since, Mike …

Mike: Yeah. I got on with my life. Um … I don't really regret my behaviour back then – obviously I shouldn't have made trouble for you, Sandra – but for myself, it didn't matter … I've done okay in spite of school.

Sandra: You have Mike, but there are lots of others in your gang who didn't make it.

Mike: Mmm … I can think of one or two … But I still think, if you know what you want out of life, you'll get there. I mean, look at me, I didn't pass many exams … I even walked out of some, like science … wrote my name at the top of the paper and thought, I can't do this … oh, what the heck, the sun's shining, I'm off.

Sandra: Incredible. I was totally stressed out during exams, spent hours revising, and Mike managed to fail virtually everything and still be successful.

Int: Should you have been more relaxed at school, Sandra?

Sandra: That's easy to say now. I had a lot of pressure on me to do well. My parents, my brothers … all my family expected … the best.

Mike: Same here. But my dad sort of looked beyond school. He knew I'd be okay – he'd left school himself at 14 and he always felt that I'd sort things out for myself, somehow.

Int: And how did you get the company started? No careers advice from school, I imagine?

Mike: Careers teachers? They didn't have a clue! I got things started in a small way while I was still at school, actually – I used to help out in a local travel agency, buying and selling cheap tickets on the phone. In my final year, I sometimes spent my lunchtimes checking the Internet on the school computer. I found some good deals for flights, that I managed to sell on. Then, when I left school, my dad gave me a bit of money and I set up an office … and it all … like … took off.

Int: So school did help you a little …or its facilities did?

Mike: Yeah …

Int: Okay, well we'll have to leave it there. One final thing, Mike. Why did Sandra get the job?

Mike: Oh, university education, languages, a good communicator – she's great, just what the company needed.

Sandra: All thanks to school, Mike.

  © Cambridge University Press, 2000

Exam folder 7 photocopiable tapescript

Int: Good morning and welcome to the Food and Drink Show. In the studio today we have Christine Whitelaw who works as a Personal Assistant to the world famous chef Patrick Millar. Christine has worked for him for the past 18 months and has loved every minute of it. Her boss has many interests ranging from a cookery school for professionals and amateurs, to a catering service and a range of luxury food items. Christine's organisational skills have to be faultless as a result. She also considers a good memory, confident phone manner and fast typing speeds to be vital to her job. So Christine, how did you become PA to such an important figure in the food and drink industry?

Christine: Well, I always wanted to work in catering, so after leaving school I completed a year on a cookery course before spending another year at secretarial college. My first job came about following a visit to London. I went to lunch at the Palace Hotel and thought, 'I would really like to work here', so I wrote to see if they had any positions, and it just so happened they did.

Int: That was a lucky break, wasn't it?

Christine: It certainly was. I worked as a PA to the executive director of the hotel group for more than three years before hearing that Patrick Millar was advertising for a new PA. I applied, had to go to two interviews, and got the job.

Int: How does an ordinary day go?

Christine: I usually meet Patrick first of all to run through his diary and letters. If clients are expected for lunch, I may take them on a pre-lunch tour of the cookery school. It has a collection of 6,000 cookery books, which many people are keen to see. Then I take them to the restaurant. In the afternoons I usually do letters and make phone calls. I have an assistant to help me. Each day is fairly different, however. If Patrick is busy in the morning we sometimes have a working lunch together in the chef's office, never in the restaurant or kitchen.

Int: Did you find your previous experience in the hotel business useful?

Christine: Yes, especially in learning how to deal with the public, both face to face and over the phone. One thing it didn't prepare me for was the long hours, as, nowadays, I often have to work until 7pm and then go on to a reception or function.

Int: You often hear about how difficult these top chefs are to work for. Is Patrick very moody or do you get along well?

Christine: Oh, he's terrific and he involves me in most of the decision-making. The worst part of working for him is that I'm surrounded by delicious food all day. I try not to be tempted!

Int: Can you cook yourself?

Christine: Well, I do enjoy cooking and I have tried a few things from his recipe books. However, I have no plans to work as a cook. The job I have combines everything I love: food, meeting people and being at someone's right hand.

Int: Thank you, Christine for coming in to talk to us today. Next week we'll be interviewing …

Unit 15, 15.1 Exercise 2 photocopiable tapescript

Situated in the northwestern part of Arizona, the Grand Canyon is one of the natural wonders of the world. Contrary to popular belief, the Grand Canyon is not the longest, deepest, or widest canyon in the world. But it is accessible, and with little vegetation to hide it, it feels big. Nothing prepares you for that first sight of it. From the top it drops 1.6 kilometres to the desert floor below. But however vast it seems, it is not big enough to support the millions of people who visit it every year.

When one section of the Grand Canyon was declared a national park in 1919, three years after the creation of the National Park Service, visitor numbers were 44,000. Today, with five million visitors a year, the Park Service is finding it difficult to keep the Canyon accessible to the public and to safeguard it for future generations.

The pressures on the Grand Canyon National Park have forced the Park Service to draw up a management plan. One of the first problems it has tackled is that of the large number of visitors' cars. Options included the introduction of an electric bus service and a light railway system in and around Grand Canyon village.

Some of the other problems faced by the park are the result of things happening outside its boundaries. Take air pollution. On summer days, when there are southwesterly winds, the pollution blown in from Southern California can restrict the views over the Canyon.

Then, another of the big problems is the availability of water resources in the park, as, at present, there is a drought. The Park cannot draw water from the river but only from a spring on the north side of the canyon, using a pipeline. If this pipeline is damaged, then water has to be brought in by truck. This last happened in 1995 when floods caused a landslide, which destroyed the pipeline.

The Colorado River, which created the Canyon, looks wild but in fact, is managed intensely. Twenty-four kilometres upstream is the Glen Canyon Dam which has had a profound impact on the river. Now the river flow is about a tenth of what it was previously.

The Colorado used to reach temperatures of twenty-four degrees in summer. Today, it is a cold seven degrees all year as water release comes from deep within the reservoir. As a result, some species of fish have become extinct. In addition, the rapids are getting bigger, as the river is too weak to move the boulders washed out of the canyons downstream.

Visitors are proving to be powerful allies of the park. Those who once thought that the Grand Canyon was just an awesome hole in the ground soon learn that however big it is, its popularity is in danger of destroying the very qualities that made it one of the seven natural wonders in the world.

Unit 20, 20.2 Exercise 1 photocopiable tapescript

The long corridors of cell block B were buzzing. Behind cell doors, convicts were calling to each other, or getting undressed and ready for bed. Everyone had to stop talking at half past nine, when the lights were switched off. Frank Morris, bank robber and burglar, stared at the ceiling, alone in his cell. His world measured three paces by five. Day one of his ten-year sentence on Alcatraz Top Security Island Penitentiary was over. All around him were men regarded as the most hardened desperate criminals in the entire USA.

After lights out, the stillness was broken only by the distant boom of a foghorn and the footsteps of a patrolling guard. Morris noted the time it took the guard to walk the length of the corridor before he turned around. Already he was planning his escape.

Morris's pleasant face and friendly manner hid a ruthless determination and a brilliant brain. As the days went by he became accustomed to the routine of Alcatraz. After the evening meal the men were locked in their cells. They had four hours to themselves before the lights went out. Some liked to paint, others to try to learn to play a musical instrument.

In conversation with another prisoner, Morris learned that three years before, a large fan motor had been removed from a rooftop ventilator shaft above his cell block. It had never been replaced. He immediately saw a way of escape. Morris began to plot. It seemed impossible to reach the shaft from his locked cell but one day he saw a way.

He tried picking at the concrete around a small air vent in his cell. It was slow work and he had to hide the hole he was making with a large accordion, a musical instrument that he had bought with money he'd made in the prison workshop.

The more he plotted, the more he realised that the plan would work better if he had others to escape with. He recruited three other inmates. One of them worked as a cleaner and Morris got him to steal a vacuum cleaner, which Morris turned into a drill. This made digging much faster, but they could only use it during the music practice hour.

They knew that if they managed to get down to the shore, it would mean swimming across the Bay. So one of the four managed to steal plastic raincoats to make into water wings.

Seven days before they were all due to escape, one of the four decided he could wait no longer. He forced the others to climb through the holes they had made in their cells and climb up to the roof. They remembered to keep absolutely quiet but as they were crossing the roof a slate was dislodged and fell to the ground. Below, one of the guards heard it and stopped to listen. However, he heard nothing more and continued walking.

The route from rooftop to shore passed by brightly floodlit areas, overlooked by gun towers. Carefully, they moved forward. Crouching in the damp sand, the escapees inflated their raincoat water wings, then waded through a sharp wind into the dark, freezing waters of San Francisco Bay.

Nothing was ever heard of them again. Whether they are still alive or were swept far out to sea, no one ever found out.

 © Cambridge University Press, 2000

Unit 21, 21.1 Exercise 6 photocopiable tapescript

1

Some people only buy flowers very occasionally, on impulse, but to me, a house looks bare without flowers. They brighten up your living space and they've always been important in my life. When I was small, my father travelled a lot in his job. Whenever he came home, he was always carrying an armful of flowers for my mother, even though sometimes he'd only been away for a couple of days. So I grew up with fresh flowers. After I left home, I was a penniless student. Despite being hard-up, I would still try to buy flowers, though my limit was usually a pound bunch of daffodils. Now, with a steady income, I spend at least £20 a week and I wouldn't dream of cutting back on this – I've been doing it for so long that the outlay has become part of my life, like the phone bill or food shopping.

2

For two years now, I've been going to a private gym. I used to be really unfit – I er … liked my food rather, and I smoked quite heavily, too. My doctor told me I had to get myself in better shape and suggested dieting. Well, even though I cut down on what I ate – and cut out the cigarettes entirely – I still didn't feel particularly healthy, so I enrolled at this gym. The joining fee was quite steep, and I pay a monthly membership. While not exactly loaded, I can afford it – and I can't imagine life without my twice-weekly visit! If I do a full work-out, I use the pool afterwards. It's nice to be able to socialise a bit. When I walk out of the place I feel great, you know, totally relaxed. It's a small price to pay for feeling good about yourself.

3

There is nothing more wonderful after a difficult day than sinking into a well-made bed with freshly laundered sheets. Utter bliss! It's an indulgence I picked up when I was young. Every year we would travel to Europe as a family and always stayed in delightful hotels, with excellent bedding. After buying my own place, I was broke. My grandmother gave me all her handmade cotton sheets and pillow-cases, dating from around 1910. In spite of being given all this, I didn't use any of it for ages, because I was frightened that it might get damaged in the wash. Finally, I decided it was crazy to have it all sitting there in the cupboard, while I was in an old sleeping bag! Having it laundered gives me confidence it's in safe hands. They collect every Friday morning, and I get it back the following Friday, beautifully packed in a box. Well worth the expense, definitely.

4

My girlfriend and I work really long days, plus it takes us over two hours to get home some evenings, as the traffic's so bad. So, the last thing either of us wants to do is rush out again and do the weekly shopping. We used to, of course. It was terrible – more often than not we'd have some silly row about what to buy. We were just too tired and it got to us, whereas now it's much more civilised. Armed with a glass of wine, we sit in front of the computer in the flat, and dial up the Tesco Internet site. We can usually decide on our order quite quickly, even if we still argue over some things! It's all delivered to the door for a weekly charge of £5. I consider it's money very well spent. Anyway, with our joint spending power, money isn't exactly tight.

5

I can't remember the last time I went on public transport. I can't stand it – it's so crowded and dirty. I do own a car, although I much prefer taking a taxi. To begin with, I only used to get one after being out late with friends, because I wanted to be safe. But as my spare cash grew, so did my taxi habit. Now I have an account with Dial-a-Cab, who are very reliable. Much as I appreciate the convenience of taxis, it's the luxurious side that really appeals to me – the exclusiveness, if you like. I jump in and shut the door – and I'm in my own little stress-free world. And if I'm taking my son out for the day somewhere and can't easily park, I just add the cost of the fare to the day out without a second thought, even if it's a lot.

Unit 25, 25.1 Exercise 3, 4, and 5 photocopiable tapescript

Part 2

Gareth: Right, well it's as you've said really. I walk past these awful 60s concrete blocks every day and I just can't believe the mistakes that have been made...people have been uprooted and forced to live in high-rise buildings against their will. Architects and planners have never talked to the public, er, they feel they have the right to decide what's best for us.

Presenter: Is that how you operate, Jennifer?

Jennifer: Not at all, and in my view, lack of consultation over new buildings is not an issue with the public. Gareth, you're describing a time when many people wanted to be rehoused, because their living conditions were so bad. Uh, this was a policy upheld by government, rather than decided by architects.

Gareth: But the fact is that people still have to live in high-rise accommodation. I grew up in the suburbs where everyone had a garden, it was a pleasant environment. How can you expect people to enjoy life on the twenty-third floor with a bleak view and a lift that's out of order? If we were meant to live up in the sky, we would have been born with wings!

Jennifer: Well, joking apart, I was in a tower block in a run-down part of Bristol for six years of my childhood, so I do know what it's like. That's largely what drove me to become an architect, actually. Yes, some 60s architecture is poor, but the point is, if it hadn't happened, we would be making similar mistakes today, whereas ...

Gareth: They are being made!

Presenter: Gareth, let Jennifer finish!

Jennifer: ... whereas, as it is, we have been able to learn from the recent past. Look, we do have a serious problem: our cities are getting bigger, we call it urban sprawl, with suburbs that go on for ever. Okay, everyone has a garden, but at a huge cost to the tax-paying public, in terms of basic services and upkeep.

Gareth: You mean drainage, road-maintenance, that sort of thing? I hadn't thought of that ... And I suppose city expansion isn't very good news for the countryside either, it's sort of ... disappearing?

Jennifer: Absolutely. And at the same time, there's sometimes appalling decay in the middle of our cities as a direct result of the move outwards. Shops have closed because of out-of-town shopping facilities, and people often have little left to support them locally.

Presenter: Gareth, do you fancy living right in the city centre?

Gareth: Hmm. I must confess I would really like to move further in one day, there's so much going on, you know, entertainment, concerts and stuff, but any housing in central London that's nice to live in is so upmarket that it's completely unaffordable for someone like me.

Jennifer: That depends, Gareth, on whether you would be prepared to live up in the sky. What I believe in – and what many architects are trying to work towards – is the regeneration of our cities' core, and this can only happen if we build vertically – there's no space to do anything else! It's a really exciting development that could give city centres the uplift they so badly need. Gareth, imagine if your building was a multi-use one, where you could just go downstairs to see your live music, or pick up some shopping late at night...this is the housing of the future, where everything is on the doorstep. No-one will need to own a car.

Gareth: Yes, but again is that what people want? I mean having a car is every person's dream, isn't it? I know traffic's a problem, but you can't change how people are, how they want to live.

Jennifer: Well, it may surprise you that in a recent TV phone-in, 67% of callers thought that the car should be banned altogether from central London – one example of public consultation, incidentally. I think people are ready for this, Gareth, they understand that traffic congestion is killing us. Living in the city has to become a healthier and more acceptable option.

Gareth: Oh I don't know, you do sound as though you know what you're talking about.

Presenter: Gareth, Jennifer, good to see you getting on so well now! I'm going to have to stop you briefly, while we take a few calls on this topic from listeners, but ...

© Cambridge University Press, 2000

Unit 28, 28.2 Exercise 5 photocopiable tapescript

Presenter: Good morning. And it's now official – blondes really do have more fun. New research has revealed that a woman's hair colour reflects her personality; redheads are wild and fiery, while brunettes have a lot of common sense and are eager to please.

University psychologists believe they have proved that the classic stereotypes attributed to a woman's hair colour have a scientific basis, and that changing the colour of your hair may even help change your personality. According to the research, to be published later this year, dyed blondes – typified most famously by Marilyn Monroe – start having more fun and appear to worry less about money.

Dr Tony Farmer who carried out the study, said it showed for the first time that there are key personality differences between women of different natural hair colour. Whether the differences are genetic or simply a consequence of expectation is less clear. Apparently, people who dye their hair blonde are making a real gesture of rebellion. The researchers interviewed 93 women with natural hair colour, who answered 48 questions to establish their personality traits. They then conducted the same personality analysis on 30 women before and after they changed their hair colour.

Natural redheads were less likely to care about what other people thought of them and had more significant mood swings.

I decided to ask some redheads whether they agreed. First of all, Jenny Alton, the actress. What do you think, Jenny?

Jenny: Well, having red hair has caused me some problems. I remember when I was younger, my classmates would call me 'carrots'. Later on people would shout at me in the street – maybe that's why redheads become so bad-tempered.

Presenter: I wondered if this stereotyping was only aimed at women so I asked the redheaded writer Peter Jameson what he thought.

Peter: Well, I'm fairly famous for being irritable and intolerant, but I do think stereotyping can lead to discrimination. On my first day at school I was surrounded by a group of boys who attacked me so I retaliated. Of course, when a teacher appeared he immediately blamed me.

Presenter: Well, my thanks to both Jenny and Peter. Fortunately, I'm going bald so none of this applies to me. In the studio next week we …

Unit 29, 29.1 Exercises 3, 4, and 5 photocopiable tapescript

Speaker 1: The first we knew about it was when the paper phoned us up and asked for an interview. Cathy had said she'd be staying with a friend in London for the weekend. She'd phoned us on her arrival – as we thought – and we were expecting her back on the Sunday evening. To get the call like that out of the blue was terrible. Did we know that our daughter was sailing round the Mediterranean with a bunch of drug-crazed rock musicians? How old was she? Could we let the paper have a school photo to put in Monday's edition? It was a young chap and he went on and on – I mean, he must have known that he was breaking bad news to us, but he just didn't care.

Speaker 2: I was an idiot, but at the time I suppose I was flattered, it went to my head. You know, this famous singer was interested in me, some nobody from the suburbs. I would have phoned my parents again on the Sunday evening and come clean – the yacht had all the technology obviously. I'd just turned 18 the week before anyway, so I was an adult – but where's the story in that? I had to become a silly little thing, a total lie of course, but then that's their trademark, isn't it? We knew something was wrong when this speedboat kept cruising round the yacht on the Saturday afternoon. Nat – the bass player – noticed one guy had a camera with a long lens. It turned out that they'd bribed one of the bodyguards the night before, who got my name and address from my passport and radioed it all through. And the rest is history – a big juicy scandal!

Speaker 3: They run stories on us the whole time – we've got this bad boy image and any dirt they can rake up on us sells newspapers – or so they believe. I feel really bad about Cathy. She's a nice kid and she didn't deserve any of this – nor did her folks. Course the paper deliberately got her age wrong, making it look as though she was this innocent young schoolgirl who was being led astray by the big bad band. You get sick to the back teeth with it, you really do. Nat's got a better attitude, he doesn't let it get to him, but I hate it – I hate them, hounding us the whole time. They never give up, no way. Don't suppose they ever will, while we're flavour of the month.

Speaker 4: Cathy's put a brave face on the whole thing and admits she made a mistake. When she got back last week, I visited her at home – the school's on holiday until Monday next. The family all probably thought I was going to ban her from coming back next term, but I wanted to reassure her really. I mean, the whole thing has been blown rather out of proportion, a three-day wonder. Typical media sensationalism! Cathy's a promising student who should get very good grades in her A-levels. Why let all that go to waste? Everything will have died down soon, and I've every confidence that she'll be able to concentrate on her work again.

Speaker 5: Well, I genuinely believe the public has a right to know these things, I mean it could have been anyone's daughter. It's almost a duty if you like, you know, we don't shy away from the truth, even if it is hard to find. We're ready to show these people up for what they really are. Who knows, if we hadn't got to Cathy when we did, she might not be safely back home now. Perhaps some of the people involved should think about what might have happened, then they might have a change of tune, rather than criticise us as they have done. As for the band, well they're in the public eye, so if they choose to behave as they do, they've got it coming to them. And let's face it, there's no such thing as bad publicity, is there?